T5-BPY-301

Library of
Davidson College

The
Lawyer in Literature

BY

JOHN MARSHALL GEST

Judge of the Orphans' Court
Philadelphia, Penn.

BOSTON
THE BOSTON BOOK COMPANY
1913

Wm. W. Gaunt & Sons, Inc.
1982

809.933
G393 L

WM. W. GAUNT & SONS, INC.

International Standard Book Number: 912004-21-5
Library of Congress Catalog Card Number: 82-81089

Reprint 1982

WM. W. GAUNT & SONS, INC.

Gaunt Building
3011 Gulf Drive
Holmes Beach, Florida 33510-2199
U.S.A.

92-5423
ACF-6784

The Lawyer in Literature

The
Lawyer in Literature

BY

JOHN MARSHALL GEST

Judge of the Orphans' Court
Philadelphia, Penn.

BOSTON
THE BOSTON BOOK COMPANY
1913

COPYRIGHT, 1913
BY JOHN MARSHALL GEST

The Riverdale Press, Brookline, Mass., U.S.A.

To George Stuart Fullerton

Professor of Philosophy in Columbia University

That F marches just before G in the familiar pro-cession of the alphabet may not be considered by the careless crowd a matter of any special moment, yet it was due to this that you and I rubbed elbows in the class room many years ago. You, as a Philosopher, may resolve the problem of cause and effect, or reason high of Fix'd fate, free will, foreknowledge absolute; I, as the Plain Man for whom you have written, am content with the assurance that the passage of Time and separation in Space have not lessened the friendship that then and there began.

J. M. G.

Preface

THE papers contained in this volume were written in the leisure intervals of professional work, partly for my own amusement, and partly to interest members of my profession in the literary aspect of the law. I have been led to hope that they may interest a wider public in the legal aspect of literature.

The Law and Lawyers of Dickens was read before the students of the Law School of the University of Pennsylvania in April, 1905; The Law and Lawyers of Pickwick, before the Law Club of Pittsburgh in May, 1908; The Law and Lawyers of Scott, before the Law Association of Philadelphia in March, 1906; The Law and Lawyers of Balzac, before the Sharswood Law Club of Philadelphia in April, 1911, and afterwards before the Pennsylvania Bar Association at its annual convention in June, 1911; The Influence of Biblical Texts upon English Law, before the Societies of Phi Beta Kappa and Sigma Xi, at Philadelphia in June, 1910; and all of these were published in the University of Pennsylvania Law Review. The paper on the Writings of Sir Edward Coke appeared in the Yale Law Journal of May, 1909; and the address on the Historical Method of the Study of the Law was delivered to the students of the Law School of Temple College, Philadelphia, in February, 1902.

The republication of the papers that have already appeared in the University of Pennsylvania Law Review and in the Yale Law Journal is with the approval of their publishers, whose courtesy is gratefully acknowledged.

JOHN MARSHALL GEST.

City Hall, Philadelphia,
January 1, 1913.

Introduction

By John H. Wigmore[1]

THE compliment is an agreeable one, to be allowed to figure as the Introducer of so accomplished a legal scholar as the Author of these essays. When they first saw the light in the Pennsylvania Law Review, I was among those who urged that they receive a more permanent form in our literature; and it is a satisfaction to see this proper destiny now shaped for them.

Who, that has already made acquaintance with these characters of the law in Dickens and the rest, will not take pleasure in comparing notes upon them with Judge Gest? Who, that has his favorites and his aversions among them, will not be interested in the author's new points of view, his fuller survey, his keen judgment, his trenchant wit, his generous sympathies, his illuminating comments?

And yet a main use of the book ought to be to send those readers to the originals who have never been there. Can a lawyer — I mean one of self-respect, of aspiration, of devotion to his art and science, — can he afford to ignore his profession as it is glassed in the literature of life?

Why should a lawyer, *as* a lawyer, be familiar with literature, particularly the literature of the novelists?

Well, in the first place, there are episodes of fact and types of character in professional life whose descriptions by famous novelists have become classical in literature, —

---

[1] Professor of Law in Northwestern University.

Serjeant Buzfuz in *Pickwick Papers;* the Chancery suit in *Bleak House;* Effie Dean's trial in *The Heart of Mid-lothian;* and many more. With these every lawyer must be acquainted, — not merely as a cultivated man, but as one bound to know what features of his professional life have been taken up into general thought. "The first thing we do, let's kill all the lawyers!" said Dick the Butcher to Jack Cade. If you do not know, from your Shakespeare or elsewhere, that this sentiment was once — and more than once — a rabid popular demand, then you cannot gauge the possibilities of popular thought in these very days of ours.

Then, again, there is the history of law, — that is, the scenes and movements in legal annals which history has made famous. To know the spirit of those times — to realize the operation of the old rules now gone — to feel their meaning in human life — to appreciate the bitter conflicts and their lessons for today — this deepest sense of reality for the past we shall get only in the novels, not in the statute books or the reports of cases. It is one thing to read the trial of Lord George Gordon in good old Howell's State Trials, but it is a different thing to read about the very same events in *Barnaby Rudge.* We must go to *Bleak House* to learn the living meaning of Chancery's delays; to *Oliver Twist* to see the actual system of police justice in London; to *Pickwick Papers* to appreciate the other side of Baron Parke's technical rulings reported in Meeson & Welsby's volumes, — those sixteen volumes of which Erle said, "It is a lucky thing that there was not a seventeenth volume, — for, if there had been, the common law itself would have disappeared altogether amidst the jeers of mankind." Read Lady Lisle's trial by the savage Jeffreys, in Howell's State Trials, and then Conan Doyle's account of it in *Micah Clarke;* read some book on the early real property statutes of New York, and then Fenimore Cooper's portrayal of them in *Satanstoe* and *Chainbearer;* read the chill technical reports of bankruptcy proceedings in the Federal Reporter, and then Balzac's story of the downfall of *César Birotteau.* The living side of the rules of law is often to be found in fiction alone.

But there is a further service, and a higher one, to be rendered to the lawyer by literature. For literature, and especially the novel, is a catalogue of life's characters. And human nature is what the lawyer *must* know. He must deal understandingly with its types, its motives. These he cannot find — all of them — close around him; life is not long enough, the variety is not broad enough for him to learn them by personal experience before he needs to use them. For this learning, then, he must go to fiction, which is the gallery of life's portraits. When Balzac's great design dawned on him, to form a complete series of characters and motives, he conceived his novels as conveying just such learning. He even enumerated the total number of characters. His task was, he says:[1]

"To paint the three or four thousand salient figures of an epoch — for that is about the number of types presented by the generation of which this human comedy is the contemporary and the exponent, this number of figures, of characters, this multitude of portraits, needed frames. Out of this necessarily grew the classification of my work into Scenes. Under these heads I have classed all those studies of manners and morals which form the general history of Society. . . If the meaning of my work is understood, my readers will see that I give to the recurring events of daily life (secret or manifest), and to actions of individuals, with their hidden springs and motives, as much importance as the historian bestows on the public life of a nation."

---

[1] Preface of 1848 — "one of the world's great prefaces," Brunetière calls it.

In this view, the work of the novelist is to provide
a museum of human characters, traits and motives —
just as we might go to a museum of zoölogy to observe
an animal which we desired to understand but had never
yet seen alive; this was Balzac's idea:

> "There have always been, and always will be, social species, just
> as there are zoölogical species. If Buffon achieved a great work
> when he put together in one book the whole scheme of zoölogy, is
> there not a work of the same kind to be done for Society? . . . There
> are as many different men as there are species in zoölogy. The differ-
> ences between a soldier, a workman, a merchant, a sailor, a poet,
> a beggar, a priest, though more difficult to decipher, are at least as
> marked as those which separate the wolf, the lion, the ass, the crow,
> the shark, the seal, the lamb, and so on."

And so the lawyer, whose highest problems call for
a perfect understanding of human character and a skillful use of this knowledge, must ever expect to seek in
fiction as in an enclyclopedia that learning which he
cannot hope to compass in his own limited experience
of the humans whom chance enables him to observe at
close range.

This learning has been sought, possessed, and valued
by many great advocates. Perhaps they have seldom
openly inculcated its value. But I know of one singularly direct exposition of this theme, which must here
be quoted:[1]

> "Read the literature of human nature. . . . To my mind Balzac
> is the greatest judge of human nature, after Shakespeare. I think
> I learned more of human nature (outside of my own experience)
> from Balzac than I have from any other author except Shakespeare.
> I recall especially *Eugénie Grandet*, the history of a miser. I have

---

[1] Address of Frank J. Loesch, Esq., President of the Chicago Bar
Association, in 1905, at Northwestern University Law School;
printed in the *Illinois Law Review* (1907), Vol I, p. 455; entitled,
"The Acquisition and Retention of a Clientage."

read that book two or three times, and this is how it profited me afterwards. I was retained in a very serious case of fraud. I studied the party on the other side. I made up my mind that if ever there was a miser out of the pages in literature, that was the man, and that Grandet was his literary father-in-law. I studied *Eugénie Grandet* again, and then I attacked that opponent. It was an eight years' task. But the image of Grandet helped me to hound that man so, that at the end of eight years there was not anything left but his hide. The greatest admirer of the work I did is that man's own lawyer; but he will not give me credit for having any legal acumen. He maintains that I knew all the facts beforehand. Yet the truth of the matter was that I did not; I drew the bill before I had the facts. I merely judged the man's character from what I had read of *Eugénie Grandet*. That experience was to me a life lesson.

"Let me allude also to another case, one that nearly broke me down with the mental and physical strain. I had bought every printed trial I could find on that particular subject. I had a year to prepare for the actual trial of the case. There were very eminent lawyers on the other side. I will not mention names, for the parties are living. But I did not receive from all these books as much light as I did from a certain classical novel, one that characterized exactly the plaintiff's object and put that party in the lime-light. With that aid I was able to follow all the ins and outs of his maneuvers, and finally to win the case. It was a work of fiction that guided me to a right solution of that person's character, and a knowledge of his character that was essential to victory.

"Still another lesson I now recall which I learned from reading — a lesson I shall never forget. It related to a gentleman by the name of Gil Blas. Gil had various and sundry adventures, and among others he was made secretary to the Archbishop of Toledo. The Archbishop said to him one day: 'Gil, I look upon you as a very likely young man, I like your intelligence and acumen. Now I am getting old. I have to preach once a month. Make it your duty to let me know when you see any failing signs in my mental powers. I will trust you as a friend to tell me about it.' So Gil noted the character of the sermon the next month. Then he heard the ensuing sermon; and he thought the Archbishop showed signs of age and senility. At the third sermon he was more satisfied of this, and the fourth was shockingly significant. He complimented the Archbishop on the first sermon, and spoke fairly of the second, but of the others he did not. The Archbishop asked, 'Now, Gil, what is the truth?' Gil said: 'Your Eminence, your mental powers

are failing rapidly.' 'Gil,' responded the Archbishop, 'I find that
I am mistaken in your acumen. The treasurer will pay you and
you will leave the house.' I have never forgotten the moral of that
story. Such incidents of literature add to your knowledge."

And so the best literature — drama or poetry, philosophy or fiction — must always be an arsenal for the
lawyer. That is why I offer the hope that this volume
may whet the zest of all devoted members of our profession to follow the example of our author, and to seek
in literature its manifold message to the lawyer.

Contents

I

The Law and Lawyers of Charles Dickens

The Lawyer in Literature

The Law and Lawyers of Charles Dickens[1]

In selecting a subject for this address I found myself somewhat in the predicament of Solomon John Peterkin, who, having been selected by the family to write a book, and having surrounded himself with a supply of ink, pens, and paper, was puzzled to know what to write about. For one who is honored with an invitation to address the students of a law school is expected, I suppose, to speak upon a subject having at least some nominal connection with the law, while, if he attempts the discussion of a technical question, he exposes himself to the danger of having his theories dissected or his conclusions disproved in the class rooms on the morrow. Then it occurred to me that, perhaps, in your devotion to Bracton, the Year Books, and Coke on Littleton, you might be neglecting some of the more modern writers, who have been bold enough to borrow from Justinian the title of Novels for their books, which looks very much like what is called Unfair Trade Competition. So, these literary pirates sometimes call their productions Fiction, though everyone knows that the real, genuine, original Fictions are the fictions of law, which Jeremy

[1] An address read before the students of the Law School of the University of Pennsylvania on April 5, 1905.

Bentham says are the most pernicious and basest sort of lying, while Blackstone says that, though at first they may startle the student, he will find them, on further consideration, to be highly beneficial and useful.

Now, you may learn a great deal of law in a very agreeable way by reading novels. Thus, in *Ten Thousand a Year*, you find the old action of ejectment, with all its fictions and prolixities, fully described; the plot of *Felix Holt* turns upon a base fee, and I believe George Eliot obtained professional advice upon her book before it was published. In *César Birotteau*, Balzac explains in detail the French law of bankruptcy; while in other books, forged wills and murder trials of the most thrilling sort abound. Sometimes these legal novelists are not very accurate in their law, but that should only serve to stimulate the reader's criticism. Shakespeare's plays, as we all know, are crammed with legal allusions; and Sir Walter Scott, who was a lawyer by profession, and a well-read lawyer too, made good use of his legal learning. Nothing of the kind is more amusing than his account of the great case of *Peebles* v. *Planestanes* in *Redgauntlet* while *Anne of Geierstein* is worth reading for the sake of the *Vehmgericht*.

But today we may be able to find enough in Dickens to occupy the time. Indeed, it makes little difference what subject is selected, provided we don't stick too closely to it. As Mrs. Squeers used to say to the boys when they labored under extraordinary ill usage, "It will be all the same a hundred years hence."

I shall neither sketch the life of Dickens, nor attempt any criticism of his work; but it is well to recall a few important facts and dates. He was born February 7, 1812; he died June 9, 1870. He began writing his *Sketches by Boz* in 1835, at the age of twenty-three, and until the day of his death, thirty-five years after, delighted and astonished the readers of two continents with thirteen elaborate works and numerous shorter stories and sketches, introducing over five hundred characters, many of whom are, indeed, Household Words.

At the age of ten he was employed in a factory, pasting labels on blacking pots at six shillings a week, undergoing experiences which would have crushed a weaker spirit, as he said in later years, with "no advice, no counsel, no encouragement, no consolation, no support from anyone that I can call to mind, so help me God." His father was a prisoner for debt in the Marshalsea prison, and Dickens spent his Sundays there, getting the impressions which he reproduced so vividly in *Little Dorrit*. At fifteen he entered the office of one Molloy, an attorney, in New Square, Lincoln's Inn, and, later, the office of Ellis & Blackmore, attorneys, of Gray's Inn. Here he remained until November, 1828, receiving a salary of fifteen shillings a week. His experience, though short, must have been crowded. He saw the seamy side of the law, the Fleet Prison, Newgate, and the Marshalsea.

He doubtless slipped many a time into the Old Bailey and saw there tried many an Artful Dodger; that Old Bailey of which Lord Brampton says, in his *Reminiscences*, "Its associations were enough to strike a chill of horror into you. It was the very cesspool for the off-scourings of humanity." And Dickens had a wonderful memory for all these things. He used to say that he remembered his old home at Portsmouth, from which he was taken when two years old. This must be true, because he said it, and he ought to know. Like a good Churchman, *Credo quia impossibile*. At all events, he remembered everything worth remembering, and a great deal one would think worth forgetting, and everything he saw and heard, reappeared, sometimes like a photograph, sometimes like a caricature, in his books.   Then he studied shorthand, as he tells us in *David Copperfield*, and reported in the Lord Chancellor's Court; then for the newspapers; then for two years he sat in Doctors' Commons; then at the age of nineteen entered the "gallery," where he stayed for four years more, with quick eye and ears and nimble fingers, answering in a sense Browning's question, "What hand and brain went ever paired?"

Such was his education and preparation for his career, which then began with his *Sketches by Boz*, some of which are as good as anything he wrote in later life; and in 1836, at the age of twenty-four, *Pickwick* made him immortal, and has kept the whole world on a broad grin ever since.

I have said that no criticism of Dickens would be here attempted, but one thing must be said, because everybody else has said it, and it is really true in speaking of the law and lawyers of Dickens, that Dickens saw too keenly the humorous side of life to portray it as an artist; he was a caricaturist.   Life is mirrored in his pages, but the mirror was convex or warped, and he went up and down the world, holding it before everybody and everything.   He held it before his own father, and the amused world beheld the foolish figure of Mr. Micawber; he held it before his mother, and the image appeared of Mrs. Nickleby; his friend, Leigh Hunt, became Harold Skimpole; Landor was changed to Boythorn; a family friend appeared as Miss Mowcher.   So, with Dickens's reproduction of manners and institutions.   He was sentimental and emotional, but his sentiment too often becomes mawkish; his pathos is strained and artificial; the best of his writings are marred too often by blank verse, while the plots of his stories are frequently awkward, involved, and unnatural.

He was, as I said, sentimental and emotional; he was sympathetic also. He saw and appreciated the evils of society as they existed in his day, but he lacked the constructive faculty of suggesting practical reforms. His ability consisted in exciting compassion for the poor and oppressed, scorn and contempt for the oppressor, and derision for the laws which, at the time he wrote, favored poverty and oppression, and were the worn-out heritage of an earlier stage of society.

I repeat that in reading Dickens's description of the law and lawyers we must bear in mind that, first and last, his aim was to ridicule, satirize and caricature all that he disliked and despised, and he saw much in the law and lawyers of England to dislike and despise. He was not, of course, an educated lawyer. I doubt very much if he ever read any law at all. He was not a reader, like Uriah Heep, whom he found "going through *Tidd's Practice*," a great, fat book, with his lank forefinger following the lines and making tracks along the page like a snail. Dickens's knowledge was not derived from the printed page, but from what he saw and heard. He was never called to the Bar, though I believe he ate his dinners in the Middle Temple. In the guise of the *Uncommercial Traveller* Dickens says: "I was uncommercially preparing for the Bar, which is done, as everybody knows, by having a frayed old gown put on, and, so decorated, bolting a bad dinner in a party of four, whereof each individual mistrusts the other three."

Dickens's practical experience of the law was decidedly unpleasant. In 1844 Vice-Chancellor Knight-Bruce granted him an injunction against some literary pirates who published imitations of *Christmas Carol* and *Chuzzlewit*. Although successful, he had to pay the costs, a boomerang which he might have considered very funny had it happened to another. When another case of piracy occurred he wrote to his counsel, Talfourd: "It is better to suffer a great wrong than to have recourse to the much greater wrong of the law.   I shall not easily forget the expense and anxiety and horrible injustice of the *Carol* case, wherein, in asserting the plainest right on earth, I was really treated as if I were the robber instead of the robbed."   It was, doubtless, his own sentiments which he expressed in the *Battle of Life*, which he wrote soon after.

"Nothing serious in life!" said Mr. Snitchey, of the law-firm of Snitchey & Craggs, as he peeped into his blue bag.   "What do you call law?"

"A joke," replied the doctor.

"Did you ever go to law?" asked Mr. Snitchey, looking out of the blue bag.

"Never," returned the doctor.

"If you ever do," said Mr. Snitchey, "perhaps you'll alter that opinion."

Snitchey naturally took a professional view of the law.

"Take this smiling country as it stands.   Think of the laws appertaining to real property; to the bequest and devise of real property; to the mortgage and redemption of real property; to leasehold, freehold, and copyhold estate; think," said Mr. Snitchey, with such great emotion that he actually smacked his lips, "of the complicated laws relating to title and proof of title, with all the contradictory precedents and numerous Acts of Parliament connected with them; think of the infinite number of ingenious and interminable Chancery suits to which this pleasant prospect may give rise, and acknowledge that there *is* a green spot in the scheme about us!"

"The one great principle of the English law," says Dickens in *Bleak House*, "is to make business for itself. There is no other principle distinctly, certainly, and consistently maintained through all its narrow turnings. Viewed by this light, it becomes a coherent scheme, and not the monstrous maze the laity are apt to think it. Let them but once clearly perceive that its grand principle is to make business for itself, at their expense, and surely they will cease to grumble."

As Dickens viewed the law with profound contempt, so he regarded lawyers with scant favor. Most of the lawyers in his books are shysters, as we would call them, or narrow, mean, ignorant pettifoggers. His books are crowded with familiar specimens. We pass by the celebrated firm of Dodson & Fogg with sincere regret, for the present; but there are others. Here is Stryver, "the favourite at the Old Bailey and eke at the Sessions," by whose efforts Darnay was acquitted: Stryver, "stout, loud, red, bluff, and free from any drawback of delicacy, a glib man, and an unscrupulous and a ready and a bold," and Sydney Carton, his jackal, idlest and most unpromising of men, who, at the last, by the transforming touch of the novelist, is "exempted out of the number of the rascabilitie of the popular."

Of most of such men the old verses are true:

> "For fees to any form they mould a cause,
>   The worst has merits and the best has flaws;
>   Five guineas make a criminal today,
>   And ten tomorrow wipe the stain away."

Here is Jaggers, the criminal lawyer of *Great Expectations*. With Pip we may check off in detail "his large head, his dark complexion, his deep-set eyes, his bushy black eyebrows, his large watch chain, his strong black dots of beard and whisker, and even the smell of scented soap on his great hand." Mr. Jaggers's office was a most dismal place, and there were some odd objects that you would not expect to see, such as an old rusty pistol, a sword, strange-looking boxes, mementos of clients dead and gone, and on a shelf two dreadful casts of faces peculiarly swollen and twitchy about the nose. "These are two celebrated ones," as Wemmick, Jaggers's satellite, explained to Pip. "Famous clients of ours that got us a world of credit. This cast was made in Newgate, directly after he was taken down. You had a particular fancy for me, hadn't you, Old Artful?" Jaggers himself sat in a deadly black horsehair chair, with the plaster casts perched above him, and treated his clients like criminals, as in fact they were.

Here is Mr. Tulkinghorn, the sly, unscrupulous old family solicitor, "the steward of the legal mysteries, the butler of the legal cellar of the Dedlocks, surrounded by a halo of family confidences, of which he is the silent depositary." He was of the old school, and wore knee-breeches, tied with ribbons, and gaiters. He was a hard-grained man, close, dry, silent, with a priceless bin of port in some artful cellar under his chambers in Lincoln's Inn Fields, where he sits alone after dinner to enjoy his wine, with the Allegory in a Roman helmet sprawling on the painted ceiling above him, while around about are old-fashioned mahogany and horsehair chairs, and obsolete tables with spindle legs.

There are plenty of lawyers in *Bleak House* besides Tulkinghorn. Conversation Kenge, of Kenge & Carboy, Lincoln's Inn, was a portly, important looking gentleman, dressed all in black, with a white cravat, large gold watch-seals, a pair of gold eyeglasses, and a large seal ring upon his little finger. Mr. Guppy was employed in Kenge & Carboy's office, where he learned enough to file his declaration of love to Esther "without prejudice."

Mr. Vholes was another solicitor in *Jarndyce* v. *Jarndyce*. He was a sallow man, with pinched lips, that looked as if they were cold, a red eruption upon his face, tall and thin, high shouldered and stooping, always dressed in black, black gloved, and buttoned to the chin. Mr. Vholes used to say that when a client of his laid down a principle that was not of an immoral nature it devolved upon him to carry it out; the ethical force of which was rather marred by his explanation that by immoral he meant illegal.

But, of all Dickens's disreputable lawyers, Sampson Brass, Daniel Quilp's attorney, was probably the lowest. He was a tall, meagre man, with a nose like a wen, a protruding forehead, retreating eyes, and hair of a deep red, with a cringing manner and a very harsh voice — his face being, indeed, "one of nature's beacons, warning off those who navigated the shoals and breakers of the World, or of that dangerous strait, the Law." But, as he was wont to boast, he was a gentleman — by Act of Parliment. "I maintain the title by the annual payment of twelve pounds sterling for a certificate. I am not one of your writers of books, or painters of pictures, who assume a station that the laws of their country don't recognize. If any man brings an action against me he must describe me as a gentleman, or his action is null and void." Well might the words of Sir Thomas Smith apply: "Gentlemen bee made good cheape in England."

But even an Act of Parliament itself could not, for several reasons, have made a gentleman of Sampson's sister Sally. Lord Coke lays it down that women cannot be attorneys, otherwise, no doubt, Miss Sally Brass would have taken out her certificate. "This Amazon at law was a lady of thirty-five or thereabouts, of a gaunt and bony figure and a resolute bearing, which, if it repressed the softer emotions of love and kept admirers at a distance, certainly inspired a feeling akin to awe in the breasts of those male strangers who had the happiness to approach her." In face she bore a striking resemblance to her

brother Sampson. "In complexion she was sallow, rather
a dirty sallow, but this hue was agreeably relieved by the
healthy glow which mantled in the extreme tip of her
laughing nose. Her voice was exceedingly impressive,
deep and rich in quality, and, once heard, not easily forgotten. Her usual dress was a green gown, in color not
unlike the curtain of the office window, made tight to the
figure, while her head was invariably ornamented with
a brown gauze scarf, like the wing of the fabled vampire.
She was born and bred to law, and even in childhood was
noted for her exquisite manner of putting an execution
into her doll's house and taking an exact inventory of the
chairs and tables." When Shakespeare protrayed his
feminine lawyer he gave us Portia; when Dickens tried
his hand he gave us Sally Brass. The girl graduates of
the present time, the women moulded to the fuller day,
with their "star sisters answering under crescent brows,"
have thus their choice of ideals.

When Dickens began first to observe, and then to write
about what he saw, it was nominally the nineteenth century but, so far as the law was concerned, the eighteenth
century lasted until the Reform Act of 1832. The laws, a
century ago, were almost mediæval, and the trouble was
that judges and lawyers, for the most part, were satisfied with them. Not all, by any means. Here and there
a voice cried in the wilderness, and men like Bentham
marched around Jericho, blowing their rams' horns. But
it was not the first blast, nor the second, that levelled the
walls. Reform came very slowly indeed, until the middle
of the century; then the walls fell with a crash. There
were not a few defects in the law against which Dickens
shot his arrows of abuse and ridicule, and some of these
we shall now recall.

In the beginning of the last century most crimes were
felonies, and most felonies were capital. Over two hundred

offenses were punishable with death, especially those which involved a confusion of those great pronouns *meum* and *tuum*, as Lord Coke calls them. Under the Shoplifting Act, for example, to which Dickens refers in *Barnaby Rudge*, stealing in a shop to the value of five shillings was a capital offense. Stealing in a dwelling-house to the value of forty shillings was likewise capital, and the endeavors of men like Erskine and Romilly to mitigate the severity of such laws were frustrated by Lord Eldon. That great but narrow-minded man might have profited by these words of Lord Coke (not generally considered as a leader of reform), who said in the *Epilogue to the Third Institute:* "What a lamentable case it is to see so many Christian men and women strangled on that cursed tree of the gallows, insomuch as if, in a large field, a man might see together all the Christians, that but in one year throughout England, come to that untimely and ignominious death, if there were any spark of grace or charity in him, it would make his heart to bleed for pity and compassion."

When Dickens began his career, things were about as bad as they were in the latter part of the eighteenth century, the date of the *Tale of Two Cities*. "The forger was put to death; the utterer of a bad note was put to death; the unlawful opener of a letter was put to death; the coiner of a bad shilling was put to death. Not that it did the least good in the way of prevention, but it cleared off, as to this world, the trouble of each particular case, and left nothing else connected with it to be looked after." And then the heads of the victims used to be hung up at Temple Bar, as Judas Maccabeus hung Nicanor's head upon the tower as an evident and manifest sign unto all.

In one of the early *Sketches by Boz* Dickens describes a visit to Newgate. In the prison chapel was the condemned pew, in which the wretches who were condemned to death listened to their own funeral sermon on the Sunday before their execution; while at one time, not then far distant, their coffins, with a grimly terrific humor, were placed in the pew beside them. "Let us hope," said he, ";that the increase of civilization and humanity, which abolished this frightful and degrading custom, may extend itself to other usages equally barbarous."

Executions were then public, and, up to at least recent times, were attended by people of the first fashion. Boswell, Johnson's biographer, had a great taste for that sort of thing. On one occasion, he records, he saw six executed at Tyburn; on another, fifteen at Newgate. The solemn procession to Tyburn had been abrogated in 1783, much to Boswell's disgust, and Dr. Johnson observed: "The age is running mad. Men are to be hanged in a new way. The old method was most satisfactory to all parties; the public was gratified by a procession, the criminal was supported by it. Why is all this to be swept away?" The celebrated George Selwyn never missed a hanging without some legitimate excuse. When Hackman was executed for the murder of Miss Ray, the Earl of Carlisle wrote Selwyn an account of it, and added, "Everybody inquired after you." Selwyn made a trip to Paris to see Damien broken on the wheel for attempting to assassinate Louis XV. He displayed so much interest that he was asked by a French nobleman if he were a hangman. "No, sir," was his reply, "I have not that honor; I am only an amateur."

Charles Lamb wrote to a friend in Paris: "Have you seen a man guillotined yet? Is it as good as hanging?"

But times and tastes change. In 1849 Dickens saw the two Mannings, husband and wife, executed on the wall of Horsemonger Lane Jail, and, like a true-born Englishman, sat down quickly and wrote a letter to the *Times*, advocating a change, which was finally effected, I believe, in 1868.

As you well know, the goods of a stranger upon the demised premises are, with certain exceptions, liable to distress for rent. When Tommy Traddles was lodging with the Micawbers one of Micawber's financial storms broke, and forthwith Micawber wrote to Copperfield: "The present communication is penned within the personal range (I cannot call it society) of an individual in a state closely bordering on intoxication, employed by a broker. That individual is in legal possession of the premises, under a distress for rent. His inventory includes not only the chattels and effects of every description belonging to the undersigned, as yearly tenant of this habitation, but also those appertaining to Mr. Thomas Traddles, lodger, a member of the Honourable Society of the Inner Temple."

Harold Skimpole had an amusing experience with a landlord's warrant, under which his furniture was distrained upon — at least amusing to him. "The oddity of the thing," said Mr. Skimpole, with a quickened sense of the ludicrous, "is that my chairs and tables were not paid for, and yet my landlord walks off with them as composedly as possible! Now that seems droll! There is something grotesque in it. The chair and table merchant never engaged to pay my landlord my rent. Why should my landlord quarrel with him? His reasoning seems defective."

In *Oliver Twist* Dickens notices one of the common law incidents of the marriage relation. Mrs. Bumble, the helpmeet of the celebrated beadle, had unlawfully possessed herself of a certain gold locket and ring taken from Oliver's mother as she lay a-dying in the workhouse. When taxed with the crime Mr. Bumble, following the example of our common ancestor, endeavored to shift the responsibility. "It was all Mrs. Bumble. She *would* do it," urged Mr. Bumble, first looking round to ascertain that his partner had left the room.

"That is no excuse," replied Mr. Brownlow. "You were present on the occasion of the destruction of these trinkets, and indeed, are the more guilty of the two in the eye of the law; for, indeed, the law supposes that your wife acts under your direction."

"If the law supposes that," said Mr. Bumble, squeezing his hat emphatically in both hands, "the law is a ass — a idiot. If that's the eye of the law, the law's a bachelor; and the worst I wish the law is, that his eye may be opened by experience."

Dickens had doubtless seen many coroners' inquests, and he reports several. There was that held upon the supposed body of John Harmon, at the Six Jolly Fellow-ship Porters, in *Our Mutual Friend*, when Jesse Hexam, who had such remarkable luck in finding dead bodies, was the star witness. When Nemo died, in *Bleak House*, the inquest was also held at a public house, as seemed to be the custom. Indeed, it was said the coroner frequents more public houses than any man alive. Dickens describes the proceedings at the Sol's Arms very graphi-cally, where Little Swills, the comic vocalist, looks on in order to reproduce the scene at the Harmonic meeting in the evening. Little Jo is the only mourner for the dead, except Lady Dedlock, whom he afterwards guides to her lover's grave in Tom-all-Alone's. She asks the waif of the street if it is consecrated ground, perhaps fearing that, if a suicide, his body would receive outcast burial. "Is it blessed?" said she. "I'm blest if I know," said Joe. "Blest? I should think it was t'othered myself. But I don't know nothink!"

When Daniel Quilp was found drowned, and the coro-ner's jury found it a case of suicide, he was buried with a stake through his heart, in the centre of four lonely roads. This was a very old custom in England, but there seems to be no legal authority for it. Perhaps the place was so selected that, by the continual passage of the living, the burial-place might be trodden down and forgotten. It has been suggested that the stake was driven through the heart to keep the ghost from walking. The old Canon Law, I believe, simply prohibited the performance of the burial office over the bodies of those who committed suicide or were deprived of life as a penalty for crime,[1] and if you will borrow a Prayer-Book you will see this retained in the Rubric of the Burial Service of the Church of England.

The origin of the cross-roads burial is obscure and worth "a look into the antiquities, than which nothing is more venerable, profitable, and pleasant." Some think it dates from so late a period as 1600, though this seems improbable. But the custom was abolished in 1823 by 4 Geo. IV, c. 52, which shows that the story of the *Old Curiosity Shop* must antedate that time. *Bleak House* was subsequent, and so was *Nicholas Nickleby*, in which Ralph Nickleby, as he goes home to hang himself, paused to look at the grave of a suicide in whose case he himself had been of the jury.

In *Hard Times* Dickens complains, and justly, of the inequality of the law in England, which allowed divorce to the rich and forbade it to the poor. Stephen Blackpool, who found he had drawn not merely a blank in the matrimonial lottery, but the Black Spot itself, when he took Mrs. Blackpool for better or worse, applied to Bounderby for advice how to be rid of her. "It costs money," said Bounderby, "a mint of money. You'd have to go to Doctors' Commons with a suit, and you'd

---

[1] "*Placuit, ut hii qui sibi ipsis voluntarie . . . inferunt mortem; nulla prorsus pro illis in oblatione commemoratio fiat neque cum psalmis ad sepulturam eorum cadavera deducantur. . . . Similiter et de his placuit fieri qui pro suis sceleribus puniuntur.*" — Decretum Causa xxiii, Quest. V, c. 12. Gibson's Codex, 450.

have to go to a Court of Common Law with a suit, and you'd have to go to the House of Lords with a suit, and you'd have to get an Act of Parliament to enable you to marry again, and it would cost you (if it was a case of very plain sailing) I suppose from a thousand to fifteen hundred pounds: perhaps twice the money." Mr. Bounderby who afterwards married Gradgrind's daughter, found himself in a like fix: his wife leaves him, and he sends her paraphernalia after her. "I am Josiah Bounderby, and I had my bringing up. She's the daughter of Tom Gradgrind, and she had her bringing up, and the two horses wouldn't pull together."

Bounderby probably never read the Apocrypha. If he had, he might have approved the wisdom of the son of Sirach, who said, "Of woman came the beginning of sin, and through her we all die. If she go not as thou wouldst have her, cut her off from thy flesh, and give her a bill of divorce, and let her go."

Up to Justinian's time divorce might take place by mutual consent, but it is said that only one took advantage of this liberty for five hundred years. The laxity of morals which marked the decadence of Rome followed, and was caused by the idle luxury of the later period, producing a state of things which will soon be repeated with us unless some reform is effected. To elevate our marriage institutions by tinkering with our divorce laws is like putting a plaster on a cancer. The evil is not superficial, but internal, a very corruption of the blood.

But, as Lord Coke would say, let us now return to Dickens, for I know you will gladly hear him.

By the common law, an ordinary suit for a debt was begun by a *capias ad respondendum*, under which the debtor was arrested and obliged to give special bail for his appearance. If a judgment was recovered against him, and he was unable to pay the debt, or refused, as

Mr. Pickwick did, to pay it, he was arrested on a *capias ad satisfaciendum* and committed to a prison, such as the Fleet or the Marshalsea, until the debt was paid, which might mean imprisonment for life, in small, damp, crowded rooms, without beds. Pickwick mistook the underground rooms of the poor prisoners for coal cellars. The prisoner or his friends, if they had means enough, might, indeed, pay for better accommodations. Pickwick made such arrangements in the Fleet, and Dorrit had his own rooms at the Marshalsea, supported by Amy.

The law was gradually reformed in England by various statutes from 1844 to 1846, and imprisonment was finally abolished in 1869. In Pennsylvania the Act of July 12, 1842, abolished arrest in civil suits, certain cases excepted. These changes were not effected without great effort. Imprisonment for debt was considered proper and even necessary, although unknown to the early common law. Richard Steele, in No. 172 of the *Spectator*, says it is an honorable thing for a lawyer to imprison the careless debtor. There is hardly a novel of Dickens, or of Thackeray either, where someone is not imprisoned for debt. The sheriff's officer first took the defendant to a sponging-house, where he was temporarily detained while he or his friends raised the money. You may remember how Rawdon Crawley was seized at a most inopportune time, and taken to Mr. Moss's in Cursitor Street, Chancery Lane, for one hundred and sixty-six, six and eight pence, at the suit of Mr. Nathan, and, likewise, Mr. Watkins Tottle was suddenly arrested, and for a mere trifle of thirty-seven pounds found himself an inmate of the establishment of Mr. Solomon Jacobs, also of Cursitor Street, Chancery Lane.

Why they called these places sponging-houses I do not know, unless because they squeezed the debtors in them. Harold Skimpole was "took for debt," and a goodly proportion of the characters in *Pickwick*, from Pickwick himself to Jingle. Indeed, there was quite a family reunion in the Fleet.

Dickens himself knew, as a lad, what it was to be "took for debt,"' for his father underwent that painful experience, and it was in the King's Bench Prison that Micawber uttered his famous warning that, if a man had twenty pounds a year for his income, and spent nineteen pounds, nineteen shillings and six pence, he would be happy, but that if he spent twenty pounds one, he would be miserable. There was an insolvent debtors' act then, of which Micawber took advantage, and, in the meantime, enjoyed himself hugely in composing a petition to Parliament praying for an alteration in the law of imprisonment for debt.

But it was in *Little Dorrit* that Dickens described at large life in the debtor's prison, as the whole story centres about it. The Marshalsea was originally the prison of the Court of the King's Steward and Marshal, having jurisdiction of cases arising within a space of twelve miles around the King's Court, "a mere Palace Court jurisdiction," as Mr. Rugg, Arthur Clennam's professional adviser, remarked as he recommended that Clennam should be arrested by preference on a writ from the Superior Court, and be taken to the King's Bench Prison. But Clennam preferred to go to the Marshalsea, because he had there known Little Dorrit, the child of the Marshalsea.

William Dorrit was the Father of the Marshalsea, and proud of the title. He had been there so long that he regarded it as his own. He was the oldest inhabitant, and all the newcomers were presented to him at what resembled a State Drawing Room; and he was really happier there than when a turn of fortune's wheel made him wealthy and opened the prison gate. "It's freedom," said one of the residents. "Elsewhere people are restless, worried, hurried about, anxious. Nothing of the kind here. We have done all that; we know the worst of it; we have got to the bottom; we can't fall; and what have we found? Peace. That's the word for it. Peace." There is a good deal of philosophy in that. But Dorrit did not think he had got to the bottom. There was the workhouse, where old Nandy lived. The Father of the Marshalsea was disgusted with Amy because she walked with Nandy in the street. "The Workhouse," said he, "the *Union!* No privacy, no visitors, no station, no respect. Most deplorable." It was a great day in the Marshalsea when old Dorrit left it and started on his travels to Italy and Switzerland, but at last his mind fails him, and wanders back to the old days when he was the first in that humble society.

Dickens as a young man was a reporter in Doctors' Commons and in *David Copperfield* has a good deal to say about the Ecclesiastical Courts. Copperfield entered the office of Spenlow & Jorkins, the distinguished proctors, and Steerforth gave him a lucid explanation. "A proctor," he said, "is a sort of monkish attorney. I can tell you best what he is by telling you what Doctors' Commons is. It's a little, out-of-the-way place where they administer what is called ecclesiastical law, and play all kinds of tricks with obsolete old monsters of Acts of Parliament, which three-fourths of the world know nothing about, and the other fourth supposes to have been dug up in a fossil state in the days of the Edwards. It's a place that has a monopoly in suits about people's wills, and people's marriages, and disputes among ships and boats." Spenlow was a little, light-haired gentleman, with undeniable boots and the stiffest of white cravats and shirt collars. "He was buttoned up mighty trim and tight, and must have taken a great deal of pains with his whiskers, and was got up with such care that he could hardly bend himself, and, when he turned to glance at some papers on his desk, was obliged to move his whole body from the bottom of his spine, like Punch."

In *Sketches by Boz* there is an amusing account of Doctors' Commons, and the case of "The Office of the Judge promoted by *Bumple* v. *Sludberry*" in the Court of Arches. This was a brawling case; that is, Sludberry and Bumple had a falling out at a vestry meeting, by which Sludberry the aggressor, brought himself within the jurisdiction of the court, who, having heard the evidence, pronounced upon Sludberry the awful sentence of excommunication for a fortnight and payment of costs. Upon which Sludberry, a red-faced, sly-looking gingerbeer seller, asked the court to take off the costs and excommunicate him for the rest of his life, as he never went to church at all.

David Copperfield tells of another case, where a baker was excommunicated for six weeks and sentenced in no end of costs for objecting in a vestry to a paving rate; and still another excommunication case, which arose out of a scuffle between two church wardens, one of whom was alleged to have pushed the other against a pump, the handle of which projected into a school-house, which schoolhouse was under a gable of the church roof, thus making the push an ecclesiastical offense.

Another case of Spenlow's was a suit for annulment of marriage. The husband, whose name was Thomas Benjamin, took out his marriage license as Thomas only, suppressing the Benjamin in case he should not find himself as comfortable as he expected. *Not* finding himself as comfortable as he expected, he now came forward and declared that his name was Thomas Benjamin, and, therefore, he was not married at all, which the court confirmed to his great satisfaction.

But now all this miserable business is done away with in England, and the Ecclesiastical Courts deal only with clergymen of the Established Church in their professional character. Let us be thankful that, in our country, we have been saved all this.

We will now look at the picture of the Court of Chancery which Dickens gives us in *Bleak House*, a novel written for the purpose of attacking that court, as *Nicholas Nickleby* was written to expose the Yorkshire schools, and *Oliver Twist* to lay bare the English Poor Laws and the horrors of crime.

A bill in equity, in those days, was not the innocent document which with us bears the name, but a much more formidable instrument. In the first place, it was very lengthy. After the caption and names of the parties came the stating part, in which the plaintiff stated the facts of his case; then a general charge of confederacy against the defendants and divers other persons then unknown. This was originally inserted in order to lay ground for amendment by adding other parties to the bill, but soon became a mere form. The next was the charging part of the bill, in which were set out anticipated defenses, which were then denied or avoided in order to ground interrogatories. Then, after an averment that the plaintiff had no remedy at law, came the interrogatories propounded to the defendant, with prayers for relief and process. As the costs were in proportion to the length of the pleadings, it will be readily seen that the solicitors had every temptation to prolixity. Thus, a witness testified before the Chancery Commission of 1852: "If I draw a document of 120 folios, I get £6, and if I compress that into 30 folios I get only 30 shillings. In fact the worse the business is done the better it is paid for," a folio being, as I believe, fifteen lines of six words each.[1]

---

[1] Testimony, Henry Lake, First Report, Chancery Commission, 1852, Appendix A, page 180.

It frequently happened that the defendant's answer rendered it necessary or advisable to amend the bill, adding fresh interrogatories which called for a further answer. Sometimes the plaintiff would designedly refrain from making his bill full in the first instance and file what was called a fishing bill, and then on the answer coming in, would avail himself of its averments to frame his amendment. This was called *"scraping the defendant's conscience."* [1]

As the defendant very frequently filed a cross-bill against the plaintiff to scrape *his* conscience, and there were continual opportunities for exceptions, and references to a master and appeals, it will easily be seen that by the time the parties' consciences had become thoroughly scraped, the proceedings had become unconscionably complicated.

Again, the rules of the court required that every person having any interest, no matter how theoretical or contingent, must be made a party, and this added enormously to the expense, and also to the vexation of suitors. Many a man whose interest was, as a practical matter, nothing, would be made a defendant, and, fearing to disregard the suit, would be obliged to employ counsel. Forster, Dickens's biographer, mentions a case of a legacy of three hundred pounds charged on a farm worth twelve hundred pounds. There was but one defendant in reality, but seventeen according to the technical rule, and, after two years, it was discovered that an eighteenth should be added, and the suit begun *de novo*, after costs had been incurred of over eight hundred pounds. This case Dickens worked up in *Bleak House* as the story of Gridley, "the man from Shropshire."

---

[1] Testimony, James Lowe, Chancery Commission, 1826, pages 165, 166.

The testimony in a Chancery case was not oral, but taken in writing by commissioners, or examiners. The party examining prepared his questions in writing, and the other side cross-examined, if he chose, and questions were propounded to the witnesses by the examiner. This method was most unsatisfactory, tedious, and expensive. A witness before the Chancery Commission testified that in one case, where a bill had been filed against the directors of a bank to hold them liable for its debts, the expense of obtaining the testimony of one witness was over eight hundred pounds. The witness observed that "the tremendous expense expedited a compromise." [1]

Then every party had to take office copies of every paper filed or at least pay for them, on penalty of incurring the displeasure of the officials.

Then the delay caused by appeals was something of which we can have little idea at this time. In 1811 a Scotch solicitor testified before the committee on delays of suits in Chancery: "I know that there has been a great increase of appeals, and I know that appeals are entered, many of them, only for the purposes of delay. There was a remarkable instance of it this session, to prevent a person paying one thousand pounds into court; it was in the House (of Lords) seven years. I had orders to withdraw the appeal as soon as it should be called on, and when it came to the last moment I took it away upon paying the costs." [2]

In 1824 a witness before the Chancery Commission spoke of the "heart-sickening delays" in appeals, and

---

[1] Testimony, S. B. Toller, Third Report, Chancery Commission, 1856, page 38.

[2] Testimony, James Chalmers, Chancery Commission, June 18, 1811, page 24.

mentioned one important case, appealed from the Master of the Rolls to the Chancellor, which remained unheard for nearly six years.[1]

Well might poor, crazy Miss Flite say so often: "I expect a judgment. Shortly. On the day of Judgment."

Litigated or contentious suits we all expect to be somewhat protracted; but when all hands simply want their rights determined by the court, it seems cruel to prohibit them. Yet this was what the Court of Chancery did by making no distinction between contentious and merely administrative business. The disputes which arise over the interpretation of wills, the settlement of accounts, and, in short, the thousand and one things which our Orphans' Court attends to every month, would, in England, under the old practice be the subjects of bills in equity, with all their delay, expense, and vexation of spirit; as, for example, where a trustee filed a bill merely to obtain the direction of the court in the execution of the trust, or to have the terms of an obscure will construed by the court, or where a creditor was required to make formal proof of his claim: all these proceedings assumed the cumbrous and expensive character of hostile suits.[2]

In 1855 it was said before the Chancery Commission that it took the registrar six months merely to settle the decree in the settlement of an intestate estate where some of the children had been advanced. It only required somebody to do it "who understood figures," but there was "nothing that any man of business might not settle in two or three hours." [3]

[1] Testimony, John Forster, Chancery Commission, 1826, Appendix A, page 302.

[2] Chancery Commission, First Report, 1852, page 10.

[3] Testimony, R. B. Follett, Chancery Commission, Third Report, 1856, page 92.

Then when the decision of the Chancery suit involved a preliminary determination of the legal rights of the parties, the Chancellor generally considered himself bound to direct an issue to a court of law, or take the opinion of the law judges. He was concluded to be sure by neither, but took this course to assist his conscience, and it need hardly be said that it was a proceeding which did not speed the cause nor lessen its expense.

In one case, where the contest involved the determination of who were the next of kin, the Master of the Rolls heard the case for three days, and then directed an issue. The case was tried for two days, and then the Master of the Rolls, dissatisfied with the verdict, directed a new trial. The Master of the Rolls was again dissatisfied, but no further trial was awarded, for the very simple reason that the fund of five thousand pounds was just sufficient to pay the costs. [1]

How Bentham lashed the whole system. "Equity!" he exclaims. "Equity! It is a term of derision, a cruel mockery. Is it a remedy? It sweetens like sugar of lead; it lubricates and soothes like oil of vitriol." And in another place he says, "The parties, unheard of and unthought of, pay their way through the offices like half-starved flies crawling through a row of spiders."

The Court of Chancery, in some of the Colonies, was even worse, if possible. According to Parkes's "History of the Court of Chancery"— I have not seen the report of the Parliamentary Commission at first hand — the Court of Chancery in the island of Montserrat, West Indies, had several times been presented as a public nuisance; and, he says, "the tornado which periodically interrupts the sittings of the West India Courts of

---

[1] Testimony of Joseph Leech, Chancery Commission, 1852, Appendix A, page 7.

Chancery is the only temporary relief of the islanders from the visitation of equity."

A dishonest trustee sometimes used these delays as an engine of fraud. He would say, for example, to a minor coming of age: "There is a difficulty in this case, and we must get the direction of the court. If we go formally into court you will have some time to wait, but if you take the accounts as they are you will get so much immediately." Naturally, the young man would take what he could, rather than spend years in Chancery trying to get more. [1]

The pages of *Bleak House* do not disclose the details of the great case of *Jarndyce* v. *Jarndyce*, although, as the book was professedly written to show up the iniquities of the Court of Chancery, and is spun out to more than a thousand pages, surely a few might have been spared to give the reader a definite idea of what the case was about. It does appear, however, that the question was how the trusts under the Jarndyce will were to be administered, and that, while the costs were steadily increasing, the value of the estate was steadily decreasing. "It was a street of perishing blind houses, and their eyes stoned out, without a pane of glass, without so much as a window frame, with the bare blank shutters tumbling from their hinges, and the iron rails peeling away in flakes of rust; the chimneys sinking in; the stone steps to every door (and every door might be Death's Door) turning stagnant green." Meanwhile, the legatees were reduced to poverty, and everybody had to have or pay for copies of cartloads of papers, and all hands went down the middle and up again, through such an infernal country dance of costs and fees and nonsense and corruption as was never dreamed of in the widest visions of a Witch's Sabbath.

---

[1] Testimony, John Bell, Chancery Commission, 1826, Appendix A, page 252.

"And nothing ever ends. And we can't get out of the suit on any terms, for we are made parties to it, and must be parties to it, whether we like it or not."

So Tom Jarndyce committed suicide from despair. "For," said he, "it's being roasted at a slow fire, it's being stung to death by single bees, it's going mad by grains."

So Gridley, the ruined suitor, dies from sheer exhaustion. Meanwhile, the Lord High Chancellor, sitting in the very heart of the London fog, hears the interminable case, term after term, until a later will is discovered among Krook's old rubbish, and the suit collapses, just as the entire property is eaten up in costs, leaving nothing behind but what Conversation Kenge called a Monument of Chancery Practice.

All these evils of Chancery were well known, and had been exposed over and over again. But where the Blue Books, in which the evidence is contained, find one reader, Dickens's *Bleak House* will find a myriad. Even Parkes's "History of the Court of Chancery," one of the most interesting law-books ever written, does not attract the casual reader. It is a pity, therefore, not to put too fine a point on it, as Snagsby would say, that Dickens can hardly be said to have been quite fair in *Bleak House*, for at the very time it was written, the Court of Chancery had been radically changed by an Act of Parliament, of which Dickens takes no notice whatever. *Bleak House* was published in monthly numbers, from March, 1852, to September, 1853, and its preface is dated August, 1853, while, strange to say, the Acts of 15 and 16 Vict., passed July 1, 1852, c. 86 and 87, made most important alterations in the method of taking evience, substituted printed bills for engrossed bills, simplified rules as to joinder of parties, gave the Chancellor full power to determine questions of law, substituted salaries for fees, and abolished many useless expenses and offices. These acts substantially reformed the court, though it continued its separate existence until the Judicature Act of 1873, when the courts were consolidated, and (to notice one important change) it was provided that in case of any conflict between the rules of equity and the rules of the common law with reference to the same matter, the rules of equity should prevail.[1] This principle, we are proud to say, has been recognized in Pennsylvania from the earliest times, and in *Pollard* v. *Shaffer*,[2] our leading case upon the subject, Chief Justice McKean said in terms, "Equity is part of the law of Pennsylvania." The way in which our peculiar system was developed is extremely interesting, and every student should read not only Laussat's early essay on the subject, but also Mr. Sydney George Fisher's article on the "Administration of Equity, through Common Law Forms," in 1 *Law Quarterly Review*, 455.

Yet, in his preface to *Bleak House*, in August, 1853, Dickens wrote: "As it is wholesome that the public should know what has been doing, and still is doing, in this connection, I mention here that everything set forth in these pages concerning the Court of Chancery is substantially true, and within the truth."

If Dickens really intended that his readers should know the truth he should have mentioned the Act of 1852, and he certainly should have known of this act, as the Parliamentary Commission which gave rise to it could hardly have escaped his attention. This commission, appointed in 1850, was headed by Romilly, then Attorney-General, and the bill suggested by it was presented by Lord St. Leonards and approved by Lord Lyndhurst. Dickens, therefore, did not kill the Chancery snake, but only jumped on it after it was dead.

---

[1] *Pugh* v. *Heath*, 7 App. Cases, 237.
[2] 1 Dallas, 210 (1787).

I have passed over in a very cursory and digressive manner some of the Lawyers, and something of the Law, as portrayed by Charles Dickens. Did space permit, it might be interesting to speak also of other like topics, such as the Patent Laws, of his views as to the English Poor Laws as found in *Oliver Twist* and the *Uncommercial Traveller*, and what he has to say of prisons and penal systems, of solitary confinement, and his criticisms of our Philadelphia penitentiary.

There are many interesting trials in Dickens. Every one thinks at once of the most celebrated, *Bardell* v. *Pickwick*, but there are many others. Read the trial of Darnay for treason in the *Tale of Two Cities*, and his trials in Paris during the Terror; the trials of the Artful Dodger and of Fagin in *Oliver Twist*, Kit's trial at the Old Bailey in the *Old Curiosity Shop*, and the death sentence of Magwitch in *Great Expectations*. And in that one of *Dr. Marigold's Prescriptions*, called "To be Taken with a Grain of Salt," there is a description of a murder trial combined with a very good ghost story.

Then, too, Dickens often lingers over his descriptions of the Inns of Court, dear to every American lawyer's memory or imagination, recalling in their very names the associations of centuries of legal history.

These and sundry other matters of great importance I pass over with dry foot, and leave the learned and judicious reader to his own judgment thereof. But anyone who will read Dickens's books, with these things in mind, will find them as interesting as any novels — by Justinian.

II

*The Law and Lawyers of
Pickwick*

The Law and Lawyers of Pickwick [1]

When a lawyer is asked to do anything he always searches for a precedent. So when you invited me to address you upon some legal subject after dinner, I naturally turned to the ancient authorities and customs of the profession. Fortunately, we are but reviving the practice of the Inns of Court, in which our legal ancestors received their education by eating dinners and then discussing cases, and, let us hope, by digesting both; and it is even said that the dinner part of the program was the most important as well as the most agreeable.

Moreover, Lord Coke records in 12 Rep. 19, that in Michaelmas Term, 4 Jac. 1 *Post Prandium*, there was moved a question among the Judges and Serjeants, at Serjeants' Inn, if the High Commissioners in Ecclesiastical causes may by force of their commission imprison any man or no? With the resolution of the question we are not now concerned; it is as stale as the dinner which preceded it.

Three hundred years in time and three thousand miles in space separate us from that dinner of the Judges and Serjeants, at Serjeants' Inn. I will not say a corresponding difference exists between the diners, but there is a wide distinction in character between that grave constitutional question and our subject this evening. However, with the authority of what Lord Coke would call a "book-case," and supported by the glorious

---

[1] A paper read before the Law Club of Pittsburgh, *post prandium*, on the evening of May 9, 1908.

traditions of the Inns of Court, I invite your attention this evening to *The Law and Lawyers of Pickwick*.

Authors, like dogs and dogmas, have their days. Literature has its fashions, like flounces and hoopskirts, or, to use a more dignified comparison, has, like the ocean, its waves and tides. Never was a book received with wilder enthusiasm than *The Pickwick Papers*. It has been translated into twenty languages, the imitations of it were numerous, its editions almost innumerable. This popularity continued for many years. *Pickwick* was the first book on which children were taught to cut their literary teeth; when they grew up they kept on devouring it, and while the young people of this generation sometimes affect to neglect Dickens, there are decided indications of a renaissance of interest. Dickens Societies and Fellowships are increasing in number all over the world and Dickens will come into his own again, while the "best sellers" of the book factories, after their brief moment of glory, disappear forever in darkness, like the burned-out sticks of literary rockets. He won immortality through the *Posthumous Papers of the Pickwick Club*, which he produced at the age of 24.

Dickens's early ambition was to be an actor, and he was always considered a brilliant amateur. *Pickwick*, indeed, is merely a succession of scenes, like a magic-lantern show. The preface says, "The author's object in this work was to place before the reader a constant succession of characters and incidents; to paint them in as vivid colors as he could command, and to render them at the same time lifelike and amusing." There is no more plot in *Pickwick* than there is in an omelette; yet, allowing for exaggeration and caricature, the book is really important because it contains a vivid and interesting picture of life, especially low or middle class life, in England, in the Thirties, for which "histories may be searched in vain." The story is therefore valuable, for old Weller's coach has long since been supplanted by the locomotive, and his city cousin, the 'bus driver, has met his rival in the motor 'bus. Emerson says Dickens is a painter of English details, like Hogarth. And yet, in spite of the low life depicted, the book is not coarse dr vulgar. As the *Edinburgh Review*, in 1838, gravely observed, "Although the reader is led through scenes of poverty and crime, we recollect no passage which ought to cause pain to the most sensitive delicacy if read aloud in female society," [1] and Dickens himself, in the preface to the original edition of *Pickwick*, says that "he trusts that throughout this book no incident or expression occurs which would call a blush into the most delicate cheek or wound the feelings of the most sensitive person."

It is only natural that *Pickwick*, being Dickens's first book (except the *Sketches*), should reflect his early experience of law and lawyers: and it was the more natural that he should caricature the lawyers, because the men of our profession are too often regarded as the Ishmaelites of society, and the law itself as the scapegoat of our social ills.

Dickens had a marvellous memory, like the most sensitive photographic films, and so his reproductions exaggerated lights and shadows and the resulting pictures were marked by caricature and burlesque. Caricature, the humorous exaggeration of characteristics, is always popular, for every one likes to see every one else ridiculed, and burlesque renders any subject ludicrous by an incongruous manner of treating it. So when a talent for caricature and burlesque is turned loose upon the unpopular profession of the law, the result is highly edifying to the laity. But the law had its revenge on Dickens, for in his

---

[1] 68 Edin. Review, October, 1838, p. 97.

later life he had two personal experiences of litigation which probably confirmed his early impressions.

In *Dickens* v. *Lee*, 8 Jurist, 183 (1844), Charles Dickens filed a bill to restrain the defendant from publishing a fraudulent and colorable imitation of the *Christmas Carol*, which was advertised as a "Christmas Ghost Story reoriginated from the original by Charles Dickens, Esq., and analytically condensed expressly for this work." To add insult to injury the defendant dedicated the work to Charles Dickens himself. Vice-Chancellor Knight-Bruce decided substantially in favor of the plaintiff, but unfortunately Dickens had heavy costs to pay, so that the fruit of his legal victory was nothing but a Dead Sea apple. In this case the Vice-Chancellor declined to hear Serjeant Talfourd, Dickens's counsel, causing that distinguished lawyer disappointment amounting to agony, as he had sat up until three in the morning preparing his speech.

In 1858, Dickens, having had a disagreement with Bradbury & Evans, the publishers of *Household Words*, and the partnership being dissolved, advertised the publication of *All the Year Round*, stating in his advertisement that *Household Words* would be discontinued. Sir John Romilly, the Master of the Rolls, held, however, that he had no right to do this, as the right to use the title *Household Words* was an asset of the partnership and should be sold as such. It was bought in by Dickens, for £3,550, and the publication of *Household Words* ceased.[1]

But Dickens had many friends among the lawyers. He had dedicated *Pickwick* to this same James Noon Talfourd, who afterwards was his counsel, in recognition of Talfourd's efforts in the cause of authorship, for Talfourd, in spite of Macaulay's opposition, had exerted himself in

---

[1] *Bradbury* v. *Dickens*, 27 Beav. 53 (1859). 3 Forster's Dickens, 239.

the House of Commons in behalf of the Copyright Act, from 1837 to 1842, when his efforts succeeded in passing the Act of 5th Victoria, ch. 45, on which the English law of copyright now depends. Dickens was then a reporter in the "Gallery" and doubtless made there the acquaintance of Talfourd, which ripened into a warm friendship; indeed when *Pickwick* was completed, the event was celebrated at a dinner, with Talfourd in the chair.

We will now follow the footsteps of the Pickwickians in their pleasant though desultory paths.

The Pickwick Club was evidently intended as a burlesque of the British Association for the Advancement of Science, which was organized by Sir David Brewster and others in 1831, but the machinery of the Club was soon abandoned and the book records only the travels and adventures of Samuel Pickwick, the too susceptible Tracy Tupman, the poetic Augustus Snodgrass, and the sporting Nathaniel Winkle. The illustrious Pickwick was a mature bachelor who had amassed a competent fortune, apparently in the sugar business in Demerara, and Snodgrass, in his minority, had been Mr. Pickwick's ward.[1] The story is said to begin on May 13, 1827, when

---

[1] The lovely Mrs. Pott called him "a delightful old dear," and Pickwick appears throughout the tale as an old man. When he kissed his hand to her at the Eatanswill election the crowd shouted, "Oh, you wenerable sinner," and, "I see him a-vinkin at her with his vicked old eye." Mrs. Raddle called him "you old wretch"; Mrs. Cluppins called him an old brute; his counsel drew attention to his age at the trial of *Bardell* v. *Pickwick;* at Bath the ladies of an ancient and whist-like appearance immediately saw that Pickwick was precisely the very man they wanted. At the close of the book he calls himself "a lonely old man." It gives one a slight shock to find that he could not have been much over forty-five or fifty years old, for when at Dingley Dell on Christmas Day he is asked to slide on the ice, Pickwick says he used to do it when he was a boy, but he hadn't done such a thing for thirty years.

Library of
Davidson College

Pickwick and his friends, in company with Alfred Jingle, set out for Rochester, where they arrive in time for the charity ball, when Jingle, arrayed in Winkle's "Pickwick coat," quarrels with Dr. Slammer, of the 97th Regiment. May 13, 1827, fell, as all the world knows (or at least knew then), on Sunday, on which day it is obviously impossible that English people should have a ball, but as we shall see, the date is wrong by three years, and should be May 13, 1830.[1]

Then follow in rapid succession the celebrated duel of Winkle and Dr. Slammer, the visit to the Wardles at Dingley Dell, the shooting party and the cricket match, and the elopement of Jingle and Rachel Wardle, the old maiden aunt, to the White Hart Inn, High Street, Borough. Here we meet Sam Weller, who directs Jingle to Doctors' Commons, for his marriage license. But Pickwick and his lawyer, little Mr. Perker, of Gray's Inn, save the lady in the nick of time. Perker was "a little man with a dark, squeezed-up face and small restless black eyes that kept winking and twinkling on each side of his little inquisitive nose as if they were playing a perpetual game of peep-bo with that feature. He was dressed all in black, with boots as shiny as his eyes, a low white neck cloth and a *clean shirt* with a frill to it. A gold watch chain and seals depended from his fob. He carried his black kid gloves *in* his hands, not *on* them; and as he spoke, thrust his wrists beneath his coat-tails, with the air of a man who was in the habit of propounding some regular posers." The remarkable fact in this description seems to be that the lawyer wore a clean shirt![2]

---

[1] Jingle refers on the opening day of the story to the French Revolution, of July, 1830. Mr. Percy Fitzgerald, in his Pickwick Dictionary, analyzes elaborately the chronology of the story.

[2] Mr. Blackmore, of Ellis & Blackmore, who were Dickens's employers, always contended that Mr. Ellis was the original of Perker.

Library of
Davidson C

Rachel being rescued, the Pickwickians returned to Dingley Dell and found that the lovesick Tupman, after Rachel's elopement, had disappeared with suicidal intent. They follow him to the Leather Bottle, at Cobham, and find Tupman absorbing fresh life from a roast fowl, bacon, ale "and et ceteras." After discovering the stone marked with the cabalistic initials of Bill Stumps (an episode which Dickens probably borrowed from Scott's *Antiquary*), they all return to Dingley Dell and then back to London to exhibit the ancient relic at a meeting of the Pickwick Club, and prepare to visit the ancient borough of Eatanswill, at the invitation of Perker, who was agent for the Honorable Samuel Slumkey, one of the candidates.

The chronology of *Pickwick* is a little mixed, but it seems to have been early in July that a memorable occurrence took place in Mr. Pickwick's apartments in Goswell Street. Mrs. Martha Bardell, his landlady, the "relict and sole executrix of a deceased custom-house officer, was a comely woman of bustling manners and agreeable appearance, with a natural genius for cooking, improved by study and long practice into an exquisite talent."

If the narrative of Pickwick's conversation with Mrs. Bardell is to be accepted as true, that lady might well have understood it as a proposition of marriage. "Oh you kind, good, playful dear," said Mrs. Bardell, as she flung her arms about Mr. Pickwick's neck, with a cataract of tears and a chorus of sobs; (although how one person could execute a chorus is hard to understand.) "Bless my soul," cried the astonished Mr. Pickwick — "Mrs. Bardell, my good woman; dear me, what a situation — pray consider — Mrs. Bardell, don't — if anybody should come." Unfortunately somebody *did* come, for at that moment Tupman, Winkle and Snodgrass entered the room and beheld their chief supporting Mrs. Bardell in his arms. The situation was, to say the least, awkward, and Pickwick's explanation still more awkward, so that Sam Weller's entrance was very welcome to Pickwick, who at once engaged him in a capacity in which he would have "change of air, plenty to see, and little to do, which suited his complaint uncommon."

The scene shifts to Eatanswill,[1] which has been identified as Ipswich, and there Pickwick participated in the election and attended Mrs. Leo Hunter's Fête Champêtre and has his exciting adventure in the young ladies' boarding school at Bury St. Edmunds, as a result of which he spends three days in bed with the rheumatism. Just as he rallies he is handed a letter, which he found worth reading, although its perusal doubtless did not tend to restore his nerves, now greatly shattered by pain and exposure:

"Freeman's Court, Cornhill, August 28, 1827.
"*Bardell* against *Pickwick*.
"Sir:—
"Having been instructed by Mrs. Martha Bardell to commence an action against you for a breach of promise of marriage, for which the plaintiff lays her damages at fifteen hundred pounds, we beg to inform you that a writ has been issued against you in this suit, in the Court of Common Pleas; and request to know, by return of post, the name of your attorney in London, who will accept service thereof. We are, Sir,
"Your obedient servants,
"Dodson & Fogg.
"Mr. Samuel Pickwick."

"Mercy on us!" said Mr. Pickwick, "What's this? It must be a jest; it — it can't be true. It's a conspiracy.

---

[1] Pott, the editor of the *Eatanswill Gazette*, consults the files of that paper for 1828, so the year could not have been 1827.

Ridiculous." Getting little comfort from his triumvirate of friends who reminded him of the recent embarrassing occurrence, or from Wardle, who calls him a sly dog, Pickwick forms the idiotic resolve to interview the plaintiff's attorneys in person, but prepares for the event by going with the shooting party on Captain Boldwig's preserves, where he got gloriously drunk and woke up in the village pound where Boldwig has deposited him like a stray beast.

The office of Dodson & Fogg was the ground floor front of a dingy house at the very furthest end of Freeman's Court, Cornhill, and the clerk's office was a dark, mouldy, earthy-smelling room with a couple of old wooden chairs, a very loud-ticking clock, an almanack, an umbrella stand, a row of hat pegs, bundles of dirty papers, some old boxes and decayed ink bottles of various shapes and sizes. Here Pickwick presented himself on September 3, 1830 (for the date of the letter quoted is certainly wrong by three years), and after waiting a suitable number of minutes was ushered into the private room of Mr. Fogg, "an elderly, pimply-faced vegetable-diet sort of man in a black coat, dark mixture trousers and small black gaiters, who seemed to be an essential part of the desk at which he was writing and to have about as much thought or feeling." Fogg, cautiously, would not begin the interview until Dodson appeared, a plump, portly, stern-looking man, with a loud voice, and thus out-numbering poor Pickwick two to one, they proceeded to bully him and actually serve him with a copy of the writ, showing him the original.[1] Pickwick boiled with rage and called the lawyers swindlers. This was just what they wanted and they called the clerks to witness, as Pickwick threatened to assault them. The prospective suit for damages, however, was avoided by the promptness of Sam Weller.

---

[1] Chitty's Archbold's Practice, 114. Sellon's Practice, 95.

"Battledore and shuttlecock's a wery good game,"
said Sam, "vhen you ain't the shuttlecock and two lawyers the battledores, in vich case it gets too excitin'
to be pleasant."

"Sam," said Mr. Pickwick, "I will go immediately to
Mr. Perker's.' "

"That's just exactly the wery place vere you ought to
have gone last night," replied Mr. Weller.   Mr. Pickwick
felt the need of a drink of something hot, but as he remembered (perhaps) Lord Coke's dictum in 4 Inst. 57, that
"hot water spoils the stomach," he mixed it with brandy
and then betook himself to Perker's chambers, at Gray's
Inn; but he must have spent an unconscionable time at
the tavern, for our veracious narrative states that his
visit to Dodson & Fogg was in the morning and that by
the time he reached Gray's Inn it was eight o'clock.   In
those old times this appeared to be the regular hour for
lawyers to close their offices, as appeared from the unbroken stream of legal gentlemen that met him in muddy
highlows, soiled white hats, and rusty apparel.   Perker
had gone, and Lowten, his clerk, was at the Magpie and
Stump, singing comic songs.   Then old Jack Bamber told
about the Inns of Court and their "lonely rooms, where
young men shut themselves up and read and read, hour
after hour and night after night, till their reason wandered
beneath their midnight studies.   How many vain pleaders
for mercy do you think have turned away heart-sick
from the lawyer's office to find a resting place in the
Thames or a refuge in the gaol?   They are no ordinary
houses, those.   There is not a panel in the old wain-
scotting but that, if it were endowed with the powers of
speech and memory, could start from the wall and tell
its tale of horror."

Dickens then, in the story of the Queer Client, undoubtedly draws from his own childish experience of the

Marshalsea, where on Sundays he used to visit his father, a prisoner for debt. "It may be my fancy or it may be that I cannot separate the place from the old recollections associated with it, but this part of London I cannot bear. The streets around are mean and close, poverty and debauchery lie festering in the crowded alleys, want and misfortune are pent up in the narrow prison. Twenty years ago that pavement was worn with the footsteps of a mother and child who day by day presented themselves at the prison gate. No expression of interest or amusement lighted up its thin and sickly face. His recollections were few enough, but they were all of one kind, all connected with the poverty and misery of his parents. The hard realities of the world, with many of its worst privations — hunger and thirst, and cold and want — had all come home to him; and though the form of childhood was there, its light heart, its merry laugh and sparkling eyes were wanting."

Lowten, a puffy-faced young man, drew a chair "close to Mr. Pickwick in an obscure corner of the room and listened attentively to his tale of woe." Dodson & Fogg's sharp practice excited his professional admiration. "Capital men of business is Dodson & Fogg," was the eulogy of Lowten, who, in the absence from town of his principal, promised "to do the needful" for Pickwick.

Feeling as all good clients should that having handed over his case to the lawyer "to do the needful," the responsibility of the case was shifted to other shoulders, Pickwick went to the Great White Horse Inn, at Ipswich, and with a fatality which seemed to attend him wherever the ladies were concerned, had the famous adventure with Miss Witherfield, better known as the Lady in the Yellow Curl Papers. This involved him the next morning in a quarrel with Mr. Peter Magnus, the lady's fiancé, when the latter on introducing Mr. Pickwick *without* the horrors of his night cap to Miss Witherfield *without* her yellow curl papers, finds that they have met before, but where, the lady says she would not reveal for worlds. So enraged was Mr. Magnus on hearing this that the middle-aged lady made up her mind that it was the duty of the gentlemen to engage forthwith in a duel, and that it was her duty to prevent it by informing George Nupkins, Esquire, the Mayor of Ipswich. As duelling was regarded by that magistrate as a "gross infringement of His Majesty's prerogative, expressly stipulated in Magna Charta, and one of the brightest jewels in the British Crown, wrung from His Majesty by the Political Union of Barons," warrants were at once issued for the arrest of Messrs. Pickwick and Tupman, although Pickwick had no more idea of fighting a duel than he had of marrying Miss Witherfield.

Grummer, the constable who arrested Pickwick and Tupman, was "an elderly man in top boots and remarkable for a bottle nose, a hoarse voice, a snuff-colored surtout and a wandering eye." Grummer, with his satellite Dubbley, a dirty-faced man over six feet tall, apprehended Mr. Pickwick at dinner, despite Snodgrass's objection that "this is a private room." Mr. Grummer shook his head. "No room's private to His Majesty when the street door's once passed. That's law. Some people maintains that an Englishman's house is his castle. That's gammon." Mr. Grummer referred, of course, to the well-known doctrine of *Semayne's* case, 5 Co. 91 b, as to which a modern commentator, Mr. Dooley, of Chicago, has observed, "An American's home, as wan iv th' potes says, is his castle — till th' morgedge falls due." In charge of these representatives of the law, and escorted by the entire youthful population of Ipswich, the Pickwickians were brought before the Mayor who sat in front of a big bookcase in a big chair, behind a big table and before a big volume. The hearing was amusing, for Dickens had evidently in mind some bombastic and ignorant Justice, whose court he had attended. Fortunately, Pickwick was able privately to inform the Mayor that he had received as a friend, Alfred Jingle, masquerading as Captain Fitz-Marshall, and thus obtained an honorable discharge.

On his return to London, Pickwick, we may be sure, did not go to his old lodgings in Goswell Street, but took up his abode in "very good old-fashioned and comfortable quarters, to wit, the George and Vulture Tavern, Lombard Street," and immediately sent Sam with a full quarter's rent to give a month's notice to Mrs. Bardell, so as to terminate his tenancy, and to bring back his "things" which he had left in the Goswell Street house.

When Sam called, Mrs. Bardell, Mrs. Cluppins and Mrs. Sanders were engaged in a little tea party, and when Mr. Pickwick's man was announced —

"Now what *shall* I do?" said Mrs. Bardell to Mrs. Cluppins.

"*I* think you ought to see him," replied Mrs. Cluppins. "But on no account without a witness."

"*I* think two witnesses would be more lawful," said Mrs. Sanders, who like the other friend was bursting with curiosity and apparently familiar with the "two witness" rule of the civil law.

So Sam chatted with the ladies, drank a toast, "Success to Bardell against Pickwick," and obtained in the course of conversation after the wine the highly interesting information that Dodson & Fogg had taken the case entirely on speculation.

Then they all went to Dingley Dell, for the Christmas festivities, and there Bella and Trundle were married, and Winkle danced with the black-eyed young lady with fur round the top of her boots, and Pickwick under the mistletoe kissed the old lady in the lavender-colored silk dress, and all the girls kissed Mr. Pickwick, and the fat boy kept on eating pies, and after all this fun the Pick-wickians went up to town to prepare for the trial of *Bardell* v. *Pickwick.*

But they found the enemy was also preparing. Mr. Jackson, of Dodson & Fogg, "an individual in a brown coat with brass buttons, with long hair and soiled drab trousers," called with a subpœna which he served upon each of Pickwick's three friends and Sam Weller, with a shilling apiece as a fee. Pickwick slept little that night; his memory had received a very disagreeable refresher, and so he started early the next morning with Sam, for Perker's office.

"This action, Sam," said Mr. Pickwick, "is expected to come on, on the fourteenth day of next month."

"Remarkable coin*ci*dence, that 'ere, sir," said Sam.

"Why remarkable, Sam?" enquired Mr. Pickwick.

"Walentine's Day, sir," responded Sam; "regular good day for a breach o' promise trial."

Mr. Weller's smile awakened no gleam of mirth in his master's countenance, and they proceeded to Perker's office, where they found Lowten driving away a persistent client, a miserable looking man in boots without toes and gloves without fingers. "There never was such a pestering bankrupt as that, since the world began, I do believe!" said Lowten, with the air of an injured man. "His affairs haven't been in Chancery quite four years yet, and I'm damned if he don't come worrying here twice a week."

"Well," said Perker, after a professional tribute to the smartness of Dodson & Fogg, "we've done every-thing that's necessary. I have retained Serjeant Snubbin."

"Is he a good man?" enquired Mr. Pickwick.

"Good man!" replied Perker; "Bless your heart and soul, my dear sir, Serjeant Snubbin is at the very top of his profession, engaged in every case. We say, we of the profession, that Serjeant Snubbin leads the Court by the nose." (Snubbin, by the way, is said to have been intended for Serjeant Arabin.) Perker is not very encouraging to his client. "We have only one course to adopt, my dear sir, cross-examine the witnesses, trust to Snubbin's eloquence, throw dust in the eyes of the judge, and ourselves on the jury." Pickwick, being an old bachelor, had not acquired that habit of unquestioning obedience to the will of a superior intelligence which in time assumes the rank of a virtue; indeed, Perker had already complained that Pickwick, like many a client we have known, had insisted upon managing his own case. But now Pickwick, following the "crooked cord of private opinion," made up his mind that he must have a personal consultation with Serjeant Snubbin, and after overruling his attorney's objections they went to the Serjeant's office in Lincoln's Inn, Old Square. Mr. Serjeant Snubbin was a lantern-faced, sallow-complexioned man about forty-five or fifty years of age. He had a dull looking boiled eye, his hair was thin and weak, he wore an ill washed and worse tied white neckerchief, and the slovenly style of his dress and his dirty office showed that he was far too much occupied to take any heed of his personal comforts. Now Mr. Pickwick, with Perker's assistance, stated his ridiculous purpose in calling upon his counsel, namely, that there was no ground for Mrs. Bardell's action, that he was conscious he was in the right and that, unless Snubbin believed this, "I," said Mr. Pickwick, "would rather be deprived of the aid of your talents than have the advantage of them."

Not only did Pickwick make this wholly unnecessary declaration to his counsel, but he also made some remarks about the conduct of his case before a jury, which, to say the least, were gratuitous.

"Gentlemen of your profession, sir," continued Mr. Pickwick, "see the worst side of human nature — all its disputes, all its ill will and bad blood rise up before you. You know from your experience of juries how much depends on *effect*, and you are apt to attribute to others a desire to use for purposes of deception and self-interest the very instruments which you, in pure honesty and honour of purpose and with a laudable desire to do your utmost for your client, know the temper and worth of so well, *from constantly employing them yourselves*."

Mr. Serjeant Snubbin made no reply whatever to Pickwick's extraordinary harangue, but rather snappishly directed that his junior, Mr. Phunkey, be summoned, and relapsed into abstraction until he came; and then having introduced his client, told Phunkey to "take Mr. Pickwick away." So ended the consultation.

If the senior Weller had then been called on for an opinion he doubtless would have proffered his well-known advice as to the two and only two defenses, "character and an alleybi." "I've got some friends," said he, "as'll do either for him, but my advice 'ud be this here — never mind the character, and stick to the alleybi. Nothing like an alleybi, Sammy, nothing." Indeed, had Mr. Pickwick made the acquaintance of the elder Weller at an earlier date, Weller, as an old matrimonial hand, would then have given him the warning which came too late. "You're never safe with 'em, Mr. Pickwick, ven they vunce has designs on you; there's no knowin' vere to have 'em and vile you're a considerin' of it they have you. I was married fust that vay myself, and Sammy wos the consekens o' the manoover." The caution is not unlike that given by Emerson, our American philosopher, in his *Conduct of Life*. "We are not very much to blame for our bad marriages. We live amid hallucinations, and this especial trap is laid to trip up our feet with and all are tripped up first or last."

The trial took place on Valentine's Day, at the Guildhall, and was presided over by Mr. Justice Stareleigh (who is supposed to have been intended for Sir Stephen Gaselee), "a particularly short man and so fat that he seemed all face and waistcoat." We will pass over, somewhat hurriedly, the report of this celebrated trial, as it is one of the best known scenes in English fiction, and familiar to every one.[1] The jury was called and among them was a chemist, or druggist as we should say, who asked to be excused because there was no one in charge of his shop but an errand boy who thought Epsom salts meant oxalic acid, and syrup of senna, laudanum. It is more than likely that Dickens had in mind the case of *Rex* v. *Terrymond*, 1 Lewin Crown Cases 169, where a chemist's apprentice was tried for manslaughter, in 1828, for causing the death of an infant by negligently delivering laudanum for paregoric. The apprentice was convicted and fined £5. Opposed to Serjeant Snubbin and Mr. Phunkey were Serjeant Buzfuz (who is supposed to be Serjeant Bompas), and Mr. Skimpin, a promising young man of two or three and forty; the former of whom opened the case with his famous speech and then produced Mrs. Cluppins, who testified to the occurrences of that fatal July morning. Pickwick, interfering as usual, of course, actually

---

[1] Serjeant Talfourd is said to have assisted Dickens in the legal points of the trial, and Serjeant Buzfuz's great speech is said to have been founded upon an actual case, 2 Atlay's Victorian Chancellors 163.

forbade his counsel to cross-examine and instructed him to say that the account was in substance correct. Then by a bold stroke Buzfuz called from the enemy's camp, Mr. Winkle, who gave his name as Nathaniel.

"Daniel," wrote the judge. "Any other name?"

"Nathaniel, sir,— my Lord, I mean."

"Nathaniel Daniel or Daniel Nathaniel?"

"No, my Lord, only Nathaniel, not Daniel at all."

"What did you tell me it was Daniel for, then, sir?" inquired the Judge.

"I didn't, my Lord," replied Mr. Winkle.

"You did, sir," said the Judge, with a severe frown. "How could I have got Daniel on my notes unless you told me so, sir?" This argument was of course unanswerable, and the Judge had the authority of Lord Coke, who remarked in *Floyd & Barker's case*, 12 Rep. 26, "*Absurdum est affirmare (re judicata) credendum esse non judici.*" I remember hearing one of our Common Pleas Judges in Philadelphia (now deceased) say exactly the same thing. Mr. Skimpin proceeded to cross-examine his own witness, without the slightest objection from Snubbin, and when the latter's turn came for cross-examination he entrusted that delicate matter to Mr. Phunkey, who was without any experience and actually brought to light the episode of Pickwick and the Lady in the Yellow Curl Papers.

Tupman and Snodgrass were the next witnesses and both corroborated their unhappy friend; then Mrs. Susannah Sanders was examined by Buzfuz, but this time Snubbin did the cross-examination himself. Buzfuz, emboldened by his success, made his only mistake. He called Sam Weller, who seized the opportunity, in answer to an entirely incompetent question, to tell the jury of his conversation with Mrs. Bardell and her friends, in reference to Dodson & Fogg. "Yes," said Sam, "they said what a wery gen'rous thing it was o' them to have taken up the case on spec and to charge nothin' at all for costs unless they got 'em out of Mr. Pickwick."

Sam's examination called for a judicial ruling on evidence. He admitted that he was in Pickwick's service.

"Little to do, and plenty to get, I suppose?" said Serjeant Buzfuz, with jocularity.

"Oh, quite enough to get, sir, as the soldier said ven they ordered him three hundred and fifty lashes," replied Sam.

"You must not tell me what the soldier or any other man said, sir," interposed the Judge: "it's not evidence." [1]

Snubbin, undoubtedly at the instance of his client, then stated, "to save the examination of another witness," that Mr. Pickwick had retired from business and was a gentleman of considerable independent property. As this left a pretty safe margin for the jury to guess at the damages, you may be sure Buzfuz had no objection and closed his case. Snubbin offered no testimony, and at once went to the jury. The Judge delivered a jelly-fish charge, the jury retired and came back in just fifteen minutes,— a very bad quarter of an hour for Pickwick, who put on his spectacles and "gazed at the foreman with an agitated countenance and a quickly beating heart," which probably stopped beating altogether when he heard the jury give their verdict for the plaintiff, with damages in the sum of seven hundred and fifty pounds. If Pickwick had been learned in the law he might have congratulated himself that the Ecclesiastical Courts had no longer jurisdiction to compel specific performance of the contract

---

[1] The ruling is cited in Taylor on Evidence, 567, but apparently the case is not referred to by Mr. Wigmore in his work on Evidence. If so it is the only reported decision which he has failed to cite.

to marry; as it was, he immediately announced his determination never to pay a farthing of cost or damages, even if he should spend the rest of his life in prison, and having learned that execution could not issue until the next term, at the expiration of two months, resolved to enjoy his breathing spell at Bath, for which they took the "Moses Pickwick" coach the next morning.

Trinity Term commenced, Pickwick returned to London, and it is worth while to observe that Snubbin and Perker so felt the hopelessness of their case that they did not even move for a new trial. Dodson & Fogg lost no time in issuing an execution against the body of Samuel Pickwick, who was arrested in his bed-room at the George and Vulture. Namby, the sheriff's officer, a man dressed in a particularly gorgeous manner, with plenty of jewelry, called at nine in the morning, when Pickwick, who was not fond of early rising, was yet asleep. He was hurried through the sordid details of the toilet and then taken without breakfast by his captor to his sponging house, in Bell Alley, Coleman Street. Here defendants were allowed a respite in the custody of the sheriff's officers before going to prison, in order that they or their friends might have a chance to pay the judgment. Perker, who had been sent for, urged him to do this, but Pickwick as usual was obstinate and declared he would go to prison that night.

"You can't go to Whitecross Street, my dear sir," said Perker. "Impossible! There are sixty beds in a ward and the bolt's on sixteen hours out of the twenty-four. You can go to the Fleet, my dear sir, if you're determined to go somewhere." Now if a defendant in the custody of the sheriff wanted to be committed to the Fleet he could do it by means of a *Habeas corpus cum causa*, which writ operated to remove the body of the prisoner and the whole cause. The writ issued, as of course, was returnable immediately, and in obedience to it the sheriff's officer brought the defendant to the Judge in chambers, who signed the commitment. The practice, as stated by Dickens, seems to be accurate according to the books;[1] the proceedings in the Judge's chambers, the office boys and clerks, etc., are so lifelike that they were no doubt drawn from his own experience.

The Fleet Prison was destroyed about 1846. For nearly a millennium, to use the word in a very inappropriate connection, this prison had existed as an institution so horrible as to be almost picturesque. Here were gathered the poor debtors taken in execution according to the old rule, *Qui non habet in aere, luet in corpore*, and put in the charge of the Warden of the Fleet, who was answerable either for the body of the debtor or the debt that he owed. The Warden made his profit from the fees he was able to exact from the wretched inmates, and somewhat resembled the landlord of a hotel from which his unhappy guests could find no escape. Indeed the wardenship was a lucrative vested interest, an estate saleable and inheritable like a manor. The debtor, with his hopes abandoned and his ambitions forgotten, was worse off than a criminal, for the felon could serve out his term. He was worse off than a pauper, for the law made no provision for his support. Nor could the creditor, if so disposed, release his debtor without cancelling his debt, and could only hope that the debtor's family or friends would pay that debt and procure the discharge. The debtor too often became a lost and forgotten man, penniless and destitute except so far as the poor box rattled at the gate and the cry of "Pity the poor prisoners" aroused the compassion of the charitable wayfarer. And yet Newgate and the

---

[1] 2 Chitty's Archbold, 941. Mr. Fitzgerald in his "Bozland" is very much puzzled by the proceeding.

Compter [1] of London were reputed to be still worse and the wretches confined in them from early times endeavored to obtain their transfer by the simple legal fiction of confessing themselves debtors to the king, for whom the Fleet was the appropriate prison.[2]

The law of imprisonment for debt was modified in England by statute in 1844, and finally abolished in 1869, at least theoretically; but the County Courts retain the power to imprison debtors as for contempt who refuse to obey their judgments. A newspaper has stated, indeed, that in 1905 over 11,000 were imprisoned for this cause.[3]

When Pickwick went to the Fleet, the prison had been materially improved through the reforms of Howard, but it was in all conscience bad enough, for, as Coke says, "*Carcer est mala mansio;*" though we cannot feel much sympathy for a man who could escape by paying a judgment obtained by legal process, unjust though he felt it to be. He certainly was introduced to very unattractive society by Roker when he spent his first night with Smangle and Mivins, and was chummed the next day with the drunken chaplain, the disreputable butcher, and the reprobate blackleg.

But as Perker should have told Pickwick, who found it out for himself, gold and silver, those "mute but moving ambassadors," were inside the Fleet pretty much the same as they were outside of it, except that

---

[1] The Counter, or Compter, of London (from *computare*) was a city prison for debtors and minor offenders.

[2] Œconomy of the Fleete, Camden Society, XII. Cf. *Worlay* v. *Harrison*, Dyer 249 b. 8 Eliz. An interesting account of the London prisons about this time is contained in "Police and Crimes of the Metropolis" [by John Wade, London, 1829].

[3] See as to power of the Court, article by E. Bowen-Rowlands, 18 L. Q. R. 243 (1902).

their purchasing power was not quite so great. When a man was able to sequester his property or income from his creditors he could live in the Fleet in comparative comfort. There were many cases, indeed, of persons who became used to the place, lost their friends, contracted new habits of sloth and carelessness, and actually refused to leave the prison when finally the opportunity came.

"They don't mind it," said Sam, "it's a regular holiday to them, all porter and skittles. It's the other vuns as gets done over with this sort o' thing; them downhearted fellers as can't svig away at the beer, nor play skittles neither; them as vould pay if they could and gets low by being boxed up. Them as is always a idlin' in public houses it don't damage at all, and them as is always a vorkin' ven they can, it damages too much." And then Sam tells the story of the dirty-faced man in the brown coat, a prisoner for seventeen years, who was allowed to go out by the turnkey and one night got back just in time to be locked in. The turnkey threatened if he did not keep better hours to shut him out altogether, and the dirty-faced man was seized with a violent fit of trembling and never went out again.

Now there was a Chancery prisoner who had been in the Fleet long enough to have lost friends, fortune and home, and to have acquired a right to a separate room. This he agreed to let Pickwick have for twenty shillings a week, and Pickwick hired some furniture for twenty seven and six pence a week in addition. "As they struck the bargain Mr. Pickwick surveyed the prisoner with a painful interest. He was a tall, cadaverous man in an old great coat and slippers, with sunken cheeks and a restless, eager eye. His lips were bloodless and his bones sharp and thin. God help him, the iron teeth of confinement and privation had been slowly filing them down for twenty years."[1]

But the poor side of the prison was the worst. When Pickwick looked down the dark and filthy staircase which led to a range of damp and gloomy stone vaults, he mistook them for coal cellars. "You don't really mean," said he, "that human beings live down there in those wretched dungeons?" "Yes," replied Mr. Roker, "and die down there wery often; and what of that? Yes, and a wery good place it is to live in, ain't it?"

Now Sam Weller had no intention of letting Mr. Pickwick live in the Fleet without his attendance, and obtained the professional aid of Mr. Solomon Pell, who had once helped Weller, senior, through the Insolvent Court. This learned lawyer was a fat, flabby man in a coat which looked green one minute and brown the next. His forehead was narrow, his face wide, his head large and his nose on one side of his head, as if Nature had given it an angry tweak. "The last Lord Chancellor," said Pell, "was very fond of me." "Pell," said the Chancellor (who, by the way, must have been Lord Eldon), "no false delicacy, Pell. You're a man of talent, you can get anybody through the Insolvent Court, Pell, and your country shall be proud of you." "My Lord," I said, "you flatter me." "Pell," he said, "if I do I'm damned."

The scheme concocted was for Weller, senior, to lend Sam twenty-five pounds on a confession of judgment, upon which execution was issued at once by Mr. Pell, and Sam was arrested on a *capias* and committed to

---

[1] But some of the Chancery prisoners held lucrative situations in prison and one solicitor actually practised there with much success. 2 Atlay's Lives of the Victorian Chancellors, 15. Sir Edward Sugden exposed Dickens's ignorance of Chancery procedure and the Law of Contempt in *The Times*, 2 Atlay, 35.

the Fleet, not very long after he left it at Mr. Pickwick's command and very much to the astonishment of that gentleman.

Pickwick spent three months in the Fleet, and toward the close of July those sharp practitioners, Dodson & Fogg, turned their batteries on their *quondam* client Mrs. Bardell. "Just as a matter of form" they had induced her after the trial to give them a *cognovit*, or confession of judgment, for their costs, and when they lost hope of getting anything from Pickwick, they entered up judgment, issued execution, and Mrs. Bardell found herself once more under the same roof as her old lodger, Pickwick, but singularly enough was taken there directly and not from the preliminary custody of the sheriff's officer. Our hero's chivalry was aroused and once more Perker was summoned. Notwithstanding Pickwick's habitual obstinacy he finally consented to take Perker's advice. Mrs. Bardell agreed to satisfy her judgment upon Pickwick's paying to Dodson & Fogg their costs, and in addition she signed a statement that the suit was from the beginning brought about by these sharp practitioners. These costs amounted to £133.6.4, which Dodson & Fogg received with great good humor, and the jocular remark to Pickwick that he didn't seem to look quite so stout as when they last had the pleasure of seeing him. What Pickwick had to pay his own lawyers Dickens does not tell us, but presumably as much, and in view of his extra expenses in the Fleet, Mr. Pickwick paid altogether perhaps fifteen hundred dollars or more, and spent three months in prison, for the dubious pleasure of supporting the Widow Bardell in his arms for a fraction of a minute.

Perker could not undertake to say whether the evidence which could be got about the conduct of the suit would be sufficient to justify the indictment of Dodson & Fogg for conspiracy, and an ingenious writer in the *Cornhill Magazine* for July, 1890, has made a most able and amusing defence of Dodson & Fogg, showing that these gentlemen have not deserved their unhappy reputation.

There is one more legal episode in *Pickwick*, the probate of Mrs. Weller's will and the settlement of her estate by Mr. Solomon Pell. The will was written on a dirty sheet of letter paper and had been deposited by Mrs. Weller in the little black teapot on the top shelf of the bar closet, at the Marquis o' Granby, and by it she bequeathed £200 in consols to Sam and all the residue to her husband, whom she appointed her executor.

What right Mrs. Weller had at the date of the story to make a will is not very obvious, as before the Married Women's Property Act of 1882, a married woman was unable, generally speaking, to make a will, even of personalty, for her chattels belonged to her husband, and naturally she could not dispose of these by will except with his consent. Possibly it was of property settled to Mrs. Weller's separate use.[1] But an unjust law can always be evaded. Where there is a will there is a way, and as women always have their way they naturally expect to have their wills also; so Mrs. Weller made hers. However, under the circumstances, it seemed to make so little difference that Mr. Weller, having read it to Sam, was on the point of putting the testamentary paper in the fire, but Sam insisted on a more formal settlement of the estate. Pell undertook the probate. The first thing he did was to demand £5, the second was to refresh himself with three chops, and liquids both malt and spirituous, at the expense of the estate, and then the will was proved at Doctors' Commons, the legacy duty paid, the business "good vill, stock and fixters" sold, the inventory taken,

---

[1] Jarman on Wills, sec. 40.

the consols transferred, and at the end Mr. Pell remarked to his clients, "You'll find my terms very cheap and reasonable, and no man attends more to his clients than I do, and I hope I know a little law besides."

Dickens did an immense amount of good by his novels in exposing the wrongs and cruelties of the older English law and the inhumanity of the existing social order. Ridicule is stronger than argument, caricature more powerful than a bald recital of sober facts. Ten thousand men and women read his accounts of life in the Fleet, and the horrors of imprisonment for debt, as told in *Pickwick*, for every one who read the actual facts, often much more disgusting, in the reports and the works of legal reformers;[1] and without much doubt these farcical *Pickwick Papers* hastened the abolition of imprisonment for debt and the destruction of the Fleet, so that the cause of humanity owes much to his humor and pathos. Had Dickens possessed greater legal training and a mind fitted for the requisite technical detail, there were many anomalies and outgrown antiquities of the law which he could have demolished.

It would have been easy for him in the trial of *Bardell* v. *Pickwick* to show the absurdity and the injustice of the legal rules of the incompetency of parties and interested witnesses. Mrs. Bardell, under proper cross-examination, might have exposed the weakness of her case; Pickwick, if allowed to testify, would have shown the strength of his own, provided he stood the test of cross-examination. But the idea seems never to have entered Dickens's mind.[2]

---

[1] *E.g. Case of Huggins, et al.*, 17 St. Trials, 298.

[2] Although now the testimony of the parties is admissible in breach of promise cases, yet Parliament by Act of 32 and 33 Vict. c. 68, sec. 2, required that it be corroborated by some other material evidence in support of the promise.

Now there is a sober lesson for us in the *Pickwick Papers*, the iniquity of speculative agreements as to costs and fees between attorney and client. We have all read Sharswood's *Legal Ethics*, and none can read what that learned and upright lawyer has written and fail to see how the practice corrupts and degrades the profession, transforms the sworn officer of the Court into a party litigating his own claim, destroys the dignified relation of attorney and client by making them mere business partners in a commercial venture, unduly encourages litigation, and makes the lawyer become his own Satanic tempter.

Whatever was the exact agreement between Mrs. Bardell and Dodson & Fogg, it seems clear that in England it was either entirely void as against public policy, or at least was subject to the supervisory power of the Court.[1] The Act of 33 and 34 Vict. ch. 28, provides that attorneys and their clients may contract in writing for the payment of fees and disbursements in respect to business done or to be done, either for a gross sum or by a commission or percentage, *but* the amount payable under the agreement cannot be received by the attorney until the contract has been examined and allowed by the taxing officer of the Court, and if the agreement is not fair and reasonable the opinion of the Court may be obtained and the Court has power to reduce the amount or cancel the agreement altogether. The attorney, moreover, cannot acquire any interest in any suit or contentious proceeding, or stipulate for payment only in the event of success in such suit or proceeding.[2] That a contract between lawyer and client for a fee contingent upon the successful event of the case is valid has not, apparently, been doubted in Pennsylvania

---

[1] *Drax* v. *Scroope*, 2 B. & Ad., 581 (1831).
[2] *Clare* v. *Joseph*, 76 L. J. K. B. 724.

since *Patten* v. *Wilson*, 34 Pa. 299, where such an agreement was held to operate as an equitable assignment of the verdict in an action of tort, and therefore good as against an attaching creditor of the client.[1]   In *Perry* v. *Dicken*, 105 Pa. 83 (1884) the attorney, who appears to be the same who figured in *J. Charles Dickens' Case*, 67 Pa. 169 (strange coincidence of names), was the only surviving witness as to facts essential to his client's case, and undertook with other counsel of record to prosecute the case (an ejectment) for the contingent fee of $5,000.   He testified, he won the case, he sued his client for his fee and recovered; and the Supreme Court by a majority of four to three affirmed the judgment.

We must confess with sorrow that for the last twenty-five years the standard of our profession in this and other states has been steadily deteriorating.   The lawyer no longer occupies the position he formerly held as a member of a class to which on the whole others had a right to look up with respect and confidence, and the Bench is not likely to rise much higher than the average of the profession.   There are doubtless other causes, but the capital cause is this professional and degrading practice, now so prevalent, especially in actions of tort, and most of all in damage cases against corporations, which calls emphatically for an awakening of the professional conscience and for correction by the legislature.   This is the duty of the day for those of us who wish the Bar of our state and country to regain its former reputation.

---

[1] *Phila.* v. *Terry*, 17 Phila. 275; *Fenn* v. *McCarroll*, 208 Pa. 615.

III

*The Law and Lawyers of
Sir Walter Scott*

The Law and Lawyers of
Sir Walter Scott[1]

"If it isna weel bobbit
We'll bob it again."

WALTER SCOTT occupies a unique position in literature. His fame rests on his poems and novels, but he was also an historian, an antiquarian, a lawyer, a judge and a clerk of the highest Court in Scotland. No less a man than Emerson said that Scott, in the number and variety of his characters, approached Shakespeare, and Scott's flatterers were fond of making a closer comparison, but Scott himself, with the natural modesty of a Scotchman, and the true self appreciation of a genius, said he was not fit to tie Shakespeare's brogues. He surely could not have written *Hamlet*, nor indeed could he have written *Rabbi ben Ezra*, nor yet *In Memoriam;* but the *Lady of the Lake*, *Marmion* and the *Lay of the Last Minstrel*, with their smooth verse and charming ballads, have never been equalled. His novels are wonderful. No writer has produced so much that is so uniformly good. He hits the gold every time. Stevenson, no mean critic, called him, "out and away the king of the Romantics" and "the best of novelists," but maintains that Scott was wrong in his history, and picks the *Lady of the Lake* and *Guy Mannering* to tatters, for their "bad English, bad style, and abominably bad narrative." Macaulay, on the other hand, was amazed by Scott's

---

[1] An address delivered to the Law Association of Philadelphia, on March 6, 1906.

skilful use of history in his novels. "Scott has used," says Macaulay, "those fragments of truth which historians have scornfully thrown behind them, in a manner which may well excite their envy. He has constructed out of their gleanings works which, considered as histories, are scarcely less valuable than theirs." "Yet," Macaulay adds with his usual snarl, "there are in *Waverley* and *Marmion* Scotticisms at which a London apprentice would laugh." This London apprentice doubtless is elder brother to Macaulay's celebrated schoolboy; but Walter Scott, when Lockhart kindly pointed out some little slips, merely said, "I never learned grammar." De Quincey alleged that Scott utterly failed in depicting the English peasantry, nor would this be surprising, for Scott never lived among them, and so, according to other critics, he has not been absolutely correct in reproducing the colloquial Scotch of the Highlands.

We can afford to pass over his slips in grammar, his errors in style, his occasional mistakes in history, for the sake of the vivid humorous narrative and stirring verse. But vivid and stirring as they are, there is not a visible trace in the whole series that their author was conscious (though Stevenson says all Scots are thus conscious) of the fragility and unreality of that scene in which we all play our uncomprehended parts. He looked on this strange world, so infinitely pathetic, so irresistibly comic, as substantial and necessary. No doubt of its reality ever entered his mind.

As Taine said, Scott paused on the threshold of the soul. Carlyle said there was nothing spiritual in him; the Mystery of Existence (with capitals) was not great to him. He quietly acquiesced and made himself at home in a world of conventionalities. But, as Carlyle graciously concludes, "when he departed he took a Man's life along with him" — which upon the whole is not very remarkable.

As Scott took the world as he found it, so we must take Scott as we find him, and acknowledge what Emerson calls "the exceptional debt which all English speaking men have gladly owed to his character and genius." He is indeed "the delight of generous boys." He who wrote that fateful tragedy, *The Bride of Lammermoor*, ("worthy of Æschylus"), and the *Heart of Mid-Lothian*, also wrote those rattling romances, *Guy Mannering*, *Quentin Durward*, *Ivanhoe* and *The Talisman*, and whosoever reads them, old as he may be, may become for the time a boy again.

Scott was a worshipper of the God-of-things-as-they-are, a rank Tory, a valiant Jacobite from a boy, unduly deferential to the Prince Regent; but he was upright, modest and fair-minded, he was gentle and generous and truthful, (except in one egregious instance), good humor streamed from every pore, he was thoroughly in sympathy with everybody, including himself, he was sane, cool and courageous, he was born under a dancing star; and when that fateful day arrived of threatened insolvency, he wrote in his journal *Venit illa suprema dies*, and without a whimper sat down at his desk. He wrote a volume of *Woodstock* (there were three of them) in fifteen days and said he could have done it in ten, were it not for his Court of Sessions work. The motto on his sundial was: "Work for the night is coming," and in his books he often says, "Tomorrow is a new day."

> "The sun set, but set not his hope;
> Stars rose, his faith was earlier up;
> He spoke, and words more soft than rain,
> Brought the Age of Gold again;
> His action won such reverence sweet,
> As hid all measure of the feat."

But I have no desire to don the waxen wings of criticism or biography. The subject of this paper is the

Law and Lawyers of Scott, and our purpose is to portray
Walter Scott as a lawyer and to trace the influence of
his legal training and study upon his writings. No one
reading his novels and poems without this thought in
mind can realize how much of their interest, learning and
humor is derived from this source. It is safe to say that
had not Scott been a lawyer, his writings would have lost
much of their characteristic flavor.

Walter Scott, the son of Walter, was born August 15,
1771. He died September 21, 1832. In his fifteenth year
he became an industrious apprentice in the office of his
father, a Writer to the Signet, and in the little back room
underwent the toilsome, but beneficial, drudgery of an
attorney's clerk, learning, what he never forgot, the
value of work,—

"That grips together the rebellious days."

He says that he disliked the monotony of the office,
detested its confinement, and reviled the "dry and barren
wilderness of conveyances," but he was ambitious, and
said of himself that when actually at the oar, no man
could pull harder than he. He made his extra pocket
money for books and the theatre by copying papers,
and once wrote 120 folios without stopping. He then
decided to adopt the advocate's profession, and from 1789
to 1792, pursued the regular course of study, including
Heineccius' *Analysis of the Pandects* and Erskine's
Institutes. The Scots law formed a complete and interesting system, dating as a whole from the institution of
the Court of Session in 1532, by James V, having its
composite origin in the Civil, Canon and Feudal laws,
English, French and Scottish customary law, with statu-
tory modifications, a tangled skein of many colored
threads, woven into a picturesque and serviceable tartan
plaid by men inferior to none in legal ability and learning,

for as Scott himself said, although Heaven did not form the Caledonian for the gay world, a Scotchman is a born lawyer. The Court of Session, by the way, was originally modelled after the Parliament of Paris and the Scottish lawyers frequently studied in Paris and Leyden.

Scott, himself, describes Scottish law as a fabric formed originally under the strictest influence of feudal principles, but renovated and altered by the change of times, habits and manners, until it resembles some ancient castle, partly entire, partly ruinous, partly dilapidated, patched and altered, during the succession of ages, by a thousand additions and circumstances — a comparison reminding one of Blackstone's similar description of the common law in his third book.

Scott with his friend and fellow-student, William Clerk, was called to the Bar on July 11, 1792, in his 21st year. With characteristic humor and at the same time exhibiting his fondness for the history of the law, he wrote his thesis (which apparently has never been printed) on the title, *De Cadaveribus Punitorum*, (Concerning the Disposal of the Dead Bodies of Criminals,) Dig. xlviii, c. 24, and dedicated the same to Lord Braxfield, the "hanging judge," or as Scott used to allude to him, "Old Braxie." He was a well-known figure on the Scottish Bench, curious stories are told of him, and he was the original of Stevenson's *Weir of Hermiston*.

In *Redgauntlet*, Scott introduces himself as Alan Fairford, his father as Alexander or "Saunders" Fairford, and his friend William Clerk as Darsie Latimer, the hero of the story. In the novel, old Fairford writes to a friend, as Scott, senior, may well have done,—"Alan has passed his private Scots law examination with good approbation — a great relief to my mind. His public trials, which are nothing in comparison, save a mere form, are to take place by order of the Honorable Dean of Faculty on

Wednesday first; and on Friday he puts on the gown and gives a bit chack of dinner to his friends and acquaintances, as is the custom." In the novel Alan's thesis does not concern the dead bodies of criminals, but is upon the title *De periculo et commodo rei venditae*, and according to the story, Alan studied law to please old Fairford, who regarded as the proudest of all distinctions the rank and fame of a well-employed lawyer, and would have laughed with scorn at the barren laurels of literature. Scott's description of Alan was true of himself: "He had a warmth of heart which the study of the law and of the world could not chill, and talents which they had rendered unusually acute."

In Scott's first criminal case, he defended a poacher, and whispered to his client, as he heard the verdict,—not guilty —"You're a lucky scoundrel." "I am just of your mind," was the reply, "and I'll send you a hare in the morn."

But when retained in a more important case, he was not so fortunate. The General Assembly of the Kirk of Scotland sat in judgment in the case of a clergyman whose name was M'Naught, though it should have been M'Naughty, for he was accused of habitual drunkenness, celebrating irregular marriages, singing of profane songs and dancing with a "sweetie wife," that is a lassie who sold gingerbread, or "sweeties" at a country frolic.

On account of the personnel of the Court, Scott could not have prudently made the obvious defence that the reverend gentleman had at the most been guilty of mere *clerical errors*, so he was unfortunately obliged to defend the case upon its slender merits. As he quoted more at large from his client's convivial ditties than was agreeable to the General Assembly, one of that venerable Court called him sternly to order, while his chums, who filled the gallery, encouraged him with shouts of "encore."

Disconcerted by these inconsistent suggestions, Scott made somewhat of a fizzle. At any rate, Mr. M'Naughty was convicted, and his youthful advocate walked out of Court feeling, as we have all sometimes felt, that the whole azure canopy had suddenly shrivelled into a blackened scroll. He was greeted by his cronies with shouts of laughter, and dragged off to a neighboring tavern where they spent the evening in a High Jinks with which the Scottish lawyers were wont to drive away dull care.

In *Guy Mannering*, Scott describes a High Jinks in which Paulus Pleydell, Esq., was found taking a prominent part when Mannering and Dandie Dinmont sought him out for advice. In these merrymakings dice were thrown by the company and those upon whom the lot fell were obliged to assume certain fictitious characters or repeat verses. Forfeits were easily incurred, and paid by additional rounds of drinks. Pleydell was grotesquely attired as King of the Revels. "It's him," said Dandie, astounded at the sight. "Deil o' the like o' that ever I saw." Dandie wanted to retain Pleydell in a dispute with a neighbor about a lot of land worth scarcely five shillings a year. "Confound you," said Pleydell, "why don't you take good cudgels and settle it?" "Od, sir," answered the farmer, "we tried that three times already; but I dinna ken, we're baith gey good at single stick and it couldna weel be judged." "Then take broadswords and be d——d to you, as your fathers did before you," said the counsel learned in the law. Dandie was at first about to take the advice in earnest, and goes away in sorrow, but afterwards Pleydell takes his case. "I don't see, after all," said he, "why you should not have your lawsuits too, and your feuds in the Court of Session, as well as your forefathers had their manslaughters and fire raisings."

Scott himself was no anchorite; he rather prided himself on his skill in making punch, and, as he said in his journal, he thought "an occasional jolly bout improved society," and recommended a little magnesia for the "morning after."

Later on, Scott defended a young man charged with homicide and secured his acquittal. Part of his brief is given by Lockhart in Chapter VII. It is a careful and conscientious though rather labored piece of work.

It must be confessed that Scott did not score a brilliant success at the Bar, although in a letter to his fiancée in 1797, he claimed that none of his contemporaries had very far outstripped him, and on December 16, 1799, he was glad to accept the office of Sheriff or Sheriff Depute of Selkirkshire, a position which paid £250 or £300 per annum, and did not conflict with his private practice, but rather advanced it. The duties of a Scotch Sheriff are, naturally, very different from those of the English official of the same name, as they resemble those of a County Court Judge. Scott's jurisdiction included generally all civil actions, personal and possessory, and certain offenses against the criminal law; and, in addition, he returned juries and executed writs. Scott's letters and journal contain frequent references to his duties which he discharged in a humane and sensible manner.

He often procured a settlement of insignificant cases; as he said "there is something sickening in seeing poor devils drawn into great expenses about trifles, by interested attorneys." But he also admitted, doubtless recognizing the legal mind and litigious nature of the Scot, that too cheap access to litigation has its evils, on the other hand.

In 1830, a convict attempted to escape from the Court-room. Sir Walter, with sixty years on his head, leaped, game leg and all, from the Bench and stopped him with his own hand. No English Sheriff could have done more.

Even before his appointment as Sheriff, Scott was incited by the writings of Matthew Gregory Lewis, the celebrated "Monk," to try his hand at ballad writing in imitation of the German of Bürger, and soon found that the "fair fields of old romance" were ready for his cultivation. His work in ballad writing, and the *Border Minstrelsy*, culminated in 1805, when the *Lay of the Last Minstrel* marked a new epoch in literature. The general admiration of this lovely poem led Pitt to appoint Scott one of the Clerks of Session, apparently discovering some connection between poetry and a snug berth, and, although Pitt died just at that time, the appointment was confirmed by Fox, as is gratefully commemorated by Scott in the introduction to *Marmion*.

Just one hundred years ago, therefore,— to be exact, on March 8, 1806,— Scott's appointment was gazetted and he took leave of one profession to adopt another. His salaries as Sheriff and Clerk of Session, aggregated about £1500; his duties in the first office were not burdensome, while as Clerk he was only occupied during the sessions of the Court. The Clerk's duties were not so light as he modestly stated them to be, but called for diligence, accuracy and regularity, as frequent notes in his journal attest, taking up probably about one-half of his time. For twenty-five years he held this office, until retired by disability November 18, 1830, when his salary was reduced to £840.

His place in Court is still pointed out, where he wrote many a page of Waverley novels, to the accompaniment of long-winded argument, for Scott was never disturbed by his surroundings. He confesses he sometimes took a nap. "The Lords," said he, "may keep awake and mind

their own affairs"; but when Court adjourned and his
duties were over, he was his own master and would pack
up his papers in his green bag and hurry off to meet his
friends at a "Gaudeamus" or to buy a fine print of
Charles Edward. Yet sometimes this official drudgery
offended him. "Old Hutton," he relates, "*parcus et
infrequens Deorum cultor*, used to say it was worth while
going to a Presbyterian kirk for the pleasure of coming
out, and truly I am of the same opinion as to the Court
of Session."

In 1808, Scott was made Secretary of the Scottish
Judicature Commission, which was appointed at the
instance of Lord Eldon, who had no objection to innova-
tions so long as they did not affect his own Court, which
needed them most. Scott regarded this as a post of considerable difficulty, as well as distinction. The Commission
reported in 1810, a bill which made great changes in the
law and led Scott to write an essay on Judicial Reform,
an able paper, portions of which are given by Lockhart.

Scott was opposed to the introduction into Scotland
of trial by jury in civil cases, which occurred in 1815,
and expressed his disgust with the inferior character of
the jurors under the new system. He was also much
opposed to the House of Lords sitting in London as a
Supreme Court for Scotland, and predicted from it the
downfall of the Scottish Bench, Bar and Law, and in
Redgauntlet we find one of the characters, Hugh Redgauntlet, denouncing the Scottish advocates as mongrel
things that must creep, to learn the ultimate decision of
their causes, to the bar of a foreign court. In the *Heart
of Mid-Lothian* he expresses himself in favor of public
executions on account of their effect on the spectator.

But while thus generally conservative, he was in advance of his time in advocating the abolition of capital
punishment for all save a few crimes, and its infliction

with certainty in all proper cases. He disliked the Scotch verdict "not proven," that *medium quid*, saying: that one who is not proven guilty is innocent in the eye of the law. He objected to strict rules of court, *e. g.* those imposing judgments by default, which are seldom enforced because the penalty is disproportioned to the offense, so that the rule ends by being a scarecrow. He thought that attorneys ought to be fined for errors or omissions in practice.

Scott loved and honored his own profession and respected his brother lawyers. He used to say, after he had retired from practice, that intelligent barristers were the best companions in the world and their conversation amused him more than that of other professional men, because there was more of life in it, with which, in all its phases, they became acquainted.

It is not, therefore, surprising to find Scott's novels filled with his impressions of the law and lawyers. He could afford (and so can we) an occasional jest at the expense of our profession or shall we say *craft*, but there is a vast difference between Dickens's treatment of law and lawyers and Sir Walter's. Dickens saw nothing good in either, and caricatured both. Scott, on the other hand, was an artist: he knew a thousand times as much about the subject as Dickens, and, in his fair-minded manner, endeavored to give a just picture of it. But, naturally, the scamps of the law play a larger part in literature than their betters, for a good, well-behaved lawyer is in sooth a very prosaic individual. We — let us say we for the sake of euphony — do the day's work for a mere living wage, keep our clients out of the clutches of the Courts as much as we can; we labor on our briefs which nobody reads, except, of course, the Judges for whose mental improvement they are intended, and when we die, our libraries, if we have any, are generally sold at auction.

But a bad lawyer is such a picturesque villain that he is the stock character of every novelist and playwright — Judas Iscariot, if he were not a lawyer, is said to have carried a bag, the universal badge of our profession, so our enemies may regard him as an honorary member of the Bar.

Scott puts in the mouth of *The Antiquary*, an estimate of the honest lawyer: "In a profession," says he, "where unbounded trust is necessarily imposed, there is nothing surprising that fools should neglect it in their idleness and tricksters abuse it in their knavery, but it is the more to the honour of those, and I will vouch for many, who unite integrity with skill and attention, and walk honourably upright where there are so may pitfalls and stumbling blocks for those of a different character. To such men, their fellow-citizens may safely entrust the care of protecting their patrimonial rights and their country the more sacred charge of her laws and privileges." *But*, "They are best aff, however, that hae least to do with them," said Edie Ochiltree, interrupting the panegyric.

In Paulus Pleydell, "a good scholar, an excellent lawyer and a worthy man," Scott undoubtedly reproduced some lawyer of his acquaintance, and Ticknor said, that in conversing with Scott, he observed the similarity of the author's opinions with those expressed by Pleydell in *Guy Mannering*. We have already noticed how Mannering discovered Pleydell on a Saturday night at the tavern where he was celebrating a High Jinks. On the Sunday, Pleydell was a different man, piloted Mannering to church, and then took him home to dinner, where he showed Mannering his library filled with books, "the best editions of the best authors."—"These," said Pleydell, "are my tools of trade. A lawyer without history or literature is a mechanic, a mere working mason; if he possesses some knowledge of these, he may venture to call himself an architect." . . . "It is the pest of our profession," continued Pleydell, "that we seldom see the best side of human nature. People come to us with every selfish feeling newly pointed and grinded. In civilized society, law is the chimney through which all the smoke discharges itself, that used to circulate through the whole house and put every one's eyes out." He sends for his clerk, Driver, who of course was at a High Jinks. "That's a useful fellow," said the counsellor, "and he's such a steady fellow — some of them are always changing their alehouses so that they have twenty cadies sweating after them, but this is a complete fixture in Luckie Wood's, there he's to be found at all times when he is off duty: Sheer ale supports him, it is meat, drink and clothing, bed, board and washing." Then Scott gives an amusing account, too long to quote, of how Pleydell and Driver got up an appeal case on a Saturday night, during a High Jinks. "Law's like laudanum," said Pleydell, in another place, "it's much more easy to use it as a quack does, than to learn to apply it like a physician."

Even Geddes, the Quaker of *Redgauntlet*, admits that he has known may righteous men who have followed the profession in honesty and uprightness of walk, —"The greater their merit who walk erect in a path which so many find slippery."

Scott is strongest when he writes of Scotland and Scotchmen. He often admits that he knows little of English law, and when he speaks of it, he is apt to slip. But in Scots law and the feudal system, on which it was founded, he was at home. There was probably no country in which the feudal system was more deeply rooted and there is probably none in which so much of its spirit remains to this day. In no country was genealogy more generally studied; for one reason the canny

Scot, with his bonny blue een wide open for the main chance, always considered the possibility of his becoming the ultimate heir of entailed estates.

Scott was proud of his ancestry. Some of his ancestors were Quakers, so he was proud of them, some were notorious Highland thieves, so he was proud of them; he loved a villain for a hero, if only he were Scotch; he loved the freebooter's border raids, the stark moss-trooper's wild foray, he loved the stories of the dark days when Scotland's forests were filled with wild beasts pursued by wilder men, and men in turn were chased with savage hounds — men of whom he sang:

> "Wild through their red or sable hair,
> Looked out their eyes with savage glare
> On Marmion as he pass'd,
> Their legs above the knee were bare,
> Their frame was sinewy, short and spare
> And hardened to the blast."

These savages ate their venison raw, squeezing out the dripping blood between pieces of wood.

In the time of Charles I, a fellow known as Christie's Will kidnapped a Judge whose opinion was likely to be undesirable, and kept him close until the case was finished, which was considered an excellent joke. A Sheriff who had become somewhat unpopular, was plunged into a boiling cauldron and furnished broth for his murderers. Among the most ferocious of these savages were the blood-thirsty Macleods, a tribe of Scandinavian extraction, whose feud with the MacDonalds is told by Scott in the *Lord of the Isles*. These terrible wretches finally discovered the MacDonalds in a cavern, built a fire at the entrance and suffocated the whole tribe. In 1814, Scott visited the cave and found recent relics of the massacre, bringing away a MacDonald skull as a memento. Once. James VI tried to civilize the Macleods by introducing colonists among them, but the Macleods rose against the intruders and exterminated them.

Scott was a gentle spirit, but his heart warmed within him when he read and told of all these things. After all, these fellows were Scotchmen and he was a Scot and it was all as glorious and grand as the sounding verses:

> "*Regibus et legibus Scotici constantes*
> *Vos clypeis et gladiis pro patriis pugnantes,*
> *Vestra est victoria, vestri est et gloria*
> *In cantu et historia, perpes est memoria.*"

We do not ordinarily expect to find much of legal interest in poetry; not only, however, do Scott's poems contain many legal allusions, but Scott has added to them frequent annotations. He appends to the *Ballad of Johnie Armstrong* the bond of man rent, showing the feudal service by which the Armstrong held his land of Lord Maxwell, Warden of the West Marches. *Lord Maxwell's Good-night* suggests the bond of man rent between Kirkpatrick and Lord Maxwell. Scott notes in connection with the Lochmaben Harper, the peculiar allodial rights of Bruce's tenants; the bond of alliance or feud-stanching between the clans of Scot and Ker, and he also refers to numerous unusual forms of feudal tenure.

The law of Clan MacDuff granted exemption from ordinary jurisdiction, in cases of homicide without premeditation, to any member of the clan who rook refuge at MacDuff's Cross. In *Sir Tristrem*, Queen Ysonde is condemned to essay the ordeal of hot iron, and Scott appends a long note on the subject. In the *Lay of the Last Minstrel* he refers to the "neckverse" of the 51st Psalm, which was read by those claiming benefits of clergy, to save their necks. Earl Morton claims his vassals best steed as heriot, thus provoking a conflict, so that:

> "The valley of Eske from the mouth to the source
> Was lost and won for that bonny white horse."

The oath ordeal is prescribed to Deloraine for march treason; we have the mutual defiance of the English and Scottish heralds; and the trial by single combat between Musgrave and Deloraine, so characteristic of the feudal system and ancient law, of which Scott gives a long description.

In *Marmion*, Scott refers again to the trial by combat and to the feudal tenure under which land was held of the Abbot of Whitby:

> "Then Whitby's nuns exulting told
> How to their house three barons bold,
> Must menial service do."

Most interesting is the fate of Constance de Beverley, "immured" as punishment for her sin:

> "Yet well the luckless wretch might shriek,
> Well might her paleness terror speak!
> For there were seen in that dark wall,
> Two niches, narrow, deep and tall; —
> Who enters at such grisly door,
> Shall ne'er I ween find exit more.
> And now that blind old Abbot rose,
> To speak the Chapter's doom,
> On those the wall was to enclose
> Alive, within the tomb; — "

Truly a gruesome fate, recalling Poe's tale of the Cask of Amontillado and Balzac's La Grande Bretèche.

But now comes Professor Maitland, who shows us in his essay on *The Deacon and the Jewess*, that we are all wrong about the word *immuratus*; that it does not mean "walled in," but merely imprisoned for life and fed on bread and water, a very unromantic punishment; in short, that we must not "take our *Marmion* too seriously." Such is our respect for this great scholar, whose mere guess is better than a thousand arguments, that we must place this story also upon the shelf where rest our shattered illusions. So fare-thee-well, O shade of Constance de Beverley, and fall upon thy bended knees, if haply shades have knees, before thy champion, who, after four centuries, hath rescued thee from a lingering and horrible death.

In *Rokeby*, Scott gives us the Statutes of the Bucaniers by which the pirates distributed their booty:

> "When falls a mate in battle broil
> His comrade heirs his portion'd spoil;
> When dies in fight a daring foe,
> He claims his wealth who struck the blow."

In this poem Bertram unconsciously declares himself to be the murderer of Mortham, and Scott in a note speaks of the frequency with which conscience stricken men, impelled by the Imp of the Perverse, confess or allude to their crimes, and refers to the case of Eugene Aram, mentioning also another case from his personal experience.

In *Rokeby*, Scott introduces the ballad of Wild Darrell of Littlecote Hall, with which is connected the name of Sir John Popham, Chief Justice in Queen Elizabeth's time. The tradition is that Popham acquired Littlecote Hall from the owner as a bribe for his permitting Darrell to escape the penalty of his crime. Campbell, in his Life of Popham, takes the story from *Rokeby* and Scott's notes.

We will now go through the Waverley novels and extract some of the more interesting of Scott's legal references. To collect all would unduly expand this paper.

Much of the humor of *Waverley* is furnished by the Baron of Bradwardine and Bailie MacWheeble, the latter belonging either to the clan of Wheedle or that of Quibble, both having produced persons eminent in the law. Bradwardine himself had studied law, but by never engaging in practice, had to the best of his inability, discharged the debt he owed to his profession. He was fond of interlarding his conversation with legal phrases to show his knowledge of the science, and his favorite theme was the feudal tenure under which he held his barony by charter from David the First, "*cum liberali potestate habendi curias et justicias, cum fossa et furca, et saka et soka, et thol et theam, et ingangthief et outgangthief, sive hand habend sive bakbarend,*" and as no one knew the meaning of all these words, his self importance was vastly increased. His tenure would be called in England grand sergeanty, and consisted *in servitio exuendi seu detrahendi, caligas regis post battaliam,* that is, in undoing or pulling off the king's boots after a battle; and although his only child was his daughter Rose, he persisted that his barony, on account of the nature of the feudal service, was a male fief, passing at his death to a distant cousin. After the battle of Preston Pans, in which the Baron fought on the side of Charles Edward, he insisted on performing the ceremony, despite the fact that Charles Edward was Prince, not King, and did not wear boots but brogues.

Scott describes how after Culloden, Fergus MacIvor is tried and executed for high treason — one of the blessings we are told, which England had conferred upon Scotland, whose laws in that respect had been milder, but the attainders of the Baron and Waverley were

removed by pardons secured by lawyers Clippurse &
Hookem. Colonel Talbot, in gratitude to Waverley,
purchased the estate from Inchgrabbit, the heir male,
and conveyed Tully Veolan to its old owner, burdened
only with a marriage settlement in favor of Waverley and
Rose; the story ends with Duncan MacWheeble singing
the Hymeneal anthem of how he circumvented Inchgrabbit and his lawyer, in driving the bargain; and at
the last the old man draws up "a wee minute of an ante-
nuptial contract *intuitu matrimonii,* so that it cannot
be subject to reduction hereafter as a donation *inter
virum et uxorem.*"

Scott refers in *Waverley,* and again in *Redgauntlet,* to
the leading case of Luckie Simpson's cow. It was an old
custom in Scotland for the landlord, as his parting guest
stood at the door, about to mount, to present him with
a farewell drink called the stirrup cup. Now Luckie
Jamieson had brewed a peck of malt, and set the liquor at
her door to cool. Luckie Simpson's cow came wandering
by, seeking what she might devour, was attracted by the
foaming beverage, smelt, tasted and yielded to the tempter. The unaccustomed drink mounted to the animal's
head, descended to her legs, and affected her understanding in both directions, so that her guilt was apparent
to the enraged alewife, who demanded of Luckie Simpson
the value of the brew. Litigation ensued, the Bailie
heard the case, and then enquired of the plaintiff whether
the cow had sat down to take her drink or imbibed it
standing. It being admitted that the cow had committed
the deed whilst on her feet, the Court adjudged the drink
to be a stirrup cup for which no payment could be demanded and dismissed the suit.

The plot of *Guy Mannering* was taken from the case
of *Annesley* v. *the Earl of Anglesey,* tried in 1743, 17
State Trials, 1225, and Scott appropriated the names of

many of the witnesses to characters in the novel, which contains many legal incidents. As Paulus Pleydell represents the respectable lawyer, Gilbert Glossin is the shyster. He tries to push the sale of old Bertram's property, in order to buy it in and get possession before the long-missing heir should return, it being understood that the property could not be sold for debt if the heir were living.

The examinations of Dirk Hatteraick by Glossin, sitting as a magistrate, of Vanbeest Brown by Sir Robert Hazlewood, and of Hatteraick and Glossin by Pleydell, Sir Robert Hazlewood and MacMorlan, illustrate the differences between the English and Scottish methods of procedure; the latter more resembling the French system of private examinations previous to trial, although the "third degree," as practised here, might give suggestions to both. Glossin being committed as accessory to the kidnapping of Harry Bertram, claims it to be a bailable offense and refers to a case where resurrection women, who had promised to secure a child's body for dissection, stole and murdered a child rather than break their word and disappoint their employers.

Those of us who have had the pleasure, after a funeral, of reading the will to the assembled family, will appreciate Mr. Protocol's performance of that solemn, but sometimes amusing, business.

"Mr. Procotol, having required silence, began to read the settlement aloud in a slow, steady, business-like tone. The group around, in whose eyes hope alternately awakened and faded, and who were straining their apprehensions to get at the drift of the testator's meaning, through the mist of technical language in which the conveyance had involved it, might have made a study for Hogarth." As the document was of an unexpected nature, with contingent uses to charities, the effect was startling — and produced much mortification, which is Scots law for mortmain.

In Scots law it will be noticed a testamentary disposition of lands was effected by means of a trust deed or *mortis causa* settlement, reserving a life estate to the grantor, quite different in form, however similar in effect to wills as we know them. However, a common lawyer must not venture to meddle with a Scotch will lest he be guilty of vicious intromission, and in addition expose himself to unfeeling criticism. To quote the elegant remark of Earl Douglas,—"The man sits full still that has a rent in his breeks."

In the last chapter of *Guy Mannering*, a reference is made to the macer's court, composed of tipstaves, as we should call them, who constituted a special court for trying questions of relationship and descent, the judges acting as assessors to their own doorkeepers. When Dinmont visits Bertram in jail, the keeper wants to lock up the jail, refusing to allow Dinmont to stay because he had committed no malefaction. "I'll break your head," was Dandie's reply, "if ye say ony mair about it, and that will be malefaction enough to entitle me to ae night's lodging wi' you ony way." The argument was successful, for as the jailer remarked, "A wilful man maun hae his way."

The plot of *The Antiquary* turns on the legality of the marriage of Lord Glenallan and Eveline Neville, but its chief interest to the lawyer will be found in the entertaining conversation of the Antiquary, Jonathan Oldbuck. The Antiquary had read law and made himself master of the learning of the feudal law, but being under no necessity to practise, had followed his natural bent and cultivated his taste for old books and ancient learning. He would ponder over an old black-letter copy of the Acts of Parliament for days rather than play golf; he would trace the vestiges of an old Roman camp; and he discovered a curious stone inscribed with initials interpreted in a learned manner by the Antiquary, and in a trivial fashion by Edie Ochiltree, reminding us of the similar story of the stone discovered by the Pickwick Club which, indeed, Dickens may have borrowed from Scott.

The Antiquary is ready to remind Dousterswivel of the Act of 9 George II, c. 5, against cheats and imposters, warns Hector M'Intyre not to interfere with the Sheriff's officer, on account of the Statute of William the Lion, against deforcement, and in the entertaining examination of Edie Ochiltree before Bailie Littlejohn, cites the Act of 1701, regulating bailbonds and so obtains Ochiltree's release on nominal bail. So he gives us an amusing account of the law of imprisonment for debt in Scotland, which, technically, was not permitted; but any one who disobeyed the king's writ requiring payment, was proclaimed, by three blasts of a horn at Edinburgh market place, to be a rebel and imprisoned by an elegant legal fiction, for his ungrateful contempt of the royal mandate.

The Antiquary delighted in the old-fashioned nick sticks or tallies used by bakers to record the number of loaves sold to their customers, just as accounts used to be kept by the Exchequer. The writer can remember, as a boy, that this ancient method was used by bakers in this city.

In the *Antiquary* we are told the story of the ghost who appeared to the despairing litigant and showed him the secret depository of the old deed, the missing link in his chain of title; and in the opening of the book, mine host Mackitchinson, speaks of *Hutchison* v. *Mackitchinson* — "a weel kenn'd plea, about our backyard; a ganging plea my father left me and his father afore left him. It's been four times in afore the

Fifteen, and deil ony thing the wisest o' them could make o't but just to send it out again to the Outer house. O, it's a beautiful thing to see how long and how carefully justice is considered in this country!"

"The clergy," says the Antiquary, "live by our sins, the medical faculty by our diseases, and the law gentry by our misfortunes." — But much of the Antiquary's conversation is like certain flowers that lose their perfume when cut. You must enjoy them where they grow.

In *Rob Roy*, frequent allusion is made to the contracts of blackmail, an ingenious arrangement on the Border, by which the most powerful scoundrel, such as Rob Roy, agreed to insure his customers or clients against thefts, for an annual sum. He then employed one half of his thieves to steal and the other half to recover stolen cattle. Those who received or paid money under contract of blackmail, were guilty of a capital offense under a statute of 1567, but as Nicol Jarvie observed, "if the law canna protect my barn and byre what for suld I no' engage wi' a Hieland gentleman that can? Answer me that."

Squire Inglewood and his clerk, Jobson, the rascally attorney, figure in this book; the former being one of the *Quorum* and *Custos Rotulorum*, an office of which Sir Edward Coke wisely saith, "The whole Christian world hath not the like of it, so it be duly executed." The examination of Frank Osbaldistone by these worthies is well told. Jobson has the statute law at his tongue's end, but it is a relief to know that finally he is struck off the list of attorneys.

Bailie Nicol Jarvie is one of the best of Scott's characters, and his description of life in the Highlands is amusing. "Never another law hae they but the length o' their dirks; the broadsword's pursuer or plaintiff as

you Englishers ca' it, and the target is defender; the
stoutest head bears langest out; and there's a Hieland
plea for ye." Rob, himself, cared little for legal forms,
for when he paid his debt, Jarvie signed the receipt, but
could not find two witnesses, as required by law. Rob
remarked that no man within three miles knew how to
write, and threw the bond in the fire with the words,
"That's a Hieland settlement of accounts."

In *Old Mortality*, our attention is arrested by the
examination and torture of Ephraim MacBriar, the
Cameronian zealot, by the Privy Council of Scotland, in
which both judicial and executive powers were vested.
Scott gives a most graphic description of MacBriar's
dauntless refusal to incriminate other persons than himself, his fearful torture with the boot, his persistent
defiance and his speedy execution for treason. It is
hard to realize that such things were done with the sanc-
tion of law little more than two hundred years ago.

The Heart of Mid-Lothian, that great prose drama,
marred only by its strange anticlimax (for Scott was
generally artistic enough to stop when he was done) is
replete with interest to the lawyer. Jeanie Deans is one
of the greatest heroines of fiction — yet not of fiction,
for she really lived as Helen Walker; and Scott truly
says, "in the State Trials or in the Books of Adjournal,
every now and then you read new pages of the human
heart and turns of fortune far beyond what the boldest
novelist ever attempted to produce from the coinage of
his brain."

The story is familiar. Effie Deans was indicted under
the Statute of 1690, c. 21, which in case of child murder,
enacted that certain facts should constitute legal pre-
sumptions of guilt, to wit: the concealment by the
mother of her condition, and the death of the child or
failure to produce it. The Act was passed apparently

upon the suggestion of the Court *Re Smith* (1679); 1 Fountainhall, 47, who referred with favor to the English Statute 21 Jac. I, c. 27, on the subject; and though afterwards modified in practice, the law was not repealed until 1803.

Passing over the preliminary examination of David Deans, and that wonderful and pathetic scene between Jeanie and Effie, on the eve of the trial — Scott never wrote a stronger chapter — we come to the trial itself. Scott disclaims the ability to describe the forms of a Scottish criminal trial so accurately as to abide a lawyer's criticism, but we must assume that this statement was intended to disguise his authorship, then anonymous,[1] and that his account is technically correct.

Scots law, more liberal than the English, allowed counsel to the panel or defendant, and Effie's attorney was Mr. Nichil Novit, her advocate was Mr. Fairbrother. According to the practice in Scotland, the witnesses were "enclosed," or separated from all information of what was passing, and called into Court when their testimony was desired. The writer has seen this practice followed in Jamaica, even in a civil case. When the Court opened, Effie, between two sentinels with bayonets, was arraigned to the indictment; she pleaded not guilty and both counsel addressed the Court, speaking to the indictment and the defense, viz. that the prisoner had communicated her condition to her sister. The Court then pronounced the indictment and the defense relevant and the jury was empanelled; the prisoner again pleaded, and then the witnesses were heard. It will be noted that in Scotland the accused is subjected to a preliminary examination. He may

---

[1] An anonymous writer, however, evidently an English lawyer, in 5 Law Review 44 (1846), severely criticises Scott for his inaccuracy in legal allusions, particularly in his account of this case.

refuse to answer, but if he answers, the record of the examination may be used as corroborative evidence against him at the trial.   Effie's declaration, accordingly, is read in full.   Her counsel first offered proof of character and then called Jeanie as his principal witness. She was sworn and certain formal questions were put to her, including "whether any one had instructed her what evidence she had to deliver."   It seems possible from this, that in the Scottish practice, counsel are not at liberty to confer personally with their witnesses, for Fairbrother to his great mortification, when he puts the crucial question, receives the reply that Effie had said nothing to her.   This ruins the case, for Fairbrother can do nothing but argue as to the legal effect of the prisoner's declaration, as to which he cites learned authorities, laying stress on the highly penal nature of the statute.

The Court charges the jury, who retire for conference; upon their return, they render a sealed verdict, a lighted candle is extinguished and the verdict of "Guilty, with a recommendation to mercy" is read.   The Court, in pronouncing sentence, calls the Doomster, a tall, haggard figure, dressed in a fantastic garment of black and grey, to repeat the sentence of death, and he adds the words, "And this I pronounce for Doom."

But there is another vein in *The Heart of Mid-Lothian.* Indeed this masterpiece contains many illustrations of the close connection of tender sympathy and genuine humor.   Bartoline Saddletree — called Bartoline perhaps after Bartolus, a learned Doctor of the Law, or perhaps after Bartolinus, another less celebrated Jurist, is an amateur lawyer, who throughout the story freely gives his opinion upon all legal questions.   His favorite book was Balfour's *Practiques*, his genius lay towards the weightier matter of the law, and he regularly attended the courts to the great neglect of his business, which Mrs. Saddletree conducted, a lady well qualified by nature and experience to assume at a moment's notice the leading soprano rôle in the matrimonial duet. Bartoline, indeed, was like a Territorial Delegate in Congress, permitted to talk but not to vote. His conversation is always interlarded with legal terms, he discusses in a masterly way the guilt of Captain Porteous, of whose case Scott gives a full account; and explains to Mrs. Saddletree the theory of legal presumption in Effie's case. "The crime is rather a favorite of the law, this species of murther being one of its ain creation." "Then if the law makes murders," said Mrs. Saddletree, "the law should be hanged for them; or if they wad hang a lawyer instead, the country wad find nae faut."

His account of the pleadings in *Marsport* v. *Lackland*, is unfortunately too long to quote; but we must notice his remark that the better the pleadings the fewer understand them, and his cold-blooded criticism of lawyers' fees: "After a', its but the wind of their mouth, it costs them naething, whereas in my wretched occupation of a saddler, we are out unconscionable sums just for hides and leather." Nor should we overlook the case of *Crombie* v. *MacPhail*, involving the law of stillicide or easement of dripping water. Mrs. Crombie owned the inferior tenement, "obligated to receive the natural water drap of the superior tenement, sae far as the same fa's frae the heavens on the roof of the neighbor's house and from thence, by the gutters or eaves, upon the inferior tenement. But the other night comes a Highland quean of a lass and she flashes God kens what out at the eastmost window of Mrs. MacPhail's house — that's the superior tenement. I believe the auld women wad hae agreed, for Luckie MacPhail sent down the lass to tell my friend Mrs. Crombie that

she had made the gardyloo out of the wrang window, out
of respect for twa Highland gentlemen that were speaking Gaelic in the close below the right one.   But, luckily
for Mrs. Crombie, I just chanced to come in in time to
break aff the communing, for it's a pity the point suldna
be tried.   We had Mrs. MacPhail into the Ten mark
Court.   The Hieland limmer of a lass wanted to swear
herself free — but haud ye there, says I."—Unfortunately here Saddletree is interrupted and we shall
never know whether he was able to have this delicate
question of easement settled by the Court.

That sombre and fateful tragedy, *The Bride of Lammermoor*, is drawn from the family history of James Dal-
rymple, who, as Lord Stair, was one of the most
conspicuous figures in Scottish jurisprudence.   His
daughter had engaged herself without the knowledge of
her parents and was compelled by them to marry the
suitor of their choice, with the fatal results closely copied
by Scott in his novel.

Edgar, the Master of Ravenswood, and Lucy Ashton
likewise become betrothed in secret and she, it seems,
was under age.   Sir William Ashton, her father, a lawyer,
was Lord Keeper, a politic, proud, wary and timid man,
who had come into possession of the ancestral estates of
the Ravenswoods by means of certain transactions with
the old Lord, Edgar's father.   While it is not clearly
stated, he had apparently advanced money to Ravenswood and had taken technical, though legal, advantage
of non-payment to obtain decisions of the Scottish
Courts in his favor.   These judgments, however, were
open to attack in the British House of Lords, upon
equitable grounds, and Ravenswood was encouraged to
appeal by his kinsman and patron, the Marquis of A—.

The engagement of Lucy was repudiated by her parents
upon the authority of the Levitical Law, as stated in the

30th chapter of Numbers, to the alleged effect that a woman is not bound by a vow from which her parents dissent. Ravenswood leaves the country upon a mission for his patron, the Marquis; Lucy, under command of her mother, writes to break her engagement, no answer is received, the day appointed for her marriage to Bucklaw is fixed, and finally arrives. Just too late, as the marriage contract is signed, Ravenswood appears, and to him the Reverend Mr. Bide-the-bent reads the text upon the authority of which he had declared the nullity of the prior engagement. "If a woman vow a vow unto the Lord and bind herself by a bond being in her father's house in her youth; and her father hear her vow and her bond wherewith she hath bound her soul and her father shall hold his peace at her; then all her vows shall stand, and every vow wherewith she hath bound her soul shall stand. But if her father disallow her in the day that he heareth; not any of her vows or of her bonds wherewith she hath bound her soul shall stand; and the Lord shall forgive her, because her father disallowed her."

In *Ivanhoe*, we pass over Scott's references to the Forest laws, the legal status of the Jews, *temp*. Richard I and other topics, incidentally mentioned, until we reach the trial of Rebecca for sorcery, in the conclusion of the book. Bois Guilbert had rescued Rebecca from the blazing castle, and brought her to the Templar's Preceptory of Templestowe, with the connivance of Malvoisin the Preceptor. Beaumanoir, the Grand Master, making an unexpected visit, is induced to believe that Rebecca had bewitched Bois Guilbert by her magical art, and the Grand Master at once asserts his power and intention to try Rebecca for witchcraft.

The trial is conducted by the Grand Master with elaborate ceremonial. He refers to the rules of the Templar order, as stated by St. Bernard, recites their infraction by Bois Guilbert, especially the chapter "*Ut fugiantur oscula*," and attributes his fall to Rebecca's witchcraft. Rebecca, interrogated in her defence and acting upon the secret suggestion of Bois Guilbert, demands a trial by combat, and throws down her glove which is given to Bois Guilbert, appointed to do battle in behalf of the order; all of which is engrossed at length in the official minutes of the Chapter. The trial by combat is appointed for the third day and Rebecca sends word to Isaac of York to send Ivanhoe to be her champion. Upon the fateful day the lists are ready, and all the preparations described by Scott, with his usual zest. Ivanhoe, of course, gallops up at the psychological moment, and the Grand Master throws Rebecca's glove into the ring with the fatal signal words, "*Laissez aller*"; or as we might say, "Let her go!" After the combat and the Templar's death, King Richard appears. Malvoisin is arrested on a charge of treason and the Templars, Grand Master and all, are expelled from their castle.

What powers the Knights Templar arrogated to themselves in England, and what jurisdiction they assumed to try and condemn persons who were not members of their order, are questions which Scott does not attempt to answer, and we are in the position of the Scotch minister who, when asked what he did when confronted by difficult theological problems, replied, "I look them straight in the face and pass them by."

In *The Monastery*, Scott, in speaking of the rural superstitions concerning fairies, mentions a case which came before him as Sheriff, in which a shepherd mistook the figures in a Punch and Judy show for the "good neighbors." He also refers to the old feudal rights of the Church in Scotland, and the obligation of tenants to have their corn ground at the mill of the barony, and using the technical phrases of *intown* and *dry multures* and *thirlage invecta et illata*, intimates that he talked not without book, nor does he hesitate to quote a sentence from the Decretals.

In *The Pirate*, Scott refers to the trial of Gow, the pirate, before the Admiralty Court in 1725, where Gow refused to plead, whereupon the Court ordered his thumbs to be squeezed with whip cord as a mild preparation for the *peine fort et dure;* upon which the pirate finally consented to bring himself within the jurisdiction of the Court. Scott notices the Udallers or allodial possessors of the land in Zetland where the Norwegian law prevailed, and the scat and wattle, hawkhen, and hagelef or dues from the peasants to the lords. He refers to the law of wreck, to flotsam and jetsam, to the right of property in a stranded whale, and to treasure trove, though all his statements are not entirely in agreement with the English law.

In *The Fortunes of Nigel*, the hero is about to lose his estates by eviction, under an overdue wadset, which is the attractive name of a Scotch mortgage, He came to London to ask of King James I the repayment of a large sum, which that monarch had borrowed of Nigel's father. As that wisest fool in Christendom was not such a fool as to pay his royal debts before he was reminded of them, the sympathetic aid of his banker, the celebrated George Heriot was enlisted. James then pledges his jewels to Heriot for an immediate advance of cash to Nigel for his present benefit, gives him directions to negotiate a loan to clear Nigel's mortgage and signs his royal warrant in addition, as security. Heriot repledges the jewels to old Trapbois, the usurer, for the cash, and obtained from the Lady Hermione money to pay off the mortgage or rather to procure an assignment of it, for it would seem that the mortgagee when given the money, could be required to assign.

M antime, Nigel having fought with Lord Dalgarno, his false friend, in St. James' Park, within the verge of the court, committed a breach of privilege — a Star Chamber business, he was told, which might cost him his right hand; so he fled to Whitefriars near the Temple, so called from the church of the Carmelites or White- friars. This precinct was known by the cant name of Alsatia, a name borrowed from the debatable land be- tween France and Germany, and had at this time and for nearly a century after, the privilege of sanctuary, unless against the writ of the Lord Chief Justice or Privy Council. King James I confirmed this privilege, it is said, by his charter in 1608. There is an interesting account of Alsatia in the introduction to Inderwick's *Calendar of the Inner Temple*.

In Nigel's flight he is assisted by Lowestoffe, a young Templar, chiefly distinguished by his performances on the French horn, so annoying to Counsellor Barratter, who occupies the chambers beneath. The desperadoes and vagabonds of Alsatia, living without the pale, had a semi-organized government of their own which Scott minutely describes. Nigel lodges with old Trapbois who steals the king's warrant from him, and is then murdered by an outlaw in an attempt to steal the king's jewels which Heriot had deposited with the usurer. Martha, Trapbois' daughter, however, escapes with and marries Richie Moniplies, Nigel's servant, taking with her all Trapbois' money, the jewels and the royal warrant. Nigel is sent to the Tower on a charge of treason and the king takes this opportune time to tender Heriot the amount of his loan, and demand the return of the jewels. Heriot cannot produce them, and the king, after torment- ing him for a while, produces the jewels which had been returned to him by Richie Moniplies. It then turns out that Dalgarno had formerly deceived the Lady Hermione by a mock marriage, and, the fraud being discovered, is compelled to marry her legally. This done, he claims title to her property including the mortgage which, however, Richie pays off on the last day with the old miser's money, returns the royal warrant to the king, and presents Nigel, on the latter's wedding day, with the title deeds of his estate.

In *Peveril of the Peak*, the two Peverils are accused of complicity in the notorious Popish plot. The account of Julian's arrest and examination before Justice Maulstatute, shows in an interesting manner the terror which pervaded the community at the time. Julian is committed to Newgate and afterwards we find him in the Tower with his father; whence they are soon taken to their trial before the infamous Lord Chief Justice Scroggs. Dr. Titus Oates was the chief witness for the Crown, and Scott's narrative of the trial shows that he had studied the history of the times and the State Trials. Fortunately for the Peverils, Oates was now becoming unpopular, and Scroggs, by the private connivance of Charles II, charged in favor of the Peverils, who were acquitted.

Readers of *Peveril* will also remember the trial and execution of William Christian, in the Isle of Man, who had incurred the enmity of the Countess of Derby, the island belonging at that time to the Earldom; but the limitations of this paper do not permit more than this passing reference.

Scott alludes, also, to the tenures by which real estate was held in Man. Scott states that the transfer of land was made in open court where the grantor delivered to the grantee a straw as evidence of title. Pollock & Maitland II, 184, refer to a similar custom in some parts of England. Citing Coke 4 Inst. cap. 69, Scott suggests that "stipulation" is derived from such a *traditio stipulae* or delivery of a straw, a fanciful etymology perhaps, but very much older than Coke.

In the story, the Countess of Derby purchased the girl Fenella from her master, a ropedancer, or mountebank, to whom she had been apprenticed, and Scott supports the incident by the case of *Reid* v. *Scott of Harden*, Fountainhall, Vol. I, p. 441 (1687), where Reid, who had bought a dancing girl from her mother for about twelve dollars, sued Scott, with whom the girl had taken refuge. The Court quoted the law of Moses, held that there were no slaves in Scotland, that mothers could not sell their bairns and dismissed the case. Scott adds with pride that he was directly descended of the father of this champion of humanity.

The mainspring of the plot of *Quentin Durward*, to use Scott's own words, "is that which all who know the least of the feudal system can easily understand. The right of a feudal superior was in nothing more universally acknowledged than in his power to interfere in the marriage of a female vassal." In the story, the young and beautiful Countess Isabella of Croye, a vassal of the Duke of Burgundy, invokes the protection of King Louis XI, as lord paramount. Her romantic adventures, perils and tribulations, and her safe and happy deliverance, through the bravery of Quentin, however thrilling, are many leagues distant from the subject of this paper.

Readers of that entertaining story, *St. Ronan's Well*, may remember the managing committee of that health resort: the Man of Religion, the Man of Mirth, the Man of Peace, Captain MacTurk; the Man of Medicine, Dr. Quackleben; and the Man of Law, Saunders Meiklewham. The lawyer's nose projected from the front of his broad, vulgar face, like the style of an old sundial, twisted all of one side. He was on excellent terms with Dr. Quackleben, who always recommended him to make the wills of his patients — a prudent measure, as the Doctor's method was always to "give the disease its own way at first and then watch the turn of the tide," and he used to say that "robust health was a very alarming state, as most sudden deaths happen to people in that condition."

The plot of the story turns upon the will of Lord Etherington's uncle, Scrogie Mowbray, settling the estate upon Etherington on condition that he should, before attaining the age of 25, marry a young lady of the name of Mowbray, and by preference of the house of St. Ronan's, with limitation over. Clara Mowbray, answering to this description, was engaged to Francis Tyrrel, half brother to Lord Etherington, who thereupon arranged a private marriage ceremony in which he personated Francis. The fraud was almost immediately detected and Clara returned to her home. The validity of the marriage became, naturally, a grave question, which Scott solves in rather a clumsy fashion by killing off the principals instead of obtaining a commonplace decree of the Court annulling the marriage, which a lawyer of his attainments might surely have done.

The comedy parts of the novel are sustained by the great Meg Dods and her lawyer, Mr. Bindloose, who was also Sheriff Clerk. Meg consults him professionally and he thinks she intends to write her will, which he says is the act of a careful and of a Christian woman. "Oh! it's an awful thing to die intestate if we had grace to consider it" — a survival of the ancient belief as to the danger to the soul of one dying without remembering the Church. But Bindloose was mistaken, for Meg came to report the disappearance of Francis Tyrrel and her fear that he had been murdered, with which theory Bindloose disagreed. "Be reasonable," said he, "consider that there is no *corpus delicti*" — "*Corpus delicti?* and what's that?" said Meg. "Something to be paid for,

nae doubt, for your hard words a' end in that; and what
for suld I no have a *corpus delicti* or a *habeas corpus*
or ony *corpus* that I like, sae lang as I am willing to lick
and lay down the ready siller?"   The lawyer explains
that there was no proof that the man had been slain,
and no production of his dead body. "And that is
what we call the *corpus delicti*." "Weel then, the deil
lick it out of ye," said Meg, rising in wrath and bringing
the consultation to an end by calling her counsellor an
old fool.

There is probably none of Scott's novels which contains
more legal terms and allusions than *Redgauntlet*, and
this is particularly interesting to the lawyer, by reason
of the *cause célèbre* of Peebles v. *Planestanes* (*Anglice,
Pebbles* v. *Pavement*) which supplies the comedy part
of the story.

Scott drew Alan Fairford from his own experience,
and Peter Peebles, "that dreadful piece of realism," says
Stevenson, was also drawn from life; called Poor Peter,
because a suitor *in forma pauperis*, a worn-out litigant,
half crazed by fifteen years' experience in the Courts,
with a new solicitor every year — he wished he had a
new coat as regularly — broken down with poverty and
drink, the laughing stock of the Courts and yet proud of
his notoriety, as the best known litigant in Edinburgh.
When asked for his occupation he said, "If I am laird
of naethin else I am aye a *dominus litis*"—i.e. laird of a
lawsuit.

Now, as soon as Alan had given his "bit chack of
dinner" and had put on his advocate's gown, old Fairford plunged his son into this whirlpool of a suit with
the encouraging remark that the young advocate was
like the young doctor, who must walk the hospitals and
cure Lazarus of his sores before he could be admitted to
prescribe for Dives when he has an indigestion. So

Fairford coolly tells Alan that he must argue the case on appeal upon the Tuesday following, and overrules his objection that his inexperience would be fatal. "Ye cannot spoil it, Alan," said he, "that is the very cream of the business; there have been ten or a dozen agents concerned and the case is come to that pass that Stair or Arniston could not mend it, and I do not think even you, Alan, could do it much harm." Young Domtoustie, of that ilk, had been appointed by the Court to represent the pauper suitor, and was so alarmed by the prospect that he fled the town, so Alan is forced to take his place. The case was an action for an account between former partners, with a cross action and divers complications of Scots law, including that mysterious process called a multiplepoinding which Peebles himself swore, by the *Regiam Majestatem!* was the safest *remedium juris* of all, as it might even be conjoined with a declarator of marriage. Scott in a note says that multiplepoinding is equivalent to what is called, in England, double distress, which, to the common lawyer, explains the obscure by the unknown, for double distress is itself a Scotch term for two competing executions. Peebles claimed there was not a lawyer in England that ken'd the nature of a multiplepoinding, but this creature of the law seems almost, if not exactly, our familiar friend Interpleader Bill, disguised in Highland plaid and breeks.

To add to Peter's glory, he had the good luck to provoke Planestanes to pull his nose at the very threshold of the Court, and claimed this was not a mere assault, but constituted Hamesucken, the essence of which is to strike a man in his own home, for in truth the Court might be said to be Peter's dwelling place.

It would be too long to tell the history of this famous case, how Alan, at the very moment of success, hurries away from the court room to succor his friend Latimer, how the case is remitted to an accountant to report, and how the angry Peebles serves both the Fairfords, as solicitor and advocate, with a complaint for malversation in office. He pursues Alan over Scotland and into England, demanding a "fugie warrant" of arrest to bring him back. When Justice Foxley asks him if he will take oath that Alan was a runaway apprentice: "Sir," said Peter, "I will make oath of anything in reason, when a case comes to my oath, it is a won cause. All's fair when it comes to an oath *ad litem*." But the whole book is flavored with the case, and it must be read as a whole to be appreciated.

We must pass over, with a mere reference, other passages in *Redgauntlet*, written as only a lawyer could write them; such as the law relative to the salmon-fishing with nets in the Solway, as practised by Geddes the Quaker, and the application of the law of riot to those who forcibly destroyed them; the differences between the laws of Scotland and England, by which it resulted that Darsie Latimer (or Redgauntlet) while safe in Scotland, was subject in England, where he had property, to his uncle, and guardian, Hugh Redgauntlet; the hearing of Latimer before Squire Foxley, who complained that he was expected to carry the whole law of England in his head and a *posse comitatus* to execute it in his pocket; the smuggling cases to which Scott alludes as coming before his Court in Selkirkshire; and finally the tradition that at the coronation of George III, the solemn challenge of Dymock, the hereditary champion, who flung down his gauntlet as the gage of battle, was accepted by an unknown woman, whom Scott for the sake of the story identifies as Lilias Redgauntlet, the romantic Green Mantle of the tale — all these things and many more may be read in this interesting novel, as reference being thereunto had may more fully and at large appear.

The story of *The Betrothed* was suggested to Scott by
the poem of the Noble Moringer, which he had translated
from the German many years before, and this was founded
upon that wholesome rule of the law that no man should
stay away from home for seven years, without writing
a letter to his wife to let her know that he is still *in esse*.
For if, after seven years' absence, he casually turns up
at the old homestead, he must not be surprised if he finds
that his domestic affairs are not exactly as he left them.
The Noble Moringer leaves his lady to go on pilgrimage
and pledges her to wait for his return seven years with
a day added for good measure. The time fairly flew; the
Moringer never thought of writing home, and the last
day came when the Moringer is warned in a dream of
what is going on at home, and when he wakes he finds
himself, by the kindly aid of St. Thomas, conveniently
near his own castle. In pilgrim garb and unrecognized, he
joins in the wedding festivities and drops his wedding
ring in his wife's cup.

The ring hath caught the Lady's eye, she views it close and near,
Then might you hear her shriek aloud, "The Moringer is here!"
Then might you see her start from seat, while tears in torrent fell'
But whether 'twas for joy or woe, the ladies best can tell.
"Yes, here I claim the praise," she said, "to constant matron due,
Who keep the troth that they have plight, so steadfastly and true;
For count the term howe'er you will, so that you count aright,
Seven twelvemonths and a day are out when bells toll twelve tonight.'

The Bigamy Act of 1 Jac. I, c. xi, excepted from its
penalties those who married a second time when the
first husband (or wife) had been beyond seas for seven
years — and Tennyson should have referred to this in his
poem of "Enoch Arden," where Mrs. Arden waits over
ten years for Enoch to come back. Very likely neither
Mrs. Arden nor Tennyson himself knew the law on the

subject.   Poets should always study law, as Scott did, but if more of them did so, there would be less poetry written.

The Supreme Court of Pennsylvania, in the very recent case of *McCausland's estate*, 213 Penna. 189, has applied this rule of seven years' absence in an ingenious manner, worthy of observation.

The Act of June 24, 1885, P. L. 155, has gone further. A seven years' wanderer is liable on his return not merely to find his wife married again, but his estate administered as though he were dead.   It has been said that this Act went further.   For whatever views may be entertained as to the sanctity of the marriage bond, all persons are singularly unanimous in maintaining their rights of property.   Naturally the operation of this statute met with opposition.   In the celebrated case of *Cunnius* v. *Reading School District*, 21 Pa. Sup. Court 340; 206 Penna. 469; 198 U. S. 458; its constitutionality was tested in all the judicial laboratories and came out pure gold.

It has been often stated that this rule of the presumption of death from seven years' absence is of common law origin.   Such is or was the general impression, but see notable matter hereof in the exposition of Professor Thayer in his classical work on Evidence, whereof, as Lord Coke would say, you may disport yourselves for a time.   He concludes that while death has always been inferred from long absence, the establishment of the seven-year period has been quite modern.

In the short story of *The Two Drovers*, Scott gives us a tragedy from life.   Robin, in a fit of vengeful passion, having killed his friend, Harry Wakefield, was tried for murder, and Scott, who happened to be present at the trial, which took place in Carlisle, made a very powerful story of it.   He narrates, in particular, the Judge's charge, dwelling on the fact that two hours elapsed between the injury received by the prisoner and his fatal retaliation, thus showing the prisoner's deliberate intent. The High-lander, condemned to death, acknowledged the justice of his sentence, expressing, with unconscious rhythm the old *lex talionis* —"I give a life for the life I took and what can I do more?"

In *The Talisman*, Scott refers to the Assize of Jerusalem, that compendium of feudal law compiled for the govern-ment of the kingdom of Palestine when conquered from the Saracens. As an instance of the attachment of the Frankish invaders to their feudal customs it is also said that Richard I tried to import the Forest laws into Palestine.

Readers of the novel will remember that Conrade of Montserrat stole from its place the banner of England and was detected by the sagacity of Roswal, the hound. Richard thereupon charged Montserrat with the offense. "Murderers and robbers have been convicted," said he to the King of France, "and suffered death under such evi-dence, and men have said that the finger of God was in it. In thine own land, royal brother, and upon such an oc-casion, the matter was tried by a solemn duel betwixt the dog and the man, as appellant and defendant, in a challenge of murder. The dog was victorious, the man was punished, and the crime was confessed." Scott probably referred to the celebrated case of the Dog of Montargis; but this incident is supposed to have taken place about 1371, so that a reference to it by King Richard is a clear anachronism, though excusable enough in the circumstances. Scott describes in detail, as he loved to do, the judicial combat which ensued between Sir Kenneth, as champion of King Richard, and Con-rade of Montserrat, who is defeated and confesses his treason.

The dramatic crisis of the *Fair Maid of Perth* is the ordeal of Bier right for the detection of the murderer of Oliver Proudfute. This ancient method of trial was founded on the belief that at the touch or even approach of the murderer, the body of his victim would bleed afresh. Scott refers to it in his ballad of *Earl Richard:*

> "The maiden touched that clay cauld corpse,
>   A drap it never bled,
>   The ladye laid her hand on him
>   And soon the ground was red."

This sort of evidence seems to have been recognized in Scottish jurisprudence, at least in the *Auchindrane case*, on which Scott founded his dramatic poem of *Auchindrane*, the corpse bled at the approach of the murderer's innocent daughter, and the phenomenon naturally attracted attention. As late as 1688, in the High Court of Justiciary at Edinburgh, in the Standsfield case, Philip Standsfield, suspected of having murdered his father, touched the body, when the blood instantly gushed forth, which circumstance was included in the libel or indictment against him. The case is quite fully reported in 11 State Trials, 1371, and there are some remarks concerning it in Scott's *Chronological Notes of Scottish Affairs* from the diary of Lord Fountainhall. Henry C. Lea examines the subject learnedly in *Superstition and Force* and even states that in Pennsylvania, in 1833, evidence of this kind was allowed to go to the jury. The writer remembers that, according to the newspaper reports of a murder a few years ago in New Jersey, the relatives of the deceased made an attempt to have a suspected prisoner touch the body, and Mr. Lea refers to some similar cases. Scott makes a very skillful use of this superstition in the *Fair Maid*, and his description of the ordeal in the Church of St. John is well done. Magdalen Proudfute, the wife of the murdered man, appeals Sir John Ramorny for the murder of her husband by him or one of his household. One by one they pass by the bier and make the sign of the cross on the dead man's breast. When it comes to the turn of Bonthron, the real murderer, he declines the ordeal and demands, as he had a right, the judicial combat, which is accepted by Smith, the widow's champion. The combat is minutely described, and Smith defeats Bonthron, who is condemned to be hung.

Scott utilizes in his story the feud between two powerful clans who, animated by the *perfervidum ingenium Scotorum*, seemed bent on mutual extermination. It was finally agreed to terminate the quarrel in a *quasi-*judicial manner by a battle between thirty champions on each side, which was actually fought in 1396, before King Robert III and the whole court of Scotland, and to give greater eclat to the performance, it was reserved for Palm Sunday. They were lusty champions, true to their word, especially when they threatened revenge. Simon Glover remarked of the Highland chief, Gilchrist, — "Saving that he is hasty in homicide, I have nowhere seen a man who walketh a more just and upright path." This combat between the clans Chattan and Kay is examined at length by George Neilson in his *Trial by Combat*.

Scott also alludes to the power of the magistrates of Perth to execute, without trial, a person taken red-handed, according to what was called Jedwood justice — "hang in haste and try at leisure" — something like the more peaceful maxim of our day, "Vote first and discuss it afterwards." After this fashion, Earl Douglas hangs the murderers of the Prince, and then takes the verdict of guilty from his jury of Jedwood men.

Scott, in his introduction to the *Border Minstrelsy*, speaks also of Lydford law, a similar custom in Devonshire: —

> "I oft have heard of Lydford law,
> How in the morn they hang and draw,
> And sit in judgment after."

so that the Lynch law of our own country has a very ancient and respectable pedigree.

The scene of *Anne of Geierstein* is laid in Switzerland and France in the latter part of the fifteenth century, and Scott utilizes for the framework of his story the Vehmic tribunals, which originated in Westphalia and exercised such a mysterious and potent influence. This secret and oath-bound court assumed criminal jurisdiction of the widest range. Thieves and murderers caught in the act were executed without trial and without delay by Judge Lynch's cousin-german. Other offenders, including those who committed any act alleged to offend against honor or religion, or even dared to defy the authority of the Holy Vehm, were arrested, subjected to rigorous and inquisitorial examination, tried and if found guilty, executed by a tribunal, the very members of which were often unknown to one another. In his introduction, Scott quotes from Palgrave's *English Commonwealth* an account of the origin and method of this peculiar court which is stated to be a survival from pagan times, and connected with the ancient Saxon religion. The subject had long interested Scott. He made it the subject of his dramas, *The House of Aspen* and *Goetz of Berlichingen* which he had translated from Goethe in 1799, and, thirty years after, he returned to it in *Anne of Geierstein*. Andrew D. White in his recent autobiography says that he was incited to the study of history by reading *Quentin Durward* and *Anne of Geierstein*.

In *The Surgeon's Daughter*, Scott introduces Mr. Lawford, the town clerk, a man of sense and humanity, as well as law. Mr. Gray, the surgeon, calls for his aid when the Jewess, Lilia, is about to be arrested for treason. Despite her illness and danger of death, Mr. Lawford admits that the warrant must be executed, "for these evils," he says, "are only contingent, not direct and immediate consequences." He plumes himself not a little on his knowledge of law and of the world, thanked the Lord that they had nothing to do with English practice on this side of the Border, and speaks a word in favor of the Jews — "They are well attached to Government; they hate the Pope, the Devil and the Pretender as much as any honest man among ourselves." To which the Surgeon replied that he could not admire either of those three gentlemen.

In conclusion, the object of this paper has been to show how Scott's legal learning and training influenced his writings; perhaps this object has been accomplished, although of necessity much has been omitted for want of space, as any student of Scott's writings may readily perceive. It is difficult to keep the straight path of our subject while reading those brilliant novels, so stirring in narrative, so humorous in dialogue, so interesting in historical allusions, so absorbing in their plots. They swarm with life. What characters Scott has created! Caleb Balderston, Jonathan Oldbuck, Peter Peebles, Nicol Jarvie, Dugald Dalgetty, Meg Merrilies, Jeanie Deans, Meg Dods, Diana Vernon, and Rebecca — the female faction is well represented — and there are many more. By the *Regiam Majestatem!* these are real people, they are living now, and will live forever. To read Scott is almost enough to make any man willing to be a Scotchman, quite enough to thrill those of us in whose veins runs Scottish blood, and much more than enough to make all of us lawyers feel proud that this Scott was a lawyer. What a wonderful world does this Wizard of the North show us as we gaze into his magic drop of ink! Princes and peasants, cavaliers and covenanters, priests and puritans, lords and ladies gay, monks and maidens on their palfreys white, the moated castles and the dungeons deep, the knights of long ago with "many a crest that is famous in story," and heralds "red and blue and green with all their trumpery." And as the vision fades we can almost hear the soft Scotch melodies, now merry, now mournful, echoing from the northern hills, while the poet sings:

> "Harp of the North, farewell! The hills grow dark,
>   On purple peaks a deeper shade descending;
> In twilight copse the glow-worm lights her spark,
>   The deer, half seen, are to the covert wending.
> Hark! as my lingering footsteps slow retire,
>   Some Spirit of the Air has waked thy string!
> 'Tis now a seraph bold, with touch of fire,
>   'Tis now the brush of Fairy's frolic wing.
> Receding now, the dying numbers ring
>   Fainter and fainter down the rugged dell,
> And now the mountain breezes scarcely bring
>   A wandering witch note of the distant spell —
> And now, 'tis silent all! Enchantress, fare thee well!"

IV

*The Law and Lawyers of
Honoré de Balzac*

The Law and Lawyers of Honoré de Balzac[1]

The connection between Literature and Law, while not always apparent to him who reads the first without some knowledge of the second, is nevertheless frequent and close. The history of law is the history of civilization, and law itself is only the blessed tie that binds human society together. The novel is the picture of society, and must either implicitly or explicitly be conditioned by the law of its time, just as it must reflect social conventions and customs.

A great many great authors have studied law, though comparatively few of them have known how to use their knowledge. The novels of Dickens and Scott owe much of their humor and interest to their authors' skillful use of their information, but neither Dickens nor Scott surpassed Balzac in either information or skill.

Brilliant writers, like cut diamonds, are many-sided. Balzac's characters, as portrayed in his novels, included men and women of every walk of life, of every profession and occupation, of every grade of education, of every variation of virtue and vice. He played upon a harp of a thousand strings, though not all the spirits of just men made perfect, and in so doing he, more than any other novelist, has disclosed in his writings his own views upon every phase of the social organism.

If you want to obtain a just estimate of a novelist and his work, ascertain, if it be possible, his views upon the

---

[1] A paper read before the Pennsylvania Bar Association, June 20, 1911,

four subjects which are of all the most difficult: *Religion*, or the relation of man to the spiritual life; *Science*, or the relation of man to the material world; *Woman*, or the relation of the sexes; and *Law* (including *Politics*), or the relation of man to society.

In Religion, Balzac professed himself a devoted adherent to the Catholic Church, which he styled in *Le Médecin de Campagne* (The Country Doctor), "a complete system for the repression of the depraved tendencies of mankind," rather than the cold negations of Protestantism. Yet he was fair enough to do full justice to the Jansenists, whose system had much resemblance to practical Protestantism. But it is apparent from many passages in his novels, and particularly in *The Country Doctor*, and *Le Curé de Village* (The Country Curate), that his Catholicism was political rather than religious. It was a cult rather than a belief. He admired the Church as the conservative power in the State and Society. So far as he had any personal religion he was a deist and a mystic; and, indeed, he held that mysticism was the pure essence of Christianity. It is in the vague aspirations of Louis Lambert, and the influences of Boehm and Swedenborg in *Séraphita*, that we find his real beliefs.

His views as to Science correspond with his views as to Religion. As in the latter he was a mystic, so in the former he was an idealist.

The reader of his life will be amused by his scheme to invent a substitute for paper, which he reproduced in the autobiographical part of *Lost Illusions;* by his dream of making a fortune out of the old rubbish in the Sardinian mines; by his grotesque plan to raise pineapples in his country garden; by his wild project to transport oak timber from Russia to France without counting the cost of freight; by his airy visions of wealth from dairy farming and raising grapes and walnuts. Mulberry Sellers would have embraced him as a brother. In accordance with the equitable maxim, of which he had never heard, he considered that as done which ought to have been done. He had the idea — never mind the dull details. In medical science he was led away by everything that was new and strange. He was fascinated by the theories of Mesmer, Hahnemann and Gall. He studied astrology, second sight, spiritualism, and consulted fortune tellers.

But as Lawton says: "His scientific knowledge was superficial in nearly every branch. It was his divination that was great." In *Modeste Mignon* he imagined a reaping machine that should do the work of ten men, and in *Catherine de Médicis* he anticipated some theories of modern science. "Everything here below," said Cosmo, the astrologer, "is the outcome of a slow transformation, but all the various forms are of one and the same matter"; and this idea he afterwards elaborated in *La Recherche de l'Absolu* (The Quest of the Absolute), and again in Louis Lambert: "Everything here on earth is produced by an ethereal substance which is the common element of various phenomena, known inaccurately as electricity, heat, light, the galvanic fluid, the magnetic fluid, and so forth. The sum total of the transformations of this substance under various forms constitutes what is commonly known as matter."

Balzac's opinion of Woman, like all his opinions, was essentially conservative, and perhaps best expressed in *La Femme de Trente Ans* (A Woman of Thirty), *Une Fille d'Ève* (A Daughter of Eve), and *Mémoires de Deux Jeunes Mariées* (Letters of Two Brides). Though woman is the most perfect of creations, and man a poor creature in comparison, yet she is inferior because she is ruled by her instincts and emotions, and is distinctly subordinate to man. To paraphrase the words of the great draughtsman

of the Declaration of Independence, he holds this truth to
be self-evident — that men and women are created
unequal. Men know they are the superiors of women,
and women, down in the bottom of their little boots, that
is, in their soles, know it themselves. The state of celib-
acy is contrary to perfect society; a childless woman,
he says, is a monstrosity of nature; he made all manner
of fun of old maids, and he maintained that woman's
mission was to be the mother of the family of a man, and
that through her the family must be conserved as the basic
unit of human society. The viaticum of married life is
resignation and self-sacrifice; the bonds of habit, he says,
are better than love any day, while society substitutes
a lasting sentiment for the mere passing frenzy of nature
and creates the family as the foundation of all organized
society. In short, in marriage the woman inspires, and
the man must work, the woman must sacrifice her will,
the man his selfishness.

His treatment of the sex problem was frank and free
and distinctly different from the reserve shown by English and American novelists. The sex relation is the core
of human society, and human society, alas! is generally,
like the apple of Eden, rotten at the core. Marriage is
only a part of it, and divorce, about which we hear so
much, is a still smaller fraction. That inexplicable attrac-
tion for the other sex, which characterizes men and
women, is doubtless very much the same in London or
Philadelphia as it is in Paris; and women, they say, are
all alike everywhere, even if some of them in some places
are rather more alike than others. Social conventions
however, are very different under different skies. Hence
on the one hand our critics freely charge Balzac with
immorality, while he in turn was never tired of accusing
the English people of prudery and hypocrisy. Perhaps it
is safest to say that Balzac was of the French, Frenchy.

Their thoughts are not our thoughts, nor their ways our ways.

Balzac, indeed, endeavored to refute the charge that his women were generally, not to put too fine a point on it, not quite exactly just altogether what you like to have them; and in *Le Père Goriot* (Old Man Goriot), he actually compiled a list of his "virtuous women" and his "criminal women," exulting in the result that the former class, including, however, those still to appear, numbered sixty as against thirty-eight of the latter.

If with the one hand he has given us Beatrix, Dinah and Valérie Marneffe, in the other he holds Eugénie Grandet, Ursule and Eve Séchard, who never felt a throb of the heart not inspired by husband or children.

I have taken the trouble and the time (which might perhaps have been better employed) to examine the list of the characters in the *Human Comedy*, compiled by MM. Cerfberr and Christophe in their *Compendium*. The total number of female characters is 610, and omitting those who are mentioned so casually that their morals do not appear at all, some 287, I find there are 141 who are decidedly shady as against 182 who are apparently respectable. The general impression received by the reader, however, is that the majority of his characters have no character at all.

In Law and Politics, Balzac again appears intensely conservative. He believed in a constitutional monarchy and an aristocracy of the feudal type; aristocracy, he said, was the intellect of the social system. He wrote a pamphlet in favor of primogeniture, and he did not believe in the "rights of man," human equality, or the ability of the masses of the people to govern themselves. One man should have the power to make laws. For the provincial and middle classes, the *bourgeoisie*, he had little but sneer and satire. He reiterates in his novels his aversion to the

Code Napoléon, "that Draconian work," as the leveller of all class distinctions, and particularly did he dislike those provisions relating to inheritance, whose effect was the continual subdivision of estates and the destruction of great houses. Equal rights of inheritance, he said in *A Daughter of Eve*, kill the family spirit. His doctrine was: "Let things alone." Letting things be done in their own way is the secret of good government, and the true cause of social sores is the idleness of the rich and immoral. Indeed, he even said that philanthropy, at whose roots he hints is vanity, is a sublime error, in reality the bane of society, for it harms the mass while it benefits the individual; but his deep and sincere admiration of philanthropy (in others than himself) appears throughout *The Country Doctor* and *The Country Curate*.

In the literary treatment of his subjects, Balzac at first inclined to Romanticism, but afterwards became the exponent, perhaps we should say the apostle, of Realism. As a young man he steeped himself in Scott's novels and he never lost his intense admiration for them. He called Scott "The Immortal," and often alluded to the Waverley novels as full of scenery, metaphor and dramatic situation. *Kenilworth* he praised for romance, *St. Ronan's Well* for detail and finish, *Ivanhoe* for history, *The Antiquary* for poesy, and *The Heart of Mid-Lothian* for interest. I have noted in at least eighteen of Balzac's novels frequent allusions to Scott's characters, and particularly to the women, such as Jeanie Deans, Di Vernon (from whom he evidently modeled Laurence in *Une Ténébreuse Affaire*), the Fair Maid of Perth, Queen Elizabeth, the Highland Widow, and the White Lady of Avenel. And this is curious enough, for he complains there is no passion in Scott; his heroines, Di Vernon excepted, are all alike, and nothing but duty incarnate. Accordingly, Balzac's early ambition was to write historical romances in the style of Scott, and the first book published under his own name, *Les Chouans*, shows that he was able to do it. Later on his novels, *Sur Catherine de Médicis*, *Une Ténébreuse Affaire*, and *Maître Cornelius* (the last written to rehabilitate Louis XI from Scott's description of him in *Quentin Durward*), showed that he was able to continue and improve his method. But stronger still was his call to be the painter of contemporary life and manners, and well did he depict the heterogeneous French society of the first half of the 19th century, at once so singularly attractive and repulsive, showing life as it was lived during the reactionary restoration of the Bourbons, and the *bourgeoisie* monarchy of July. Upon his background he painted in brilliant colors man's pitiful struggle against the savage cruelty of nature and society, his plots show the gradual, fateful unfolding of his puppets' characters. That every man must work out his own damnation, is not merely a profound theological dogma and a practical rule of life, but also a fundamental canon of literary art, amply illustrated in the *Human Comedy*, where over and over again we see how each actor commits the folly, crime, or sin most congenial to his own nature. Selfishness, ingratitude, avarice, egotism, vanity, idleness, folly, jealousy, hatred, cruelty and lust, the whole list of evil traits, animate his men and women, and in his own opinion the chiefest of them is avarice. Balzac called a spade a spade, and he was very fond of talking about spades; except in those books like *Ursule Mirouet* and *Pierrette*, written expressly for those whom, in deference to the French language, I shall call the June Fillies. "You young girls," said he in *Ursule*, "are a public to be dreaded." ("*Vous autres, jeunes filles, vous êtes un public redoutable.*") And again, "I write for men, not for young girls, but I defy them to cite a single page in which religion or the family is attacked."

Balzac was indeed a Realist. He seized men and women in their homes and on the highways, he tore their clothes from their backs, and planted them in the market place under the bright sunlight before the gaping crowd, naked and unashamed, not because they were innocent, but because they gloried in their guilt. There they are, with not a rag to conceal their deformities. We watch the long procession pass,

> "And trace
> A damned soul's epitaph in every face."

Scott reproduced human nature in his novels with as much accuracy and fidelity, but his characters are as different from Balzac's as Raphael's cherubs are from the infantile failures preserved in big bottles in the anatomical museums.

Balzac called himself a humble doctor of the Faculty of Social Medicine. Rather let us say a Demonstrator of Pathology and Morbid Anatomy. He takes you into the dissecting room, while Meredith and Thackeray would tell you all you need or ought to know by means of illustrations.

There is evil in life, and literature, to be truthful, cannot ignore it. But Art for Art's sake is a false maxim, if it be allowed to degenerate into Dirt for Dirt's sake. The esthetic element cannot be separated from the moral. It has been well said by Mr. Frederick Lawton in his admirable book on Balzac, that "the artistic representation of vice and crime is justifiable only in so far as the mind contemplating it is carried out and beyond into the sphere of sane emotion."

Measured by this standard, Balzac transgressed. There is no excuse for *Massimilla Doni* and other tales, and none for such a sordid story as *La Cousine Bette*, the

Limburger cheese of literature, with Baron Hulot and the Marneffes. A man with a sensitive nostril, as Milton neatly translates Horace, needs to hold his nose as he reads. Valérie Marneffe is perhaps the most loathsome character in the realm of fiction, although Balzac claims that he did not invent her. Perhaps not, it would seem impossible. Balzac, moreover, thus set a bad example for his successors of the decadent school, and those pornographic writers who out-Balzac Balzac without possessing his redeeming qualities, those authors whose books seem to be covered over with a sticky kind of dirty varnish that smells bad and comes off when you touch it. The great mass of this *pseudo*-realism is false because (to quote an anonymous critic) it treats an exceptional condition of things, and some particular aspect of life, as though they represented the general and the whole, and this is one reason why young people who lack experience and judgment should not read it. Many of Balzac's other stories are strong meat, even if not as gamy as those mentioned. But in reading Balzac we must take him as he is and extract the abundant honey stored in the lion's carcass. And he must be read and judged in the mass. No single book can be selected which would give the reader a fair idea of his genius. He must study and compare very many or all of Balzac's works, and thus derive a composite impression. As Champfleury said: "There are two ways to criticise Balzac. First, read and sit down and write an article. Second, shut yourself up for six months and study every detail." Balzac may be justly compared with Dickens for humor, but Dickens was broader in caricature; with Thackeray for satire, but Thackeray was keener; with Meredith for analysis, but Meredith was more subtle; with Poe for imagination, but Poe was more fantastic; with Swift for cynicism, but Swift was more caustic;

with De Foe for realistic narrative, but De Foe surpassed him in verisimilitude; with Scott for vivid description of nature and of men, but Scott was his master as well as his model. Yet Balzac combined in a manner altogether wonderful all these varied powers in such a way that his baptism of the children of his brain as the *Human Comedy* was justified. Everything is there.

Balzac was born on May 20, 1799. He died August 18, 1850. Some authorities say it was August 17th, but all agree that he is dead. At this time it makes very little difference to Balzac, and still less to us, which is correct. In his youth the great Revolution was recent history, and he saw disorganized society as it was rearranged by the First Consul and the Emperor. As he matured, he witnessed the reactionary monarchies of Louis XVIII, Charles X, and Louis Philippe. His father was a lawyer, and obedient to the paternal wishes he studied law, first for eighteen months with M. de Guillonet-Merville, an ardent Royalist, and for an equal period with a notary named Passez. Though duly qualified, he never practised either as lawyer or notary. The dry details of the profession were revolting to him. You cannot harness Pegasus to a plow. He said to his sister, "I should become like the horse of a treadmill which does his thirty or forty rounds an hour, eats, drinks and sleeps by rule, and they call that living!" But his time was not wasted, for it is doubtful if any writer, not even excepting Scott, found his legal knowledge more useful.

His accurate perception and marvelous memory enabled him to reproduce in imperishable words the men whom he had met and the Code which he had studied. I have counted the number of characters in Cerfberr and Christophe's *Compendium of the Human Comedy* who are connected with the law. There are 29 judges and magistrates, 23 barristers, 14 attorneys, 24 notaries and 28 office clerks, in all 118. Not all prominent to be sure: some have only a passing mention, but many of them carry on the main action of the story. There are altogether some 1540 men in the *Human Comedy*, so that approximately eight per cent of his male characters have something to do with the law. His books are crammed with legal terms and references. The Code was at his finger ends; and as modesty can hardly be called the besetting sin of us common lawyers, it will do us no harm to read these novels as a study in comparative law as well as comparative morals.

The Code Napoléon replaced a tangled complication of heterogeneous and conflicting laws and customs. The famous epigram of Voltaire was that a traveler in France changed his laws as often as he changed his horses. Napoleon fused the old French customs of the North with the more developed Roman law of the South, in the embers of the Revolution, and from them cast the five codes in their enduring symmetry. There is little in the Code Napoléon that is original. It reduced to order and simplicity the pre-existing materials, and therein is its claim to greatness. It could only have been accomplished by the exercise of a highly centralized autocratic power, and so France anticipated Germany by a century. The Code Napoléon was promulgated in 1804, the German Code in 1900.

Of course, this sort of a code is little more than a clear and methodical statement of general principles and rules of practice, and can only be successful in such countries as France, where the law is the expression of legislative intent rather than judicial construction. In France, roughly speaking, the decisions of the courts are not binding as precedents in the English and American fashion; therefore the Code is a relatively permanent thing. The most that we can satisfactorily attain is a periodical revision of the statutes. There are some present signs, however, that the French courts are paying more regard to precedent, and our own courts rather less. Perhaps we may say that the French judges follow precedent when they feel like it, and our judges disregard precedent when they feel like it so we may be approaching a judicial *entente cordiale* based upon the labor-saving formula, "Every case should be decided upon its own peculiar facts," which plan would be a great relief to seven men that can render a reason or, to speak more technically, deliver an opinion, according, of course, to the *Rule of Reason*.

There are many millions of people, such as Frenchmen, Germans, Italians, and that sort of thing, who consider themselves more than half civilized, and yet live, in their blessed ignorance, under the Civil Code, or something like it, instead of our common law, and, strange to say, seem to get along fairly well. While our law has borrowed all it cared to from the civil law, the courtesy has not been very greatly reciprocated by these foreigners. The difference between the systems is so great that it is sometimes embarrassing to ascertain the French law in cases that occur in practice, and it may perhaps assist some of you to mention a rule that I have often found useful. If you want to know what the French law would be in a given state of facts, do not waste time in trying to study it up, for you will never understand it, but apply this simple formula: First, find out, if you can, what our own law would be, or better still, ask some good lawyer. Then take the exact contrary to this, and the result will probably be a more or less accurate statement of the French law on the subject.

We shall not today adopt this practical method of studying the French law, but out of the wealth of material extract a few examples of Balzac's treatment of law and lawyers. All of his books, except a few of the slighter sketches, have in them something of interest, but many of them are really legal novels. Nor was he unmindful of his obligation. He dedicated *L'Épisode sur la Terreur* to his former preceptor Merville, his *"cher et ancien patron,"* in terms of affectionate regard, declaring that it was from him that the author had learned enough of legal procedure to manage the business of his "little world"; and from this same Merville he drew the character of Derville, as his ideal of a competent and zealous lawyer.

Balzac's personal experience with the law was not happy. He fell in with many publishers and fell out with all, or at least most of them. He had many creditors, and the feeling between him and them was one of mutual and distinct dislike. The humdrum duties of supplying MS. on time, and paying bills when they fell due, did not appeal to his artistic genius, but he was a tenacious stickler for his own legal rights.

His most important litigation was with the *Revue de Paris* in 1835, the editor of which sent the proofs of *Le Lys dans la Vallée* (The Lily in the Valley), then in course of publication, to the *Revue Française* of St. Petersburg. This, Balzac claimed, was in violation of their agreement, and he took away his novel from the *Revue de Paris* after three parts had been published. Suit was brought against him to compel him to continue the publication, and for damages caused by the delay. It was decided practically in Balzac's favor, though Buloz, the publisher, recovered the money advanced for copy not supplied; but as Buloz had to pay the costs, this was not very substantial. Inspired by this suit, Balzac drew up some years later a Code Littéraire for the Société des Gens-de-lettres which, needless to say, was never adopted by anyone but himself, and his resentment of newspaper criticism led him to lampoon the journalists in his

Distinguished Provincial and his satirical monograph of the Parisian press.

His experience with another publisher was not so happy. William Duckett obtained a judgment against him for ten thousand francs, and to escape arrest Balzac took refuge in the house of a friend. A writ server obtained admission on the pretense that he wanted to pay Balzac some money, and when the great novelist tripped down stairs to receive it, he was promptly tripped up with an arrest warrant for the debt, which his generous friend paid on the spot.

Several times Balzac was imprisoned under the conscription law for failing to serve in the National Guards, and he later on attempted to evade his creditors by executing a fictitious sale of his country place. His biographers do not record the outcome of this experiment, but the net result of his legal complications was probably summed up in *Les Proscrits* (The Exiles): "I see too much of the law not to know that it is well to have nothing to do with it."

Although, of course, Balzac never practised law, he made himself somewhat conspicuous in 1839 by his efforts to save the life of one Peytel, convicted by circumstantial evidence of the murder of his wife and servant. Thackeray, in his *Paris Sketch Book*, gives a long account of the case, which he used to illustrate the superiority of the English criminal procedure over the French. Of Balzac's letter Thackeray remarks that it was so very long, so very dull, and so very pompous, that the Parisian public gave up Peytel and his case altogether.

Notwithstanding his own experience, Balzac, in his general views of law and lawyers, more nearly resembled Scott than Dickens. Like Scott he was a well-read lawyer, and was impartial in his treatment of the profession. He could separate the evil from the good, and could contrast the upright and learned judge and lawyer with the trickster and the incompetent. Dickens, on the other hand, could see no good in either the science of the law or in the men who practised it. He scarcely mentioned law except in terms of contempt, and nearly all his lawyers are caricatures. With Balzac, I say, it was different, though, to be sure, his standard — perhaps it was the French standard — of professional ethics is not quite the same as our own. As examples of Balzac's opinions I have collected a very few of them, scattered through his writings, to illustrate his impressions of law, law students, lawyers and judges.

Justice, he says in *César Birotteau*, is the expression of society itself; beneath justice is the sovereign will, the laws by which men have agreed to live.

In *La Femme de Trente Ans* (The Woman of Thirty), he says, "Law is the doctrine, and custom the practice of society."

Henriette, in *The Lily in the Valley*, in her remarkable letter to Félix, elaborates the idea: "My dear, these laws are not all written in a book; customs also create laws; the most important are the least known. Obey the general law in all things without disputing it, whether it hurts or advances your interest."

These manners and customs are often more cruel than the law. As Balzac says in *Une Ténébreuse Affaire*: "The manners of the time are the outcome of human nature, the law is framed by the intellect of the nation; (*les mœurs, ce sont les hommes; mais la loi, c'est la raison d'un pays;*) customs which are sometimes irrational are therefore stronger than the law."

He gives some occasional suggestions as to legislation. Thus in *The Country Doctor:* "The lawmaker should be in advance of his age." "Local differences should be studied before passing laws; every place must be considered separately." This was probably a reflection upon the uniformity of the Code Napoléon. "We have something like forty thousand laws in France," said the Country Doctor. "We might as well have none at all." Of course Balzac uttered some of the conventional gibes about the law. He repeats, in *La Maison Nucingen*, Montesquieu's aphorism, "Laws are like spiders' webs; the big flies get through, while the little ones are caught." "A lawyer!" cried David Séchard in *Lost Illusions*, "the very word gives me the colic."

Indeed, Balzac is ungallant in his comparisons. In *Modeste Mignon* he says a lawsuit is like marriage, because one party is always left dissatisfied.

"Law, like medicine, has its victims. In the first case one man suffers for the many, and in the second he dies for science," said the rascally lawyer, Fraisier, in *Cousin Pons*.

Balzac often notices the developing effect of practice upon lawyers. "Society goes through our hands," said the notary, Crottat, in *The Woman of Thirty*. "We see its passion in that most revolting form, greed. Here it is the mother of a family trying to disinherit the husband's children to enrich others whom she loves better; or it is the husband who tries to leave all his property to the child who has done his best to earn his mother's hatred."

"There are," said Derville in *Le Colonel Chabert*, "in modern society three men who can never think well of it — the priest, the doctor and the man of law. And they wear black robes, because perhaps they are in mourning for every virtue and every illusion. The most hapless of the three is the lawyer. When a man comes in search of the priest he is prompted by repentance, by remorse, by beliefs which make him interesting, which elevate him and comfort the soul of the intercessor, whose task will bring him a sort of gladness; he purifies, repairs and reconciles. But we lawyers, we see the same evil feelings repeated again and again; nothing can correct them; our offices are sewers which can never be cleansed."

And so Balzac observes, in *Ursule Mirouet*, that Judge Bongrand knew life well and had acquired in his profession large-mindedness, learning, accumulated observation, shrewdness and power of conversation.

On the other hand, in *Madame Firmiani*: "There is in a lawsuit an eagerness, a passion, which may sometimes blind the most honest man alive. Lawyers know how to legitimize the most preposterous claims, there are syllogisms in law to humor the errors of conscience, and judges have a right to make mistakes."

His accounts of the courts and prison life are remarkably good, especially in reference to Vautrin's career. In the *Splendeurs et Misères des Courtisanes*, there is a most vivid description of the Palais de Justice, and the hall known as the Salles des Pas Perdus, too long to be quoted. All the minute details of the prison cells and corridors and offices are related with the accuracy of a guide-book.

Balzac had made a careful study from actual cases of crime and the criminal law, and has offered a number of thoughtful observations about both. While in opposition to Victor Hugo, he approved of the death penalty for murder, yet he does not fail to note that it may lead a criminal who has committed one murder to add another to his account. "There is no such thing," he says in *A Start in Life*, "as a criminal who is bad all through"; and in *Vautrin's Last Incarnation* he refers to the status of released convicts, who are suspicious of society as society is suspicious of them, and are doomed to starvation or crime.

"Ignorance," he says in *Cousin Betty*, "is the mother of every crime"; "a crime is in the first instance a defect of the reason"; a remark which is true only in general; and in *L'Envers de l'Histoire Contemporaine* he suggests that convicts ought to be placed in religious institutions among good men rather than their own kind.

Criminal procedure, he says, in *Un Grand Homme de Province*, (A Distinguished Provincial), is based on the rule that everything that is probable is true, which is consonant with Bordin's opinion in *Une Ténébreuse Affaire*: "If the simple truth is given, the whole thing looks transparent," and "If the truth often looks like fiction in court, fiction on the other hand looks like truth;" maxims of which Bordin availed himself freely in defending Michu.

In *L'Envers de l'Histoire* he gives a copy of the indictment in 1809 of du Vissard and others, setting forth all the circumstances in such detail that, although it was considered short, it occupies some twenty pages. He calls it *"Le Roman de Rob-Roy en France avant celui de Walter Scott."*

Balzac is frequently struck with the inequality and inadequacy of criminal punishment. "How is it," he exclaimed in *Old Man Goriot*, "that a dandy who in a night robbed a boy of half of his fortune gets only a couple of months in prison, while a poor devil who steals a bank note for a thousand francs is condemned to penal servitude?" And in *À Combien l'Amour Revient* (What Love Costs): "If a lawyer makes off with the fortunes of a hundred families it is far worse than killing a man."

Balzac remembered his student experiences. In *Z. Marcas* he mentioned a students' lodging house in the Rue Corneille, "where there is a winding staircase, quite at the back, lighted below from the street, higher up by borrowed lights, and at the top by a skylight.   There were forty furnished rooms, furnished as students' rooms are! What does youth demand more than was here supplied? A bed, a few chairs, a chest of drawers, a looking-glass and a table. As soon as the sky is blue, the student opens his windows."

And from the same story we learn that the profession was overcrowded then as now. "In all the law courts there are almost as many lawyers as there are cases. The pleader is thrown back on journalism, on politics, on literature. Work as he will with all his energy, a young man starting from zero may at the end of ten years find himself below the point he set out from. In these days, talent must have the good luck which secures success to the most incompetent; nay, more, if it scorns the base compromises which insure advancement to crawling mediocrity, it will never get on." In *Old Man Goriot*, it is said that not five advocates in Paris made 50,000 francs a year, and Peyrade, in *Les Petits Bourgeois*, said the streets of Paris were fairly paved with lawyers.

Law students were pretty much the same then as now. Rastignac, in *Old Man Goriot*, went to the lectures simply to answer to his name, and then left. Through a reasoning process familiar to most students he saw the advisability of deferring his studies to the last moment before going up for his examination, and then cramming his work into the third year when he meant to study in earnest.

Balzac gives a minute and interesting study of a law student's experience in *Un Début dans la Vie* (A Start in Life), one of his most entertaining and farcical sketches. "Live in a garret," said Old Cardot to Oscar Husson; "go straight to your lecture and from that to your office; work away morning, noon and night, and study at home; be a second clerk by the time you are two and twenty, and head clerk at four and twenty." And when he enters

Maître Desroches' office, the attorney introduces him to Godeschal, the head clerk, with these words: "He will dine with us and sleep in the little attic. Allow him exactly time enough to get to the law schools and back so that he has not five minutes to lose; see that he learns the code and does well at lectures; give him law books to read up when he has done his school work." The boy had to get up at five to go to the office, and his day lasted until bedtime; his only holiday was Sunday. They had pleasant jokes for new pupils, one of which was an elaborate scheme to make each fresh arrival pay tribute in the form of a *bienvenue*, or an elaborate breakfast to the office. A sham register of the High Festivals of the Minions of the Law (*Registre architriclino-basochien*), beginning in 1525, and containing the records of the feasts supposed to have been given by each newcomer, was unostentatiously laid on the neophyte's desk, and Frédéric Marest, whose turn it was, gave them a bacchanalian feast at the Rocher de Cancale with some young ladies of his acquaintance, which proved very unfortunate for Oscar.

The legal profession in Paris was divided, as it now is in England, into the two branches, and Balzac disapproved of the division. It is no more ascertainable, he said in *Les Petits Bourgeois* (The Middle Classes), why the law gives a client two men instead of one, than why an author needs both a printer and a bookseller, overlooking the obvious reason that it is more for the public interest to give two men a job than only one. The Association of Advocates forbade the members to do any legal act that is essentially the duty or right of the attorneys; and the advocates, who had to be householders, at least were under the supervision of a board of control like our censors, and Peyrade, the shyster lawyer, was summoned before it.

The lawyers seem to have in their fashion enjoyed life. Perhaps they had dinners together, as we do. In *The Seamy Side* it was said that M. Joseph's face bore traces of a joviality peculiar to the notaries and attorneys of Paris, and in *Modeste Mignon* the jests of a lawyer's office were considered famous. And they knew what professional courtesy meant. The attorneys of Paris, it is said in *The Middle Classes*, live in real brotherhood, and the result is a certain facility for arranging any matter than can be arranged. They obtain from each other such concessions as are admissible, applying the proverb, "one good turn deserves another," which is acted on in fact in every profession. The counterpoise to this good fellowship lies in what may be called professional conscience; no consideration can overcome the sense of honor of a lawyer.

Of course, there were both sheep and goats in the profession. In Paris, said Blondet in *La Maison Nucingen*, there are attorneys of two classes. There is the honest attorney: he abides within the law, pushes on his cases, neglects no one, never runs after business, gives his clients his honest opinion, and makes compromises in doubtful cases; he is a Derville in short. Then there is the starveling attorney, to whom anything seems good, provided he is sure of expenses; he will work to make the worse appear the better cause, and take advantage of a technical error to win the day for a rogue. Of the latter class Fraisier in *Cousin Pons* is a good example, who thus advised his client: "Unless you keep within the law, you get nothing. You know nothing of the law; I know a good deal. I will see that you keep on the right side of it, and you can hold your own in all men's sight. As for your conscience, that is your own affair."

A lawyer, says Balzac in *The Country Parson*, and again in *An Historical Mystery*, is, at the first, judge of the client and the case; but unfortunately Clousier, the lawyer in *The Country Parson*, lost his practice by his adherence to this maxim, instead of that asserted by Dr. Minoret in *Ursule*, that the glory of a clever lawyer is to gain a rotten suit. Such men are those of whom Milton speaks as "allured to the trade of law, grounding their principles not on the prudent and heavenly contemplation of justice and equity, which was never taught them, but on the promising and pleasing thoughts of litigious terms, fat contentions, and flowing fees."

Balzac pays his respects to clients as well as to their lawyers. They were conscienceless as well. "I do not know," said the Marquise d'Espard, when examined as to her affidavit in *L'Interdiction*, "what my attorney may have put into my mouth."

Attorneys, he says in *The Middle Classes*, meet with more clients who tell lies than who tell the truth; and in *Lost Illusions:* "The client before and after the lawsuit would furnish a subject worthy of Meissonier; there would be brisk bidding among attorneys for the possession of such admirable bits of *genre*."

Practical experience of litigation teaches the layman a good deal. There is nothing so little known as that which everybody is supposed to know, the law of the land, to wit, and so he shows in *Lost Illusions* how David Séchard learns something about the law of commercial paper. No wonder that, by way of illustration, he said in *L'Élixir de longue Vie* (The Elixir of Life), "thoughtful as a man in a lawsuit on his way to Court." Every one knows how sometimes we have to give our clients a good talking to, although as Latournelle, the notary in *Modeste Mignon* said, we fling their secrets into the Styx which every lawyer keeps handy for them. So, in *The Bachelor's Establishment*, Desroches, the attorney, gave the dreadful Philippe Bridau one of those unanswerable sermons, in which a lawyer places things in their true light, using the crudest language to epitomize the facts of his clients' conduct, to analyze their ideas, and to reduce them to the simplest expression.

A lawyer's apparent indifference sometimes surprises the agitated client. Derville, when consulted by Birotteau, was staid and self-possessed as is the wont of the men of law, accustomed as they are to the most harrowing disclosures. Birotteau felt as a new thing in his experience this necessary coolness; it was like ice to an excited man telling the story of his misfortunes.

But this coolness is better for the client. Balzac remarks in his description of the trial in *Une Ténébreuse Affaire*: "The lawyers' faces inspired confidence; a doctor never allows a patient to see his misgivings, and a lawyer always shows his client a hopeful countenance. These are the rare cases when insincerity becomes a virtue."

Balzac's pictures of lawyers and their offices abound in his novels, all characterized by his minute attention to detail. In *Cousin Pons*, he thus describes the shyster, Fraisier, and his offices: "The room was a complete picture of a third-rate solicitor's office, with the stained wooden cases, the letter files so old that they had grown beards, the red tape dangling limp and dejected, the pasteboard boxes covered with the gambols of mice, the dirty floor, the ceiling yellow with smoke." There is a similar uninviting description of Claparon's business office in *César Birotteau*: "Fraisier was small, thin and unwholesome looking; his red face, covered with an eruption, told of tainted blood. A wig pushed back on his head displayed a brick-colored cranium of ominous conformation. One might have thought there was pestilence in the air."

Regnault in *La Grande Bretèche* is thus depicted: "A man tall, slim, dressed in black, hat in hand, who came in like a ram ready to butt his opponent, showing a receding forehead, a small, pointed head and a colorless face of the hue of a glass of dirty water. He wore an old coat much worn at the seams, but he had a diamond in his shirt front and gold rings in his ears."

Desroches is described in *Un Ménage de Garçon* as having a harsh voice, a coarse skin, pitiless eyes, and a face like a ferret's, licking the blood of a murdered chicken from its lips.

One of the characters in *La Maison Nucingen* thus described this same Desroches: "He used to make me feel that I had met a tiger escaped from the Jardin des Plantes. He was lean and red haired, his eyes were the color of Spanish tobacco, and his complexion was harsh. He looked cold and phlegmatic. He was hard upon the widow, pitiless to the orphan, and a terror to his clerks. Learned, crafty, double-faced, honey-tongued and never flying into a passion."

The rascally Goupil in *Ursule Mirouet* had short legs, a broad face with a mottled skin, a hooked nose, twisted crosswise from right to left, and thin, reddish hair. His arms were over long, ending with huge hands that were seldom clean. With worn-out shoes and thread-bare, greasy clothes, nothing was lacking in the aggregate of sinister details.

The notary in France, and especially in Paris, is a very important personage, and middle-class men believe a notary far rather than an attorney. A Paris citizen, said Balzac, is not without some alarm when he goes to see his attorney, while he always goes with fresh pleasure to his notary, and admires his wisdom and good sense. He is the man of business *par excellence*, and enjoys a lucrative monopoly in his supervision of deeds and mortgages, marriage contracts, wills, articles of incorporation, etc. The notaries form an exclusive, self-prepetuating association, something like our Stock Exchange, and now in Paris number but 122. When a notary dies or retires, his business is sold and his successor takes over and preserves the records and papers of the office. Their clients are protected by this saleable value of their office, and apparently they are obliged to make a despoit for their clients' further protection. Balzac refers to this several times in *César Birotteau* and *Les Petits Bourgeois*. Notaries cannot speculate on their own account. Balzac frequently refers to this also and their fraudulent tricks to circumvent the law, especially in *Les Petits Bourgeois*.

Balzac has a great deal to say about judges, and most of his judges are honest men, like Popinot in *The Commission in Lunacy*, and old Blondet in *The Cabinet of Antiques*. The latter's integrity was as deeply rooted in him as his passion for flowers; he knew nothing but law and botany. He would have interviews with litigants, listen to them, chat with them and show them his flowers; he would accept rare seeds from them, but once on the bench no Judge on earth was more impartial.

The allusion here made is to the practice which up to the Revolution, permitted, or at least condoned, the personal solicitation of judges and even the making of presents to them by litigants, like the custom in England which caused Bacon's downfall. Indeed, the office of Judge in France was formerly saleable like an estate. In Balzac's novels there are frequent allusions to the influence used outside of the Courtroom upon the Judge. Judge Camusot, for example, was completely under his wife's influence, and the ladies generally seem to have been very successful in this irregular practice. In *The End of Evil Ways*, the Countess de Sérizy called on the Judge to interview him as to Lucien de Rubempré, and actually seized the notes of his examination and threw them into the fire. The ladies, said Balzac, have a code of their own, and laugh at statutes framed by men. "If that is a crime, said the countess, "well, monsieur must get his odious scrawl written out again."

To mention those of Balzac's novels that possess legal interest is almost to repeat the catalogue of all. To get over the ground we must proceed *hoppibus, skippibus, jumpibusque,* a Latin expression you may hunt for in Cicero. Of those most important may be mentioned these: *The Country Parson* derives its dramatic interest from the murder of the miser, Pingret, by Tascheron during his intrigue with Véronique Graslin. He was convicted through circumstantial evidence; and it is curious to note that the jury were not segregated, and that Graslin, who was one of the jurymen, talked the case over with Véronique, his wife, who suggested her lover's acquittal, on the ground that if Tascheron's life was spared, the relatives of the murdered man might recover his money. Seven of the jury, therefore, voted to acquit and five to convict; the judges voted with the minority, and Tascheron was convicted. (This was in 1829, before the law of May 13, 1836.) His execution took place at the time of the birth of Véronique's child, and the remainder of the book is an attempt to work out the change wrought in Véronique's character through the influence of the Country Parson. Her dramatic confession at her death reminds the reader of Hawthorne's *Scarlet Letter.*

Ursule Mirouet, one of Balzac's masterpieces, is distinctly a legal novel. Ursule, the orphan niece and ward of Dr. Minoret, and intended by him to be his universal legatee, was, naturally, the object of the enmity of his heirs at law, among whom Ursule was not included, on account of her father's illegitimacy. This gave Dionis, the notary, an opportunity to give a learned opinion to the heirs at law on the law of inheritance by illegitimates, referring to Articles 757, 908 and 911 of the Code, and

the decisions of the Court of Appeal and the Royal
Court of Paris, against which the head clerk, Goupil,
cited a judgment delivered by the Supreme Court at
Colmar in 1825. When a mortgage is given to ·Dr.
Minoret to secure his advances to Savinien, the formalities are all mentioned, even to the registration fees. And
when Dr. Minoret settles his account with Ursule, as
her guardian, a family council is held in accordance
with the Code. Dr. Minoret being aware that a will in
Ursule's favor might be disputed, and that his adoption
of her might give rise to litigation, invested her money in
consols payable to bearer, and hid them in a volume of
the *Pandects*, a book pretty sure not to be opened. He
then wrote a will in favor of the Vicomte de Portenduére,
Ursule's fiancé, and explained his plan to Ursule in
a letter hidden in a cabinet. The doctor's nephew stole
the will and letter and the certificates, and there is related
in detail the inventory and legal settlement of the estate,
and the final discovery of the theft.

In *La Recherche de l'Absolu* (The Quest of the Absolute), Balzac introduces very many points of law. The
rights of children in their parents' estate, and the eman-
cipation of a minor by marriage or by consent of the
family council if eighteen years of age under Articles 476
and 478 of the Code, and the minor's disability under
Article 484 to sell her real estate, are important in the
framework of the story. In like manner, in *Albert
Savarus*, Rosalie de Watteville was emancipated before
twenty-one.

César Birotteau is the story of the successful but
simple-minded perfumer, who amassed a fortune by his
lotions, and then ended in bankruptcy through the
. fraudulent land schemes of the notary, Rogron. They
had straw men in those days. Balzac's own financial
troubles doubtless induced him to make a special study

of the bankrupt law.   We have the filing of the petition, the publication of the decree in the *Gazette*, the filing of the schedule, the appointment of the agent, the preparation of the inventory, Birotteau's deprivation of civil rights, the meeting of creditors and appointment of trustees, the *concordat* or composition, and the bankrupt's discharge; all are set forth in such elaborate detail that the story has been styled a handbook of the Commercial Code.   Though Birotteau by his bankruptcy lost his civil rights, in the end, crushed, insulted and yet forgiving, he is rehabilitated through the efforts of his friends and dies dramatically after his triumphant return to the Exchange.   In *César Birotteau* there are also many details of landlord and tenant law, and building contracts, so intricately described that it is impossible to condense them.

Cousin Pons was a childlike old musician, with a famous collection of valuable paintings.   The novel is entirely taken up with the conspiracy of the infamous Doctor Poulain and the lawyer, Fraisier, who try to induce him to make a will in favor of his dreadful nurse, La Cibot; and after he died, leaving a will in favor of his friend Schmucke, the intrigues are related by which the legatee was defrauded of his rights.   In this story, mention is made of several points of testamentary law: that a physician in attendance on a testator cannot accept a bequest, Article 909 of the Code; that, in the absence of heirs in the direct line, a testator may dispose of his entire property by will, Article 916; and there are described different ways of making wills, which may be either dictated to a notary in the presence of witnesses, or holographic, *i.e.*, written out, dated and signed by the testator himself.   It is curious to note the fidelity to detail with which Balzac describes the formalities of the registration of death (the *Acte de Décès*) with witnesses, under Article 77 of the Code.

Les Petits Bourgeois (The Middle Classes) is so crammed throughout with the sordid legal schemes of La Peyrade and Cérizet, with constant references to many titles of the law, that it is impossible to do justice to it here. In fact it contains sufficient material for a separate paper. *Les Illusions Perdues* (Lost Illusions) abounds with commercial and patent laws, suits, executions and interpleaders, and arrests for debt. It appears that arrears of rent are a preferred claim in bankruptcy; and that articles of partnership must be filed with the Tribunal of Commerce. (See Article 42 of the Commercial Code.) We learn a good deal about the difference between the Paris and country lawyers, the law of costs and the method of protesting drafts. As old Séchard said, "See what comes of knowing how to write your name."

In *Esther*, it is noted that by writing *Bon pour* you simply promise to pay; doubtless Article 1326 of the Code is alluded to. The word *Accepté* constitutes a bill of exchange, (Article 122, Commercial Code), and makes you liable to imprisonment for five years. Cérizet in *Les Petits Bourgeois* made La Peyrade sign a bill in this way. *Le Cabinet des Antiques* (The Collection of Curiosities) is the story of Notary Chesnel's devotion to his family clients, and is filled with the law of forgery, from which we learn that in France the charge of forgery may be brought by a private individual and can be settled out of Court if the money is returned to the person defrauded. In *Le Curé de Tours* (The Abbé Birotteau), we have the simple old Abbé and his legal tangles with his landlady, the artful old maid who got him to sign an agreement to give up his furniture if he left the house, and then forced him to go. *Les Comédiens sans le Savoir* (The Unconscious Comedians), might have, as a second title, How to Win a Lawsuit. Gazonal, a man of the South, comes to Paris about his pending lawsuit, apparently a case of eminent domain as we would call it, meets his old friends de Lora and Bixiou, with whom he did the town, and discovers that the way to succeed in litigation is to reach the Court through the ladies and politicians who enjoy the judicial confidence. After Gazonal had given promissory notes to Miss Jenny Cadine, the mistress of Massol, who had the case decided in his favor, he had his notes handed back to him by de Lora, and the farce ended in a roar of laughter.

In *Eugénie Grandet*, the author takes pains to explain the difference between liquidation and bankruptcy, either voluntary on the bankrupt's own petition, or involuntary upon the petition of his creditors. Liquidation is not bankruptcy; it is a disgraceful thing to be a bankrupt but liquidation reflects no discredit, as it can be privately arranged without recourse to the Tribunal of Commerce. The old miser, Grandet, undertook to liquidate his brother's affairs, with the consent of the creditors, and managed so well by tiring them out for five years that he made a very good thing out of it for himself; but in the end, Eugénie, who inherited his fortune, paid all the debts in full for the sake of her worthless cousin, Charles. So Charles Mignon, in *Modeste Mignon*, underwent a voluntary liquidation in this way and afterwards returned to Havre a millionaire.

Un Homme d'Affaires (A Man of Business) is a little sketch showing how a sharp lawyer got the better of the sharp spendthrift de Trailles, by his greater familiarity with the procedure in attachments.

In *Cousin Betty* there are numerous legal details. Whereas a Frenchman might be imprisoned but five years for debt, a foreigner remained in prison for life, or until his debts are paid, so Cousin Betty had Steinbock, who was a Pole, arrested by a cunning little trick, in order to gratify her jealousy. Victorin Hulot appears as the type of the honest lawyer, who studied his cases thoroughly and would not accept every brief that was offered him. The unspeakable Valérie after her husband's death remains chastely a widow ten months, in accordance with Article 228 of the Code, and the provisions of her marriage contract with Crevel, drawn up by Berthier, are given in detail. He even notes that a marriage contract costs fifteen francs, and the marriage costs thirty, which expense caused many poor people to ignore the legal formalities. And in this book, as in many others, Balzac refers to Article 913 of the Code that forbids a man from giving away more than half of his estate if he leaves one child, more than a third if he leaves two children, or more than a quarter if he leaves three or more.

Pierrette is the touching story of a little orphan girl, whose ill treatment by her guardian, Rogron, gave rise to lawsuits only terminated by her death. The law regulating guardianships through the family council is discussed, including the appointment of a *tuteur subrogé*, or deputy guardian, who in Pierrette's case was Auffray, the notary, to whom the court gave the custody of Pierrette after Rogron's cruelty to her became known. Under Article 421 of the Code, the deputy summoned a family council of six members, who were appointed by the justice of the peace as their legal president. Normally, under Article 407, this should be composed of three relations on the father's side and three on the mother's; but as this was impossible, the justice, under Article 409, summoned family friends in his discretion. The council dismissed Rogron as guardian and appointed Auffray as Pierrette's guardian and Ciprey deputy guardian. But Pierrette died before her lawsuits were ended, and it was never legally determined how far her death was due to the cruelty of her unnatural guardian.

Une Ténébreuse Affaire, sometimes called *A Gondre-ville Mystery*, is the narrative of the abduction of Malin in the time of the First Empire, and a large portion of the book is occupied with the very vivid account of the trial of Michu, his conviction, the ineffectual appeal to Napoleon, and his execution, all under procedure anterior to the Criminal Code.

In *Ou Ménent les Mauvais Chemins* (The End of Evil Ways), and *La Dernière Incarnation de Vautrin*, Balzac gives us a picture of society from the viewpoint of the criminal. He relates in a manner absolutely true in its details criminal procedure, the habits and methods of the criminals of the day, their peculiar code of honor, and repeats their very slang. These books and *L' Histoire des Treize* (The History of the Thirteen), with *Ferragus*, seem to be the origin of the police novel of later times.

The examination of Lucien and Vautrin by the Juge d'Instruction in *The End of Evil Ways*, and of Tascheron in *The Country Parson*, in order to discover the facts of the case, show the source from which the police of our times may have derived the "third degree," though, indeed the English State Trials disclose a startling similarity.

Balzac approved of this method of ascertaining guilt. Innocent men, he says, are quickly released; and while public opinion condemns persons under suspicion, it is favorable to those committed for trial.

Le Contrat de Mariage (The Marriage Settlement) is the story of a very unhappy marriage with too much mother-in-law. As its title implies, the interest of the tale centers about the sordid business negotiations between young Salonet and old Mathias, the two notaries, representing respectively the bride and the groom. Balzac never wrote anything more entertaining.

In *The Country Doctor*, Balzac illustrates very neatly the French law under Article 1583 of the Code, according to which a sale is complete between the parties and the property passes as soon as the thing and the price are agreed upon, although delivery is not made nor the price paid.

In *Gobseck*, Derville the attorney, who appears to little advantage, tells the story of the old miser, with references to the law that a woman not in trade cannot make a technical bill of exchange, and that fees for settlements and compromises are not according to the fee bill. The story turns upon the law of sale with *faculté de rachat* or right of re-purchase (Article 1659 of the Code), a tempting arrangement to the needy Countess de Restaud. Derville shows how she, being a married woman, could not thus get money on her jewelry without her husband's consent (Article 217 of the Code); how he, Derville, assisted the usurer to circumvent the husband; how the Count made a deed of all his property to Gobseck, taking a counter deed as security, and how the Countess, after her husband's death, hastily destroyed the deed, thinking it was a will, so that Gobseck remained the owner of the estate, though he afterwards restored it to the Count's son.

In *Le Député d'Arcis* (The Member from Arcis), Balzac gives the law as to recognition of natural children by *Acte authentique* under Article 334, that is, by deed acknowledged before a notary. This, of course, was not equivalent to legitimation, which could be accomplished by the marriage of the parents under Article 331; but gave the children so recognized their certain shares of their parents' estates, defined by Article 756 of the Code, viz., a third of the share of a legitimate child. The law of interments is here referred to and also in *Ferrugus*. In the latter book, it is said that interments were under the charge of the police department, and that a husband has no right to the custody of his wife's dead body nor a father to his child's. In Paris there were seven classes of funerals regulated by law as to cost. In *Un Ménage de Garçon*, old Claparon was given a third-class funeral, considered very cheap, but even that was too expensive for old Goriot.

In *Les Paysans*, Balzac repeats the proverb *Charbonnier est maître chez lui* (a man's house, even a charcoal burner's, is his castle), apparently an inheritance from the Roman law (Gaius in Dig. II, 4, 18), while in *Une Ténébreuse Affaire*, Malin harangued the crowd, *"des droits du foyer, de l'habeas corpus et du domicile anglais."*

In many of his stories Balzac illustrates incidentally numerous titles of the law. In *Catherine de Médicis*, he illustrates the sumptuary laws of the period, the methods of judicial torture and execution, and even notes how modern municipal regulations have abolished the medieval gargoyles. In *Gambara*, the old musician's panharmonicon was sold in execution on the public square in accordance with Article 617 of the Code of Procedure. In *La Vendetta*, he shows the law of the marriage of minors, under which men under twenty-five years, and women under twenty-one years, cannot contract marriage without their parents' consent. After that age, if consent is withheld, an *Acte respectueux* or "respectful summons" under certain formalities (Articles 148 and 152), is held to supply the place of consent, this being a legal and formal way of saying, "We intend to do it whether you like it or not." In this way under Notary Roguin's advice Ginevra Piombo and Luigi Porta, whose families were separated by the vendetta, were finally married. In *Un Homme d'Affaires* (A Man of Business), and *La Maison Nucingen* (The Firm of Nucingen), we are given the law of confusion of debts under Article 1300 of the Code; in *Les Employés*, the law of gambling contracts under Article 1965 of the

Code, and the purchasing of a bankrupt's debts, the allowance of which rests with the committee of liquidation, as was also arranged by Diard in *Les Maranas;* in *Melmoth Réconcilié,* he notes that "P" is the usual abbreviation of "Protested" on bills of exchange; and even in *La Grande Bretèche,* that masterly tale worthy of Poe, where the story is related three times from three several viewpoints, the notary's narrative is drawn to life. M. Regnault in his description of *La Grande Bretèche* refers to the law forbidding, under heavy penalties, a trespass upon enclosed property, and says a hedge is the same as a wall. Speaking of the furniture, he says there was not enough to fill ten lines in an inventory; he explains the will of Madame de Merret, and the law forbidding a notary to accept a bequest under the will he has written; indeed, he talks throughout as though he were dictating a legal document.

Le Colonel Chabert is the pathetic story of a hero of the Napoleonic Wars, who was severely wounded at the battle of Eylau in 1807, and left senseless on the field. Supposed to be killed, his body was stripped and buried with the dead. Having revived and extricated himself he found himself in a hospital, a physical and mental wreck, and when, having suffered a total change in appearance, he recollected his name and rank, he found no one to believe him. He was alive, yet officially dead, and in something of the predicament described by Kipling in *The Strange Ride of Morrowby Jukes,* or that of Mrs. Cunnius, in *Cunnius* v. *Reading School District,* 206 Pa. 469, or Miss Mary B. Devlin, in *Devlin* v. *Commonwealth,* 101 Pa. 273. Nine years afterwards he succeeded in reaching Paris, and found that his wife had married Count Ferraud, by whom she had two children. This was bad enough, but, even worse than that, he found that his will had been proved and his estate settled and divided, his wife receiving most of it.   Apparently this was in accordance with Article 120, *et seq.*, of the Code, providing for the administration of the effects of an absentee, who is entitled to receive his property back again in its then condition, and one-fifth of the income, if he reappears within fifteen years.   Now, if a man wants to have his estate properly settled, it is absolutely necessary for him to die.   It is not enough for him to disappear, no matter for how long, if he neglects this simple preliminary.   When he comes back unexpectedly, and makes himself generally disagreeable, his return to the scene of his former activities will disarrange the most careful administration, and even if his supposed death was mourned, his reappearance will be even more sincerely lamented.   This at least was Colonel Chabert's experience, and though not a lawyer he speedily concluded that there was a jurisdictional defect; and not being of the Enoch Arden temperament, he resolved to claim his money and his wife, minus the two superfluous children.   Receiving no reply from his wife to his letters, he resolved to apply to her lawyer, Derville, and the story opens with his entry into Derville's office, Balzac's description of which is hardly attractive.   The office was a large room, furnished with the traditional stove to be seen in all these dens.   The stovepipe crossed the room diagonally to the chimney of a bricked-up fireplace, and on the marble chimney-piece were chunks of bread, triangles of Brie cheese, pork cutlets, glasses, bottles and the head clerk's cup of chocolate. The smell of these dainties blended so completely with that of the overheated stove, and the odor peculiar to old papers, that the trail of a fox would not have been perceptible.   The only decorations consisted of huge yellow posters, seizures of real estate, auction sales in partition, and all the glory of a lawyer's office.   An enormous stack of pigeonholes adorned the wall from top to bottom, crammed with papers with an infinite number of tickets hanging from them at the ends of red tape, which give a peculiar physiognomy to law papers. The lower rows were filled with cardboard boxes yellow with age, on which might be read the names of the more important clients, whose cases were juicily stewing at the time. The dirty window panes admitted but little daylight. "Were it not", says Balzac, "for the mouldy sacristies where prayers are weighed out and paid for like groceries, and for the old clothes shops with their fluttering rags, an attorney's office would be of all social marts the most loathsome." The colonel, with his singular appearance and costume, was received with ridicule by the office clerks, who were engaged in drafting an appeal from the head clerk's dictation, a greenhorn among them copying, as part of the legal form, the head clerk's instructions to dot his "i's." Derville is out, but an appointment was made for one o'clock in the morning, as this notable lawyer is apparently able to work all night. After hearing the story, Derville, notwithstanding that he was attorney for the Countess Ferraud, agreed to represent the colonel, and advanced him money for living expenses. Upon receiving affidavits from Germany which convinced Derville of Chabert's identity, the lawyer explained to his client the legal complication resulting from the wife's second marriage. The point was not covered by the Code, and could only be decided by the judges "according to conscience," who might not think the colonel in a very pretty moral position at his age to reclaim a wife who no longer cared for him. (But see Article 139 of the Code.) Derville, therefore, advised a compromise for an annuity of 24,000 francs, for, as he justly said, with so much a year you can find other women who would suit you better and make you happier.

So Derville interviewed the countess, his own client, as
though she were a stranger and an adversary, and, strange
to say, assumed to advise her, yet it seemed to be regarded
as entirely regular. The compromise fell through, the
countess fell back on Delbecq, an attorney of her own,
and completely triumphed over the old man, who spent
the rest of his life in an asylum.

I have referred particularly to this story in order to
show the standard of professional ethics followed by
Derville. In *What Love Costs an Old Man*, the Duc de
Grandlieu employed Derville to ascertain the source of
the wealth of Lucien de Rubempré, who was the suitor
of the duke's daughter. Derville visited Eve Séchard,
Lucien's sister, and deliberately misrepresented himself
as the attorney for a supposed natural brother, who
would be entitled to certain rights in old Séchard's estate,
and by her answers was assured of the falsity of Lucien's
statement that his sister had supplied him with the
money.

In *L'Interdiction* (The Commission in Lunacy), Balzac portrays Popinot, his ideal judge. The Marquise
d'Espard, who was living apart from her husband, and
was very tired of him, presented, through the attorney,
Desroches, a petition to the Court that the Marquis
should be declared incompetent to manage his business
affairs. The case was assigned to Judge Popinot, and
the Marquise, through her particular friend, Rastignac,
procured Dr. Bianchon, the judge's nephew, to invite
him to dine with her. The judge, by way of answer,
quoted the Code of Civil Procedure, Art. 378, Sec. 8,
forbidding any magistrate to eat or drink in the house of
any party to a litigation before him. The judge was a
widower with a penchant for old clothes and shabby hats,
his hands preferred pockets to gloves, and he had a distinct aversion to shaving more than twice a week. With

his huge feet, flat nose and enormous ears, his appearance did not commend itself to the casual observer, while his purity of mind and honesty of purpose made it impossible for him to enter into those schemes which political pull then made essential for professional advancement. Familiar with criminals, and knowing the life of all the poor of his district, he occupied the time not spent in his judicial duties in works of charity, so that his merits were best appreciated by those who were least able to reward them.

The petition of the Marquise, founded upon Article 489 of the Code, is set out in full by Balzac and occupies nearly a dozen pages, setting forth in detail the alleged eccentricities of the Marquis; and after reading it, Judge Popinot resolved to call upon the parties and examine them as to the facts. This procedure may seem queer to us, but the difference in practice is agreeable to the formula already given for French law. At any rate Popinot visits the Marquise, taking his friends along with him, and cross-examines her so skillfully that her dishonest motives are laid bare. He leaves as tea is served. In his subsequent visit to the Marquis, he ascertains that the real cause of the apparent extravagance of the Marquis was his endeavor to make restitution to the lawful heirs of property confiscated at the time of the Revocation of the Edict of Nantes by Louis XIV and given to the ancestors of the Marquis. Just as the judge had written his report and was about to dismiss the petition, the President of the Court dismissed him on the ground that he had taken tea with the Marquise, and Cæsar's wife must be above suspicion, so Camusot, a dependable judge, who figures in other novels, is appointed in his stead.

But Balzac is too vast. It is impossible to discuss the law and lawyers of *The Human Comedy* in an hour. It would be easier to exhaust my audience than my subject, and to accomplish the latter would violate the rule against perpetuities. Any Balzackian will see that this is only the barest sketch of the subject, but as Emerson said in his journal, "Sometimes a Scream is better than a Thesis," and as Lord Coke remarked, with one of his brilliant mixed metaphors, after a tedious discussion of the once profitable, but now happily forgotten Statute of 32 Hen. VIII c. 5 (Co. Litt. 290 a): "This little taste shall give a light to the diligent reader."

V

The Writings of Sir Edward Coke

The Writings of Sir Edward Coke [1]

ELIZABETH, Queen of England, had many claims to great distinction. Her very name was Tudor, a contraction, it seems, of Theodore, "the gift of God," an epithet of happy omen associated with the mighty rulers of the earth, among whom may be mentioned the African king, Theodore of Abyssinia. This monarch is described in the *Encyclopedia Britannica* as a "man of education and intelligence, superior to those among whom he lived, with natural talents for governing and gaining the esteem of others. He had a noble bearing, and a frame capable of enduring any amount of fatigue, and he was the best shot and the best horseman in Abyssinia. He was generous to excess and free from cupidity but subject to violent bursts of anger." [2]

Elizabeth also possessed many of these royal traits of character, although Coke said her name was not really Tudor but rather Owen or Meredith, though "God would not suffer her to have a sir name because by his grace and goodness she should deserve for her imperial vertues to be called Elizabeth the great." [3] "She was," said Coke, "the phoenix of her sex; [4] she was *Angliae Amor;* [5] familiar with French, Italian and Spanish and learned in Latin and Greek; [6] and "as the rose is the queen of flowers

---

[1] Reprinted from the *Yale Law Journal*, May, 1909.

[2] *Encyclopedia Britannica*, Art. Abyssinia.

[3] 4 Inst. 239.   The references to 2, 3 and 4 Inst. are to the London Ed. of 1809.

[4] 8 Rep. 77a.   The references to the reports are to Thomas and Frazer's edition.

[5] 2 Inst. 578.

[6] 4 Inst. 227.

. . . she was the Queen of Queens. You cannot question what rose I mean: for take the red or the white she was not only by royal descent and inherent birthright, but by roseal beauty also, heir to both." [1]

Whether or not Elizabeth deserved this praise, and even if she had no right to bear the royal name of Theodore, she was fortunate enough to lend her own to the most glorious period of her country's history. Never before was thought more effervescing or life more iridescent and vivid. There was a volcanic eruption of brilliant men; Coke was born in 1552, Bacon in 1561, Shakespeare in 1564. Why it was that these men, unequalled respectively as lawyer, philosopher and poet, should have appeared within the narrow limits of a dozen years is certainly strange, but as writers always say of what they cannot explain, we shall not stop here to inquire.

Among these and other men who graced the complex Elizabethan Age, Coke was by no means the least important. He was the oracle and ornament of the common law: a lawyer of prodigious learning, untiring industry and singular acumen, with an accurate knowledge of human nature. He was a Judge of perfect purity, a patriotic and independent statesman and a man of upright life; and to bring us to the subject of this paper, his writings have had more influence upon the law than those of any other law writer — certainly in England — who ever lived. And yet there are some who, while admitting his learning, would deny every other claim just made for him. It is indeed hard to estimate correctly even after three centuries, those mighty men who then occupied the center of the stage. Every one who reads the fascinating

---

[1] Co. Litt. Pref.   Coke often alluded to his service as Elizabeth's Attorney General.   3 Inst. 79, 112, 164, 191, 236; 4 Inst. 110, 257, 341, 347.

Elizabethan story becomes insensibly a Baconian or a Cokian, a partisan of one or the other of those wonderful men. They were indeed antipathetic, each doubtless feeling for the other intellectual compassion rather than sympathy.

We are finding out in the twentieth century what the English lawyers discovered in the sixteenth, that the old common law, with its unsurpassed powers of adaptability and expansion contains within it the solution of present-day problems, and in our renewed study upon historical lines we cannot have a better motto than "Back to Coke." As he himself said: "Out of the old fields must come the new corne."[1] There are few principles of the common law that can be studied without an examination of Coke's *Institutes* and *Reports*, which summed up the legal learning of his time. From this study the student is deterred by the too common abuse of Coke's character and the general criticism of his writings as dry, crabbed, verbose and pedantic. Much of this criticism is incorrect, for his severest critics, I am sure, are the least familiar with his writings; much of it is unfair, for Coke, like every man, was necessarily a product of the age in which he lived. His faults were the faults of his time, his excellencies those of all time. He was diffuse; he loved metaphor, literary quibbles and verbal conceits; so did Bacon, and so did Shakespeare. So did all the writers of his day. They were creative, not critical. But Coke as a law writer was as far superior in importance and merit to his predecessors, at least if we except Bracton, as the Elizabethan writers in general were superior to those whom they succeeded, and, as the great Elizabethans fixed the standard of our English tongue, so Coke established the common law on its firm foundation. A modern lawyer

---

[1] 2 Inst. 22; Pref. 1 Rep. xxx.

who heaps his abuse on Coke and his writings seems as
ungrateful as a man who climbs a high wall by the aid of
the sturdy shoulders of another and then gives his friend
a parting kick in the face as he makes the final leap.

The two writers who are responsible for most of the
unfair criticism of Coke as a man and a lawyer are Lord
Macaulay and Lord Campbell, the former exhibiting all
his violent prejudice and the latter his inaccurate super-
ficiality.   Just criticism requires sympathy with its subject and these men did not walk with Coke.   They stood
on the other side of the street and called him names.
It is not the present purpose of the writer to defend
Coke's personality, but only the literary characteristics
of his writings, and in this mere sketch, I shall, after
quoting the charges of Macaulay and Campbell, endeavor
to prove their unfairness and then to show by quotations
from Coke himself that his literary taste and abilities
have been underrated, and that his writings possess a
certain characteristic charm.

Macaulay, in his *Essay on Lord Bacon*, attacked Coke
with the same "rancorous insolence" of which he accuses
Coke.   He calls Coke a "stupid sergeant,[1] pedant, bigot
and brute," although Macaulay grudgingly admits that
"he had qualities which bore a strong, though a very disagreeable, resemblance to some of the highest virtues
which a public man can possess."[2]

Again Macaulay says: "Coke's opposition to the
Court, we fear, was the effect, not of good principles, but
of a bad temper,"[3] and in recounting Bacon's downfall,
Macaulay says: "Coke, for the first time in his life,

---

[1] Macaulay's *Works* in 12 vols.   Longmans, Green & Co., Vol. viii.,
p. 516.   Coke was not made a sergeant until he went on the Bench.
1 Johnson's *Coke*, p. 215.

[2] Vol. viii., p. 547.

[3] Vol. viii., p. 562.

behaved like a gentleman."[1] Lord Campbell, on the
first page of his *Life of Coke*,[2] praises him in no slight
language for his knowledge of the law, his ability and
independence as a Judge,[3] and his great services to his
country in framing the *Petition of Right*,[4] but throughout his biography severely criticises Coke's personal
characteristics. These criticisms can best be refuted by
a calm consideration of his life and the opinions of those
more capable of correct judgment than these brilliant but
prejudiced men who wrote two centuries after their victim died. But what is more important for us just now
is Campbell's criticism of the method and style of Coke's
writings. Collected from various portions of the biography, these charges are about as follows: "His reasoning," says Campbell, "is narrow minded"; he had an
"utter contempt for method and style in his composi-
tions";[5] he had "no genuine taste for elegant literature";[6]
"his mind was wholly unimbued with literature or
science";[7] he knew "hardly anything beyond the weari-
some and crabbed learning of his own *craft*,"[8] although
Campbell elsewhere says of Coke: "He is uniformly
perspicuous and gives amusing glimpses of history and

---

[1] Vol. viii., p. 583.

[2] *Lives of the Chief Justices*, Vol. i. Murray's Ed.

[3] Campbell emphasizes this frequently; see pp. 257, 268, 277, 279,
282, 286, 293, 346.

[4] Vol. i., pp. 330, 339.

[5] Vol. i., p. 239. On p. 345 he calls Coke a "deep but narrow-
minded lawyer," but says on p. 289 his *Reports* "were executed with
great accuracy and ability, though tinctured with quaintness and
pedantry."

[6] Vol. i., 239. Campbell, however, gives several good examples
of Coke's style; pp. 341, 342.

[7] Vol. i., p. 337.

[8] Vol. i., p. 345. It is interesting to observe how Campbell speaks
of his own profession.

manners." [1]   He endeavors to prove Coke's distaste for
literature by saying that at school "he was more remarkable for memory than imagination and he had as much
delight in cramming the rules of prosody in doggrel verse
as in perusing the finest passages of Virgil." [2] If Campbell had any authority for this, he fails to give it, and it is
probable that he displayed his own imagination rather
than his memory when he made this silly statement.
But he makes another statement quite as foolish. [3]
"Coke," he says, "values the father of English poetry
only in so far as the Canon's *Yeoman's Tale* illustrates
the Stat. 5 H. IV, c. 4 against alchemy or the craft of
the multiplication of metals; — and he classes the worshipper of the Muses with the most worthless and foolish
of mankind: — The fatal end of these five is beggary, —
the alchemist, the monopolist, the concealer, the informer
and the poetaster.

Saepe pater dixit, studium quid inutile tentas?
Maeonides nullas ipse reliquit opes." [4]

This is indeed a curious innuendo.   It would not prove
that a lawyer does not care for literature, to show that he
does not quote poetry in his law books.   Coke was not
obliged to quote Chaucer at all, but if he did, he would
naturally cite him to illustrate some point of law.   But
in fact Coke quoted Chaucer no less than four times.
In speaking of good pleading, Coke refers to Chaucer's
sergeant-at-law:

"Thereto he could indite and make a thing,
There was no wight could pinch at his writing." [5]

[1] Hardcastle's *Life*, Vol. ii., p. 26.
[2] Vol. i., p. 241.
[3] Vol. i., p. 337.
[4] 3 Inst. 74.
[5] 2 Inst. 123.

and he applies the same verses to Littleton in the preface to *Co. Litt.* from which it appears that Campbell never read or had forgotten the very interesting and well-written preface to Coke's most famous work.[1] Coke, in explaining the meaning of Vavasor, cites Chaucer "our English poet" in the *Franklyn's Prologue*,[2] and he illustrates the meaning of Lusheburghs, a kind of base coin, by a quotation from the *Prologue to the Monk's Tale*.[3] Lord Campbell would have been fairer also had he noted that Coke quoted from Chaucer *"in libro meo,"*[4] showing that he thought enough of Chaucer to own a copy. Prejudiced statements like this have widespreading influence. Emerson in his *Essay on Culture* evidently adopted Campbell's remark about Coke and Chaucer.

Nor does Coke "class the worshipper of the Muses with the most worthless and foolish of mankind." He classes the "poetaster" with the alchemist *et al.*, but "poetaster" is not equivalent to "poet," for it means a "trifling" or "foolish" poet. It would be as just to say that Ben Jonson, in ridiculing such a one in his play *"The Poetaster,"* meant to decry his own profession. Coke, as I shall endeavor to show, had a great respect for poets and was fond of poetry, and the Latin verses which he quotes from Ovid,[5] simply express the obvious truth that poetry is not a money-making business, for even Homer left no fortune.

It seems almost certain indeed that Coke, in this passage about the "poetaster," alluded to Ben Jonson's play of that name, for in the *Apologetical Dialogue* which

---

[1] Hardcastle's *Life*, i., 62, 71. As a student, Campbell does not seem to have read Co. Litt. very industriously.

[2] 2 Inst. 667.

[3] 3 Inst. 1.

[4] 3 Inst. 74.

[5] Tristia, Lib. 4, Eleg. 10.

follows it, the dramatist defends himself from the charge
that he had intended to ridicule the profession of the law,
by saying:

> "Indeed, I brought in Ovid,
> Chid by his angry father for neglecting
> The study of their laws for poetry;
> And I am warranted by his own words:
> '*Saepe pater dixit, studium quid inutile tentas?*
> *Maeonides nullas ipse reliquit opes.*'
> But how this should relate unto our laws,
> Or the just ministers, with least abuse,
> I reverence both too much to understand!"

Campbell's citation, therefore, proves the exact opposite
of his proposition, for it shows that Coke had read at
least this much of Jonson.

Coke was a lover of learning, a Cambridge man and
very loyal to his university. His allusions to Cambridge
are always devoted and affectionate. Thus he says:
"That famous University of Cambridge, *alma mater mea.*[1]
In remembrance of my love and duty *almae matri Acade-
miae Cantabrigiae.*"[2]   "The liberal arts and sciences," he
says in his chapter on the University Courts, "are the
lumina reipublicae," and the Act of 13 Eliz., confirming
the universities in their rights, he called, "this blessed
Act."[3]

But to return to Campbell: "The Globe and other
theatres were rising into repute, but he never would appear at any of them; . . . *it is supposed* that in the whole
course of his life he never saw a play acted, or read a play,
or was in company with a player."[4]   This must have

---

[1] Co. Litt. Pref.

[2] Co. Litt. 109 b.

[3] 4 Inst. 227.   Holt, C. J., in I Ld. Ray. I., 468, speaks of Coke's
loyalty to Cambridge as shown in Bonham's Case, 8 Rep. 107 a.

[4] Campbell's *Lives*, Vol. i., p. 243.

been "supposed" by Campbell himself, for no authority is given for the statement, and, as shown above, Coke, it is almost certain, had read Jonson's *The Poetaster*. Even if it were true that Coke did not attend the theatre, the fact would not prove that he did not care for literature or poetry. Very likely the leader of the bar, an indefatigable worker in his profession, could not spare the time. But Campbell makes a more serious charge. "He shunned the society of Shakespeare and Ben Jonson as of *vagrants* who ought to be set in the stocks or whipped from tithing to tithing. The Bankside company having one summer opened a theatre at Norwich while he was recorder of that city, in his next charge to the grand jury he thus launched out against them: 'I will request that you carefully put in execution the statute against *vagrants*; since the making whereof I have found fewer thieves and the gaol less pestered than before. The abuse of *stage players*, wherewith I find the country much troubled, may easily be reformed, they having no commission to play in any place without leave, and therefore, if by your willingness they be not entertained, you may soon be rid of them.'" And Campbell adds a note: "It is supposed to be out of revenge for this charge that Shakespeare parodied his (Coke's) invective against Sir Walter Raleigh in the challenge of Sir Andrew Aguecheek."[1]

There is no foundation whatever for the statement that Coke regarded Shakespeare and Jonson as vagrants, and shunned their society, nor can any such inference be fairly drawn from Coke's Norwich charge. This was delivered on August 4, 1606, when Coke was Chief Justice of the Common Pleas and not during his recordership, which office he had held nearly twenty years before. The charge was piratically published by one Pricket, and in the

---

[1] Campbell's *Lives*, Vol. i., pp. 337–338.

preface to 7 Rep., Coke explains that it was printed without authority with many errors and omissions. But even if he was correctly reported, it must be remembered that theatres and actors were strictly regulated by the Statutes of 14 Eliz. c. 5, and 39 Eliz. c. 4, by which "Common Players in Enterludes & Minstrels with Fencers Bearwardes" and other undesirables were classed as "Rogues, Vagabonds and Sturdie Beggers" and punished accordingly, unless belonging to a "Baron or other honorable Personage or having licenses of two Justices of the Peace."[1]

It was perfectly proper that the grand jury should have their attention called to these statutes and their violation by companies of irresponsible strolling players. Jonson himself was accused of having ridiculed actors in *The Poetaster*, and Coke might have defended himself from the charge of persecution in Jonson's own words:

> "Now for the players, it is true I tax'd them
> And yet but some; and those so sparingly,
> As all the rest might have sat still unquestioned,
> Had they but the wit or conscience
> To think well of themselves."[2]

More than this, we have Jonson's own words to show the great respect he entertained for Coke. In his *Underwoods*, Jonson addressed Coke when the latter was Lord Chief Justice, in part as follows:

> "He that should search all glories of the gown,
> And steps of all raised servants of the crown,
> He could not find than thee, of all that store,
> Whom fortune aided less, or virtue more,

---

[1] The statute is alluded to in *The Poetaster*, Act I, Sc. 1.
[2] Apologetical Dialogue, *Poetaster*.

Such, Coke, were thy beginnings when thy good
In others' evil best was understood:
When, being the stranger's help, the poor man's aid,
Thy just defences made th' oppressor afraid.

. . . .

And now such is thy stand, while thou dost deal
Deservèd justice to the public weal,
Like Solon's self, — " [1]

The Norwich charge was delivered August 4, 1606, Coke having been made Chief Justice of the Common Pleas on June 20th of the same year. As Gifford, Jonson's editor, points out, Coke is addressed as Lord Chief Justice of England, and as Coke was not promoted, or, as he considered it, demoted to the King's Bench until October 25, 1613, at which time he assumed the title of Lord Chief Justice, the above lines must have been written on or after that date, and therefore subsequent to the charge at Norwich. It is incredible that Jonson would have addressed such praise to Lord Coke if in fact Coke was the persecutor of play-actors or had abused them in his charge.

The reference to Coke's conduct at the Raleigh trial and Shakespeare's alleged resentment is without foundation. Sir Walter Raleigh's trial took place November 17, 1603,[2] at which Coke, who as Attorney General was the prosecutor, addressed Raleigh in the celebrated invective: "All that Cobham did was by thy inspiration, thou viper, for I thou thee, thou traitor." The editor of the State Trials adds in a note that Shakespeare in all probability alludes to this when he makes Sir Toby Belch, in *Twelfth Night*, Act. III, Scene 2, say, in giving directions to Ague-cheek for his challenge to Viola: "If thou thou'st him some thrice it may not be amiss." This mistake has been repeated by every detractor of Coke (including

---

[1] *Underwoods*, LXV.
[2] 2 St. Tr. 1.

Campbell) ever since, none of them stopping long enough
to note that *Twelfth Night* was produced long before Raleigh's trial.   It was almost certainly acted in the Temple
before February, 1601-2.[1]   It is of course possible to
argue that the words were a later addition after the trial
and before the folio was printed in 1623, but this is very
unlikely.   Shakespeare died, it will be remembered, in
1616.   Dr. Furness in his *Variorum* edition observes, on
this passage, that he has small faith in those contemporary
allusions.   Coke, therefore, more probably took the
phrase from Shakespeare, or indeed it was probably a
common expression of disdain.[2]

Campbell is still more unfortunate in his disparagement
of Coke's scientific attainments.   "His progress in science
we may judge of by his *dogmatic assertion* that the metals
are six, and no more: — gold, silver, copper, tin, lead and
iron; and they all proceed originally from sulphur and
quicksilver as from their father and mother."[3]   Campbell, however, does not quote Coke accurately or fairly.
Coke said: "There are six kinds of metals, viz.: aurum,
argentum, aes, sive cuprum (*quia inventum fuit in Cypro*)
stannum, plumbum et ferrum.   That is to say, gold,
silver, copper, tynne, lead, and iron; for *chalybs*, steel, is
but the harder part of iron, and orichalcum, aurichalcum,
viz.: lattyn or brasse, is compounded of copper and other
things. . . .   How these several kinds of metalls as *is
supposed*, proceed originally from sulphur and quicksilver

---

[1] Singer's *Shakespeare*, preliminary remarks.

[2] *Cf.* Epistolae Obscurorum Vivorum I. 14, "*Dixit ei multa superba
dicta et tibisavit eum.*"   II. 58, "*Tunc rebellavit mihi et statim
tibisavit mihi.*"   In the edition by Francis Griffin Stokes, a reference is noted to the passage in *Twelfth Night* and to the French
verb, *tutoyer*.

[3] 3 Inst. ch. xx.   Campbell i., 338.   Plowden says the same.   Case
of Mines, Plowd. 339.

as from their father and mother, and other things concerning the same, you may at your leisure read in Georg Agricola, lib. 10, ca. 1." &c.

Coke made no professions to scientific attainments and merely adopted on this question, and as to the quintessence, in the same chapter, the views current in his day under the authority of Paracelsus and others. He evidently accepted the common opinion with some distrust, and at any rate may certainly be excused for not knowing any more than Sir Thomas Browne and Sir Francis Bacon, the former of whom was willing to encourage the experiments of alchemists even if he distrusted them.[1]

Georg Agricola was the foremost mineralogist of his day, and Coke was quite right in referring to him as an authority. Bacon speaks of Agricola with respect as *"scriptor recens, diligenter admodum in mineralibus."*[2] Sir Thomas Browne owned a copy of Agricola, and in writing to his son Edward, in Vienna, refers him to that author;[3] and Dr. Edward Browne, in his letter to his father, Feb. 3, 1669, encloses several inquiries from the secretary of the Royal Society, such as: "Whether in all the mines of gold, silver, copper, iron and lead of Hungary, there be found everywhere quicksilver and sulphur?" showing that the question was a live one.

Bacon himself, although he believed alchemy to be an imposture,[4] seems to have believed in the transmutation of metals,[5] and he thought it would be easier to make silver than gold because both quicksilver and lead are weightier

---

[1] 1 Browne's *Works*, Ed. Simon Wilkin, xcvi.

[2] *De Augmentis*, Lib. iii.; 1 Spedding 572. Plowden 339.

[3] 1 Browne 183, 188.

[4] *In Praise of Knowledge*, 1 Montagu's *Bacon*, 253.

[5] *Advancement of Learning*, Book II; 2 Montagu 147; 4 Spedding 367; *Natural History*, Century iv.; 4 Montagu 159; 2 Spedding 448; *Physiological Remains*, 7 Montagu 209, 212; 3 Spedding 809.

than silver,[1] and he expressly says that "mercury and sulphur are the principal materials of metals."[2] This all shows that Coke relied upon recognized authority in matters of science, as he generally did in everything else, and surely is not to be blamed if he accepted the views of the day, especially when a professed philosopher and scientist like Bacon expressed pretty much the same theories. It is not a little curious, by the way, that the latest theory of modern scientists indicates the ultimate unity of all matter and the possibility of its change from one form to another.

Finally, Campbell charges Coke with "a contempt for all philosophical speculation."

"Having received a copy of Bacon's *Novum Organum* from the author, he wrote on the fly leaf: 'Edw. C., *ex dono auctoris*,' and he vented his spleen in the following sarcastic lines which he subjoined:

" '*AUCTORI CONSILIUM.*

" '*Instaurare paras veterum documenta sophorum;
Instaura leges, justitamque prius.*'

"In the title page, which bore the device of a ship passing under a press of sail through the Pillars of Hercules, he marked his contempt of all philosophical speculations by adding a distich in English:

" 'It deserves not to be read in schools,
But to be freighted in the Ship of Fools.' "[3]

This book was Bacon's *Instauratio Magna*, printed in 1620, and its title page is reproduced by Spedding.[4]

---

[1] *Physiological Remains*, 7 Montagu 193; 3 Spedding 803.

[2] *Natural History*, Century iv.; 4 Montagu 175; 2 Spedding 459. See also *Novum Organum*, 2nd *Book of Aphorisms*, L; 4 Spedding 242.

[3] Campbell's Lives i., 307. Campbell takes this from Bacon's collected works. See 7 Montagu 380.

[4] 1 Spedding, 119.

After all the enmity which Bacon had for years openly exhibited to Coke, it strikes one as remarkable that he should have presented Coke with a copy of his great book. Whatever might have been his motive, he could hardly expect the donee to look on his production with an indulgent eye. Coke was born, like John the Baptist and all the rest of us, of a woman; he was only human, and the "sarcastic" but truthful advice may well have been written by Coke six months afterwards, when Bacon fell from his high estate. The ship sailing triumphantly through the Pillars of Hercules was of course intended by Bacon to typify a comparison between the recent discovery of the new material world and his own anticipated discovery of a new intellectual world,[1] and Coke's verses, comparing Bacon's ship to the well-known Ship of Fools,[2] were doubtless provoked by a claim which he, and others since his time, thought too boastful. But to say that Coke had a "contempt for all philosophical speculation" is an incorrect inference.

In taking leave of Campbell it is only fair to add that he bestows high praise upon the technical merits and great value of Coke's writings. Thus he says: "Coke's *magnum opus* is his *Commentary on Littleton*, which in itself may be said to contain the whole common law of England as it then existed. Notwithstanding its want of method and its quaintness, the author writes from such a full mind, with such mastery over his subject and with such unbroken spirit, that every law student who has made, or is ever likely to make, any proficiency must peruse him with delight,"[3] and the other *Institutes* are "wonderful monuments of his learning and industry."[4]

---

[1] Abbott's *Francis Bacon*, 377.
[2] By Sebastian Brand. Translated from Latin and German into English, 1508.
[3] Campbell i., 340. See Hardcastle's *Life*, ii., 261.
[4] Campbell, i., 335.

Of Coke's *Reports* Campbell says: "He presents a great many questions to be 'resolved' which were quite irrelevant, or never arose at all in the case, and these he disposes of according to his own fancy. Therefore he is often rather a codifier or legislator than a reporter, and this mode of settling or reforming the law would not now be endured, even if another lawyer of his learning and authority should arise. Yet all that he recorded as having been adjudged was received with reverence."[1] The criticism is not wholly deserved, at least is too strongly stated, and Coke has made his own defense. He explains the length of some of his reports by the number of questions argued at the Bar in cases involving large sums,[2] and says that he purposely endeavored to avoid the omission of authorities cited or arguments made,[3] while in Mountjoy's case[4] he says: "Many other matters were moved by the counsel on both sides at the Bar in this case, which I purposely omit because the court gave no resolution of them." A fair and careful reading of his *Reports* will lead to the conclusion that Coke conscientiously tried to pay the debt which he owed to his profession,[5] and further, that it was the frequent habit of the judges of the time to decide, as though part of the case, questions which were only collaterally involved. How well upon the whole Coke discharged his debt, Campbell eloquently admits: "Belonging to an age of gigantic intellect and gigantic attainments, he was admired by his contemporaries and time has in no degree impaired his fame. For a profound knowledge of the common law of England he stands

---

[1] Campbell, i., 340.
[2] 10 Rep. Pref. xxi.
[3] 9 Rep. Pref. xxxix.; 7 Rep. Pref. ix.
[4] 5 Rep. 6 b.
[5] 9 Rep. Pref. xl.

unrivalled. As a judge he was not only above suspicion of corruption but at every risk he displayed an independence and dignity of deportment which would have deserved the highest credit (even) if he had held his office during good behavior, and could have defied the displeasure of the government. To his exertions as a parliamentary leader we are in no small degree indebted for the free constitution under which it is our happiness to live. . . . There were other public-spirited men who were ready to stand up in defence of freedom, but Coke alone, from his energy of character and from his constitutional learning, was able to carry the *Petition of Right*, and upon his model were formed Pym and the patriots who vindicated that noble law on the meeting of the Long Parliament."[1]

I now pass to the evidence, collected from the writings of Coke, which shows the extent of his acquaintance with literature, and his own literary taste. Coke was perfectly familiar with classical literature, both prose and poetry, and his marvellous memory suggested on almost every page some parallel passage from the best Latin writers. The Greek authors he quotes less frequently and nearly always from Latin translations. Of course, in his day, Latin was the language of all learning, and every educated man understood it. To a lawyer it was indispensable, as was also the law French. Coke knew both languages as his mother tongue, and as a matter of course quoted sentences and pages from the Year Books, the Parliamentary Rolls or old records or authors like Bracton, Britton and others, without thinking it necessary to translate. Bacon, it is well known, committed to Latin, in preference to English, those of his writings which he considered of permanent value. Perhaps Coke's fondness

---

[1] Campbell i., 339.

for the Latin and his discursive habit in writing has given rise to the charge that he was a pedant. But pedantry is a useless display of learning, or perhaps a display of useless learning—at any rate, the term involves the double idea of display or affectation and uselessness. Holofernes was a type of pedant. King James I was probably another. Coke, however, was no pedant any more than Ben Jonson or Jeremy Taylor; as he said in one place, he took all in his way and omitted little or nothing, "for there is no knowledge (seemeth it at the first of never so little moment) but it will stand the diligent student in stead at one time or other." [1]

To illustrate the breadth of Coke's acquaintance with the classics and Latin authors I have noted in his works: from Juvenal, three citations; from Tacitus, eleven; Virgil, twenty-eight; Cicero, twenty-four; Ovid, five; Cato, three; Aristotle, thirteen; Sallust, three; Seneca, nine; Horace, eight; Pliny, three; writers on civil law, thirteen; Lyndwood and writers on canon law, twenty; St. Augustine, five; and he has quoted less frequently from Homer, Terence, Euripides, Martial, Strabo, Suetonius, Cæsar and a number of post-classical writers including Thomas Aquinas, Jerome and St. Ambrose. As Coke remarked: "*Authoritates philosophorum, medicorum et poetarum sunt in causis allegandae et tenendae*," [2] and he notes with pleasure: "This is the fourth time that our author (Littleton) hath cited verses." [3] "Verses," he says, "were invented for the helpe of memorie and it standeth well with gravitie of our lawyer to cite them." [4] Did space permit, it might perhaps be interesting, at least to some, to note the very many instances in which

[1] 4 Inst. *Proeme. Cf.* Co. Litt. 9 a; 4 Inst. 98.
[2] Co. Litt., 264 a.
[3] Co. Litt., 236 b; 263 b; 308 b; 395 a.
[4] Co. Litt. 237 a; Co. Litt. 264 a.

he makes an apposite poetical quotation. Following
are a few only. In the case of *Swans*, he quotes the
verses about the death song:

> "*Dulcia defecta modulatur carmina lingua
> Cantator cygnus funeris ipse sui.*" [1]

After quoting Virgil, he says: "But fearing that one
of Virgil's verses should be applied to us:

> " '*Sed jam age, carpe viam, susceptum perfice munus.*' " [2]

When he speaks of a right *in nubibus*, as the phrase
was, he quotes the description of Juno from *Æneid*, B.
IV:

> " *Insequiturque solo, et caput inter nubila condit.*' " [3]

He mentions younger sons, and the lines of Horace
occur to him:

> " *Haud facile emergunt quorum virtutibus obstat,
> Res angusta domi.*" [4]

In Twyne's case, he gives us the well-known verses:

> "*Quaeritur, ut crescunt tot magna volumina legis ?
> In promptu causa est, crescit in orbe dolus.*" [5]

The right of every accused person to be heard in his
defense recalls the "damnable and damned" proceedings of Rhadamanthus in Virgil:

> "*Gnosius hic Rhadamanthus habet durissima regna
> Castigatque, auditque dolos, subigitque fateri.*" [6]

---

[1] 7 Rep. 17 a.
[2] *Æneid* v.   2 Inst. 574.
[3] Co. Litt. 342 b.
[4] Co. Litt. 140 b.
[5] 3 Rep. 82 a.
[6] 2 Inst. 55.

And every one knows the ancient verses he has made familiar, as to the distribution of time:

> *"Sex horas somno, totidem des legibus aequis,*
> *Quatuor orabis, des epulisque duas.*
> *Quod superest ultro sacris largire camaenis."* [1]

Again:

> "For true it is that neither fraud nor might,
> Can make a title where there wanteth right." [2]

In his chapter on Witchcraft,[3] Coke himself dips into poetry.   He translates:

> *"Carminibus Circe socios mutavit Ulyssis —"*
>
> "By charmes in rhyme (O cruel fates!)
> Circe transform'd Ulysses' mates."

And again:

> *"Carmina de coelo possunt detrudere lunem —"*
>
> "By rhyme they can pull down full soon,
> From lofty sky the wandring moon." [4]

There are many entertaining literary chapters in Coke. The entire preface to *Co. Litt.* is well worth reading. Then there is the chapter Of Diet, 3 Inst. 200, in which Coke speaks of the statutes regulating the eating of flesh, and taking these as his text, warns his readers against "the dainty and disorderly excess of meat and drink" as opposed to orderly hospitality, illustrating his topic with quotations from the Bible, Cicero and Horace, and the customs of the Danes, Normans, English and the Ancient Britons.   Likewise in his chapter Of Buildings,

---

[1] Co. Litt. 64 b.
[2] 8 Rep, 153 b.
[3] 3 Inst. 43.
[4] See a longer poetical translation, 3 Inst. 156.

3 Inst. 201, Coke laments the elaborate and costly style of building then fashionable, and quotes Sir Thomas More's translation of Euripides:

> "*Aedificare domos multas, et pascere multos*
> *Est ad pauperiem semita laxa nimis.*"

> "To build many houses, and many to feed
> To poverty that way doth readily lead."

He gives us much curious and entertaining learning about the building of tombs and actions for their deface-ment, church pews and funeral expenses, the seven wonders of the world in six Latin verses, the uses of funeral monuments, the "burial of the dead," the con-secration of churches, the subterranean buildings of the ancient Germans related by Tacitus. Then he talks of lighthouses:

> "*Lumina noctivagae tollit pharus aemula lunae.*"

> "In light-house top is rear'd the light
> As high as the moon that walks by night," [1]

of restrictions against building, and the derivation of certain words.

Chapter 73 of 4 Inst. treats of the Forest law. "And seeing," says Coke, "we are to treat of matters of game and hunting, let us (to the end we may proceed the more cheerfully) recreate ourselves with the excellent description of Didoes doe of the forest wounded with a deadly arrow sticken in her, and not impertinent to our purpose."

> " *Uritur infoelix Dido, totaque vagatur*
> *Urbe furens, &c.*"

And then he goes on to tell of forests, and the forest courts, "the false and furious officers," vert and venison,

---

[1] See parallel passages in 4 Inst. 148.

the survey of dogs, the court of swanimote, and verderors, hue and cry, dog-draw, stable-stand, back-bear and bloody-hand, purlieus, scotale, the duties of wood-wards, and much more. Coke delights in explaining the technical terms of venary. What is a pretty pleasing pricket, you may here see, and what is venison, and why a hare and a boar are venison and a bear is not; and all with copious references to Bracton, the Year Books, old charters, Virgil, Lyndwood, Aristotle, Martial, the Bible, Suetonius and many notable records. "Recreations," says Coke, "should not be used as professions and trades, but to be used as medicines to make men more able and fit for higher and greater affairs . . . and thus have we wandered in the wilderness of the laws of the forest . . . wherein (as the studious reader may well perceive) we have respected matter more than method."

Coke's writings abound with quaint, axiomatic, idiomatic, and pithy expressions. The following may serve as examples (the reader may look for others, and, seeking, will find them):

"The life of a man is much favoured in law, but the life of the law itself ought to be more favoured." [1]

"The general custom of the realm is the common law." [2]

"Questions (are) like spirits which may be raised with much ease but vanquished with much difficulty." [3]

"Perpetuities were born under some unfortunate constellation." [4]

"All the sons of Adam must die." [5]

[1] 9 Rep. 68 b.
[2] 9 Rep. 75 b.
[3] 10 Rep. 29 a.
[4] 10 Rep. 42 b.
[5] 10 Rep. 50 b.

"Idleness is the mother of all vice and wickedness." [1]

Of death-bed wills he says: "Few men pinched with the messengers of death have a disposing memory." [2]

Of rebutter Coke says: "A title of the law, in my opinion, excellently curious and curiously excellent"; [3] so he speaks of "the great weightinesse and weighty greatness" of *Magna Charta*. [4]

Of a hog stye as a nuisance he says: "One ought not to have so delicate a nose that he cannot bear the smell of a hog." [5]

Fraud Coke compares to "birds closely hatched in hollow trees," or *"in arbore cava et opaca."* [6]

"The common law is an old, true and faithful servant to this commonwealth." [7]

"I am not afraid of gnats that can prick and cannot hurt, nor of drones that keep a-buzzing and would but cannot sting." [8]

Of certain books he said: "They are like to apothecaries' boxes whose titles promise remedies, but the boxes themselves contain poison." [9]

Of ignorant physicians, "Who more hurt the body of man than the disease itself, one of which said of one of their patients, *fugiens morbum incidit in medicum*." [10]

"To proceed farther were but to gild gold or to add a little drop to the great ocean." [11]

---

[1] 10 Rep. Pref. vii., 11 Rep. 53 b. *Cf.* 11 Rep. 162.

[2] 10 Rep. Pref. xiv.; Co. Litt. 111 b.

[3] 10 Rep. Pref. xvi.   .

[4] Co. Litt. 81 a.

[5] 9 Rep. 58 a.

[6] 4 Inst. 63; 5 Rep. 60 b.

[7] 6 Rep. 42 b.

[8] 7 Rep. Pref. vii.

[9] 7 Rep. Pref. vi. Coke hated medicine, and boasted that he never took it.

[10] 8 Rep. 117 a.

[11] 9 Rep. Pref. xxiv.

A certain statute, he says, "is cousin German to another." [1]

"It is the worst oppression that is done by colour of justice." [2]

"There is no greater injustice than when under colour of justice injury is done." [3]

"Sometime when the public good is pretended, a private benefit is intended." [4]

"This case is calculated for the meridian of the Court of Wards." [5]

Of the *ex-officio* oath: "No man shall be examined upon secret thoughts of his heart or of his secret opinion." [6]

"Thought is free." [7]

"The law and custom of England is the inheritance of the subject, which he cannot be deprived of without his assent in Parliament." [8]

"Trade and traffic is the life of every island." [9]

"The Judges cannot create offences nor do as Hannibal did to make his way over the Alps when he could find none." [10]

"Ambition rideth without reins." [11]

Of Ranulph, Bishop of Durham: "He lived without love and died without pity, saving of those who thought it pity he lived so long." [12]

---

[1] 10 Rep. 60 b.
[2] 2 Inst. 48.
[3] 2 Inst. 112; 2 Inst. 388.
[4] 10 Rep. 142 b.
[5] 11 Rep. Pref. iv.
[6] 12 Rep. 26.
[7] 13 Rep. 10.
[8] 12 Rep. 29.   *Cf*. Co. Litt. 95 b.
[9] 12 Rep. 79.
[10] 12 Rep. 122.
[11] 2 Inst. *Proeme* 4.
[12] 2 Inst. 15.

"Every one thirsteth after gaine." [1]

"No man can carry the words of a positive law by Parliament in his head." [2]

Of attendance at several courts on the same day: "A man can be but in one place at one time." [3]

"Elections are free." [4]

"They which gladly heare false reports and newes will be also as ready to publish them." [5]

"Once forsworne, and ever forlorne." [6]

"Preventing justice is better than punishing justice." [7]

"The devil deviseth delays." [8]

"Odious in law is waste and destruction." [9]

"The debts of cruelty are never unpaid, *respice finem.*" [10]

"Truth is the mother of justice." [11]

"A law worthy to be written in letters of gold, but more worthy to be put in due execution." [12]

"It is good chance to obtaine, but great wisdome to keep." [13]

"They that buy deare, must sell deare." [14]

"Those two great pronouns, *meum et tuum.*" [15]

---

[1] 3 Inst. 196.

[2] 2 Inst. 88.

[3] 2 Inst. 9. A remark having some present-day application.

[4] 2 Inst. 169.

[5] 2 Inst. 225, on Stat. West. 1, ch. xxxiv., as to devisors of tales.

[6] 2 Inst. 238.

[7] 2 Inst. 248, 299.

[8] 2 Inst. 260.

[9] 2 Inst. 329.

[10] 4 Inst. 12; 2 Inst. 508.

[11] 2 Inst. 524.

[12] Co. Litt. 234a; 2 Inst. 526, 625; Co. Litt. 3 b.

[13] 2 Inst. 527.

[14] 2 Inst. 566.

[15] 3 Inst. *Proeme.*

Of flattery: "It getteth away much and giveth smoke." [1]

Of bribery: "They that buy will sell." [2]

"Though the bribe be small, yet the fault is great." [3]

"Where shall a man be safe, if it be not in his house?" [4]

"The house of every man is his castle and fortress." [5]

"The King can never be poor when his subjects are rich." [6]

"Three costly things do much impoverish the subjects of England, viz.: costly apparell: costly diet, and costly building." [7]

"The sins of the soul are turned to fire." [8]

"Parliaments, palaces of princes, and pulpits should be free from adulation and flattery." [9]

"Good bills in Parliament seldom die." [10]

"No man ought to be condemned without answer." [11]

"The golden and streight metwand of the law, and not the uncertain and crooked cord of discretion." [12]

"Peace is the mother of plenty, and plenty the nurse of suits." [13]

"Execution is the life of the law." [14]

---

[1] 3 Inst. 207.
[2] 3 Inst. 148.
[3] 3 Inst. 147.
[4] 3 Inst. 162.
[5] 5 Rep. 91 b; 11 Rep. 82 b.
[6] 3 Inst. 194.
[7] 3 Inst. 199.
[8] 3 Inst. 200.
[9] 3 Inst. 209.
[10] 4 Inst. 32; 4 Inst. 83.
[11] 4 Inst. 41; Co. Litt. 227 b.
[12] 4 Inst. 38.
[13] 4 Inst. 76.
[14] 4 Inst. 130; 5 Rep. 88 b; 2 Inst. 729.

In the chapter on Ambassadors, speaking of gold and silver money, he calls them "mute but moving ambassadors." [1]

"Hope is the dream of a waking man." [2]

"Earth is the suburbs of heaven." [3]

"The agreement of the parties cannot make that good which the law maketh void." [4]

"Three things be favoured in law: life, liberty and dower." [5]

"The law is the rule but it is mute. The Judges are the speaking law." [6]

"Justice is the daughter of the law, for the law bringeth her forth." [7]

"Certainty is the mother of quietness and repose." [8]

"When the courts of justice be open, it is time of peace." [9]

"A right cannot die: trodden down it may be, but never trodden out." [10]

"Everie man is presumed to make the best of his owne case." [11]

"Warranties are favoured in law, but estoppels are odious." [12]

"Extortion is no other than robbery but is more odious." [13]

---

[1] 4 Inst. 157.

[2] 4 Inst. 203.   The same thought is ascribed to Aristotle, Plato and Quintilian.

[3] Co. Litt. 4 a.

[4] Co. Litt. 51 b.

[5] Co. Litt. 124 b.

[6] Co. Litt. 130 a.

[7] Co. Litt. 142 a.

[8] Co. Litt. 212 a.

[9] Co. Litt. 249 b.

[10] Co. Litt. 279 a.

[11] Co. Litt. 303 b.

[12] Co. Litt. 365 b.

[13] 10 Rep. 101 b.   *Cf.* Plowden 68.

"Robbery is apparent and hath the face of a crime, but extortion puts on the visure of vertue for the expedition of justice." [1]

"Copyholders though very meanly descended, yet come of an ancient house." [2]

"A mischief is rather to be suffered than an inconvenience." [3]

"Nothing that is contrary to reason is consonant to law." [4]

"These informers were best trusted where they were least known." [5]

"Corporations have no souls." [6]

"Reason is the life of the law." [7]

"The realm of England is an Empire." [8]

"There be three kinds of unhappy men: He that hath knowledge and teacheth not; He that teacheth and liveth not thereafter; He that knoweth not and doth not enquire to understand." [9]

"The King's treasure is the sinews of warre."[10]

"Three marks of a libeller: Increase of lewdness, decrease of money, and shipwreck of conscience." [11]

"It is less than a dream of a shadow or a shadow of a dream." [12]

---

[1] Co. Litt. 368 b. *Cf.* Plowden 68.

[2] Comp. Copy. § xxxii.

[3] Of Bail, ch. xiii.

[4] Co. Litt. 56 b.

[5] 4 Inst. 172.

[6] 10 Rep. 32 b.

[7] Co. Litt. 319 b.

[8] 4 Inst. 342.

[9] Co. Litt. 232.

[10] Co. Litt. 90 b. Probably an ancient saying, apparently from Plutarch.

[11] 5 Rep. 126 a.

[12] 7 Rep, 27 a.

"As was excellently shadowed by the Trojan horse in Virgil's Second book of his *Æneid*." [1]

"The real worth of anything, is just as much as it will bring." [2]

And Coke's loyalty prompted this praise of England's navy: "The king's navy excels all others in the world: for beauty they are so many royal palaces; for strength, so many moving castles, and for safety they are the most defensive walls of the realm. Among the ships of other nations they are like lions amongst silly beasts, or falcons amongst fearful fowle." [3]

"Every member of Parliament," he says, "should have three properties of the elephant; first, that he hath no gall; secondly, that he is inflexible and cannot bow; thirdly, that he of a most ripe and perfect memory." [4]

The "dull and crabbed" Coke was not, however, altogether devoid of a sense of humor, albeit of a somewhat dry vintage. His works are not exactly jest books, nevertheless there is an occasional word in lighter vein. It takes two, remember, to make a quarrel or a joke, him who speaks and him who hears, — the vibration of a note and the tuning fork in sympathy. He that hath ears to hear, let him hear.

Coke doubtless noted with pleasure the names "Catcher and Skinner," as the sheriffs in Westby's case, [5] and in another case he observed that "the land lying near the ditch is drowned *ad dampnum*." [6]

Of conflicting sumptuary laws against excess of apparel, he says: "Some of them fighting with and

---

[1] 7 Rep. 18 b.
[2] 3 Inst. 105.
[3] 4 Inst. 50; *cf.* 4 Inst. 147.
[4] 4 Inst. 3.
[5] 3 Rep. 67 a.
[6] 9 Rep. 54 b.

cuffing one another." [1]   He says: "The temporal Judge commits the party convict to the gaoler, but the spiritual Judge commits the person excommunicate to the devil," [2] but notes that excommunication had no effect upon the wheat crop of the excommunicate. [3]

He derives *placitum* or plea, "*a placendo, quia bene placitare super omnia placet*, and not, as some have said, so called *quia non placet*." [4]

Of precedency among women: "The contention about precedency between persons of that sex is ever fiery, furious and sometimes fatall." [5]

In speaking of the posterity of Littleton, Coke said: "It quartereth many fair coats and enjoyeth fruitful and opulent inheritances thereby," and he added in the margin: "The best kind of quartering of arms." [6]

Of the white staff, the Lord Treasurer's badge of office: "When treasure failed, the white staff served to rest him upon it, or to drive away importunate suitors." [7]

An infant being permitted to levy a fine before commissioners who knew she was within age, the commissioners were every one of them *fined*, but the *fine* stands. [8]

He said as to ecclesiastical patronage which he exercised himself, says Campbell, with perfect purity: "Livings ought to pass by Livery and Seisin and not by Bargain and Sale." [9]

Lord Bacon tells us that Coke was wont to say, when a great man came to dinner to him, and gave him no notice

---

[1] 3 Inst. 199.
[2] 12 Rep. 79.
[3] 3 Inst. 42.
[4] Co. Litt. 17 a; Co. Litt. 303 a.
[5] 4 Inst. 363.
[6] Co. Litt. Pref.
[7] 4 Inst. 104.
[8] 12 Rep. 123.
[9] 1 Campbell, 343.

of his coming: "Well, since you sent me no word of your coming, you shall dine with me; but if I had known of your coming, I would have dined with you." [1]

Partington's case he mentions as, "the honorable funeral of fond and new found perpetuities, a monstrous brood *carved out* of mere invention and never known to the ancient sages of the law . . . at whose solemn funeral I was present and accompanied the dead to the grave of oblivion but mourned not." [2]

"An oratour having spoken much in commendation of Hercules, it was demanded of one that stood by, *Quis vituperavit? Ad quod non fuit responsum.*" [3]

Occasionally Coke gives us some amusing mixed metaphors. — Of certain statutes: "They were so like labyrinths with such intricate windings and turnings, as little or no fruit proceeded of them." [4]

"To wind up the thred of this discourse with three acts of Parliament." [5]

"We have broken the ice, and out of our owne industry and observation framed this high and honorable building of the jurisdiction of courts." [6]

"This little taste shall give a light to the diligent reader." [7]

"But I perceive myself rashly running into an inextricable labyrinth; I will therefore sail no longer in these unknown coasts, but will hasten homewards." [8] But mixing metaphors was common enough in those days.

---

[1] *Apothegms* No. 133; **7** Spedding, 143.

[2] 10 Rep. Pref. x.

[3] 4 Inst. 12.

[4] 3 Inst. 204.

[5] 3 Inst. 224.

[6] 4 Inst. Epilogue.

[7] Co. Litt. 290 a.

[8] Co. Litt. 110 a; 9 Rep. Pref. xxv.

Shakespeare "took up arms against a sea of troubles."
The language was plastic. A man who had two images
in his mind at once did not hesitate to utter them
together.

Coke was fond of etymology and liked to give or guess
at the derivation of words. Of course he was wrong as
often as correct, and as Lord Campbell said: "Some of
his etymologies are as good for a laugh as Joe Miller or
'Punch.' " [1] There was no science of philology in his
day, so he innocently supposed that the suffix *ment*
was the root of *mens*, the mind.[2] Testament he derives
from *testis* and *mens*, just as Parliament was supposed
to be "*parler la ment*," "speak the mind," &c.[3] But
this definition of testament is given in Justinian's *Institutes*,[4] and Coke may be pardoned for assuming that
the compiler of the *Institutes* understood the Latin
language. Pages might be filled with funny specimens
such as "Gavelkind," from "gave all kinde," [5] *terra
a terendo, quia vomere teritur*,[6] and "cadaver" from the
first syllables of the words *caro data vermibus*.[7]

Coke gives us some entertaining stories from Hollings-
hed and others: "King Edward IV called before him
the wealthiest of his subjects and demanded of each of
them a certain sum of money. Amongst the rest there
was a widow of a very good estate, of whom the king
merely asked what she would willingly give him for the
maintenance of his wars. 'By my faith,' quoth she, 'for

---

[1] Hardcastle's *Life*, ii, 261.
[2] Co. Litt. 322 b; Co. Litt. 112 a; 10 Rep. 57 a.
[3] Co. Litt. 110 a.; Rep. Pref. xxv.
[4] B. ii, Tit. x.
[5] Co. Litt. 140 a.   The common etymology when Coke wrote;
Butler's note 224.
[6] 4 Rep. 37 b.
[7] 3 Inst. 203.

your lovely countenance' sake, you shall have twenty pounds'; which was more than the king expected. The king thanked her and vouchsafed to kiss her, upon which she presently swore he should have twenty pounds more." [1]

Then there is the rare and strange case of Margaret de Camoys, who was by deed of her husband given to Sir William Paynel. Coke recites at large the deed for the strangeness thereof, styling it *"concessio mirabilis et inaudita."* [2]

He gives the stories of Prince Henry and Chief Justice Gascoyne,[3] of Robin Hood and Little John;[4] John Langton, Lord Chancellor, *temp.* Ed. I,[5] and of King Canute and the sea;[6] the story of how the Abbot of Westminster and forty-eight of his monks broke into the Exchequer and feloniously robbed the king of a hundred thousand pounds, *"ad damnum inaestimabile,"* saith the record,[7] and the story of Radulphus de Ingham, Chief Justice of England, who altered the record of a fine after the term had passed, out of pity for a poor defendant, and was compelled, by way of fine, to erect Westminster clock and clock house at a cost of £800.[8]

Coke is often accused of narrow-mindedness by those who have not studied or have not appreciated his life and works. He was doubtless a conservative, as all great lawyers are apt to be, but in many ways he was

---

[1] 12 Rep. 119.

[2] 2 Inst. 435.

[3] 3 Inst. 225.

[4] 3 Inst. 197.

[5] 2 Inst. 574.

[6] 3 Inst. 207.

[7] 4 Inst. 112.

[8] 4 Inst. 255. See as to Hengham's clock, Holdsworth's *History*, i, 91 n. 3; ii, 244.

far ahead of his day and generation.   He advocated the
humane treatment of criminals in an age when barbarity
was the rule, and that they should be speedily tried and
encouraged to answer without fear.[1] He urged that
prisoners should not be put in irons, or tortured or punished before hearing, citing Virgil's verses about Rhadamanthus, contrasting this with the Divine method,
"*innocentem.*" he says, "*cogit mentiri dolor.*" [2]

"There are two great adversaries to the due execution
of these laws, especially in criminal causes, viz.: *pre-
cipitatio et morosa cunctatio.* As for a man or woman
to be committed to prison and within so short a time to
be indicted and arraigned as it is not possible for them
to procure their witnesses . . . . *in criminalibus, pro-
bationes debent esse luce clariores.*" [3] And again: . . . .
"*de morte hominis nulla est cunctatio longa.*" [4]

He advocated humanity to the criminal insane,[5] and
calls attention by an oft-quoted illustration to the
danger of circumstantial evidence.[6]

In other of his suggestions he shows broad-minded
wisdom. Surely it was no harsh and narrow-minded
man who said: "True it is that we have found by careful experience that it is not frequent and often punishment that doth prevent like offences, *praestat cautela
quam medela;* those offences are often committed that
are often punished, for the frequency of the punishment
makes it so familiar that it is not feared. For example,
what a lamentable case it is to see so many Christian
men and women strangled on that cursed tree of the

---

[1] 2 Inst. 316, 381, 386; 3 Inst. 91.
[2] 3 Inst. 35; Luke xvi. 1; John vii. 51.
[3] 3 Inst. 210.
[4] Co. Litt. 134 b.
[5] 3 Inst. 6.
[6] 3 Inst. 232.

gallows, in so much as if in a large field a man might see together all the Christians that but in one year throughout England, come to that untimely and ignominious death, if there were any spark of grace or charity in him, it would make his heart to bleed for pity and compassion." Coke then advocates preventive justice; first, in the good education of youth, and their learning a trade in their tender years; secondly, in the execution of good laws; and thirdly, as many offend in the hope of pardon, that pardons be rarely granted.[1]

"Laws," he says, "without extreme punishment or penalty are better obeyed than laws made with great punishment,"[2] and "too severe laws are never duly executed."[3]

Coke was in favor of allowing the accused defendant in criminal cases the right to produce witnesses, and maintains that there was no authority in the common law for the contrary practice. This, he says, is for the better discovery of the truth, and he tells the story of his introduction by Lord Burleigh to the queen as her Attorney General. "Madame," said the Lord Treasurer, "here is your Attorney General, *Qui pro Domina regina sequitur*," whereupon Elizabeth said the form should be: "*Attornatus Generalis, qui pro Domina veritate sequitur*."[4]

Something should be said about Coke's use of legal maxims. All the law books and reports abounded with them, *regulae* as they were called, short, pithy sentences

---

[1] 3 Inst. Epilogue.

[2] 3 Inst. 24.

[3] 3 Inst. 163.

[4] 3 Inst. 79. The writer is informed by Charles C. Binney, Esq., that this anecdote suggested to Judge Jeremiah S. Black, when Attorney General, the legend on the seal of the Department; *Qui pro Domina Justitia sequitur*.

generally in Latin, and intended to express or emphasize a general principle of law. They were like popular proverbs in common conversation. They point the argument and adorn the opinion. Coke's writings are filled with them and it would be interesting if it were possible to trace their origin. Some were taken from the civil law; some from the canonists; some from the writings of Greek and Latin authors; some were familiar sayings, and it is more than likely that many were the coinage of Coke's private mint. Some modern writers deprecate their use, regarding them as inaccurate or misleading.[1] Undoubtedly they are the most general of general rules and often indicate little more than the point of view of him who uses them, and should be employed with judgment in the light of experience, like texts of Scripture. They are the result, however, of a serious attempt to reduce the law to scientific principles like axioms in geometry, and in many cases do really express general rules of law or public policy in a crystallized form. No one need hesitate to use such maxims as the following: *"Id certum est, quod certum reddi potest,"* [2] *"Nemo punitur pro alieno delicto,"* [3] "No one can take advantage of his own wrong," [4] *"Qui sentit commodum sentire debet et onus,"* [5] *"Qui facit per alium, facit per se,"* [6] *"Vigilantibus non dormientibus jura subveniunt,"* [7] *"Communis error facit jus,"* [8] *"Nemo debet bis puniri pro uno delicto,"* [9] *"Inclusio unius est exclusio alterius,"* [10]

---

[1] Lord Esher in *Yarmouth v. France*, 19 Q. B. D. 647.
[2] Co. Litt. 96 a; 142 a.
[3] Co. Litt. 145 b.
[4] Co. Litt. 148.
[5] Co. Litt. 231 a.
[6] Co. Litt. 258 a.
[7] 2 Inst. 690.
[8] 4 Inst. 240.
[9] 11 Rep. 59 b.
[10] 11 Rep. 59 a.

"No man can be a judge in his own cause," [1] "*Melior est conditio possidentis*," [2] "*Malus usus abolendus est*." [3]

Such maxims Coke would call "a sure foundation or ground of art and a conclusion of reason." [4]

It is very easy for us, with the fruits of historical research at our hand, so painfully gathered by generations of students, to condemn Coke's errors, and even to call him, as did Maitland, "the credulous Coke." [5] We may smile or frown at his etymologies, his belief in witchcraft, his views of trial by jury, his implicit faith in *The Mirror* and its stories about King Alfred and King Arthur. [6] Coke himself closed his labors with the words: "Blessed be the amending hand, *Deo gloria et gratia*," and would repeat the sentiment now. [7] His faults, I have said, were the faults of his time, his excellencies those of all time. Let us overlook his errors in our gratitude for the mighty things which he accomplished for the common law.

This paper might readily be expanded to many times its length, but I shall conclude with something of what Coke said upon the subject which he loved most of all — the practice and the study of the law.

"No man can be a compleat lawyer by universalitie of knowledge without experience in particular cases, nor

---

[1] 12 Rep. 114.

[2] 2 Inst. 391; 2 Inst. 477; 4 Inst. 180.

[3] 4 Inst. 274.

[4] Co. Litt. 11 a. Bacon made a collection of "Maxims of the Law."

[5] The Mirror, 7 Seld. Soc. ix.

[6] 9 Rep. Pref.; 10 Rep. Pref.; 3 Inst. 224; 2 Inst. 498; 4 Inst. 78 &c. But Coke criticises *The Mirror* upon occasion. 2 Inst. 339; 2 Inst. 377.

[7] 4 Inst. Epilogue, citing Plowden.

by bare experience without universalitie of knowledge; he must be both speculative & active, for the science of the laws, I assure you, must join hands with experience. *Experientia* (saith the great philosopher) *est cognitio singularium, ars vero universalium.* The learned sages of the law doe found their judgment upon legall reason and judiciall president.

"But it is safe for the client and for the councellor also (if he respects his conscience) to follow presidents formerly approved and allowed, and not to trust to any new frame carved out of his owne invention, for *Nihil simul inventum et perfectum est.*

"Read these presidents (learned reader) and reape this faire and large field, the delectable and profitable fruits of reverend experience and knowledge; which you may doe with greater ease, for that more easily shall you learne by patterne than by precept; and they have beene so painfully and diligently weeded, as it cannot be sayd, that in this fruitfull field, *Infoelix lolium aut steriles dominantur avenae.*[1]

"Common law is nothing else but common reason, and yet we mean not thereby that common reason wherewith a man is naturally endued, but that perfection of reason which is gotten by long and continuall study.[2]

"The knowledge of the law is like a deepe well, out of which each man draweth according to the strength of his understanding. He that reacheth deepest, he seeth the amiable and admirable secrets of the law, wherein, I assure you, the sages of the law in former times have had the deepest reach. And as the bucket in the depth is easily drawne to the uppermost part of the water, but

---

[1] Co. Entries, Preface.
[2] *Cf.* Co. Litt. 394 b.; 97 b; Co. Litt. 191 a; Co. Litt. 232 b; Co. Litt. 319 b.   2 Inst. 179; 3 Inst. 100.

take it from the water it cannot be drawne up but with a great difficultie; so albeit beginnings of this study seem difficult, yet when the professor of the law can dive into the depth it is delightfull, easie and without any heavy burthen, so long as he keepe himself in his owne proper element. [1]

"Whilest we were in hand with these foure parts of the *Institutes*, we often having occasion to go into the city and from thence into the country, did in some sort envy the state of the honest plowman and other mechanics; for the one when he was at his work would merrily sing, and the plowman whistle some selfpleasing tune, and yet their work both proceeded and succeeded; but he that takes upon him to write, doth captivate all the faculties and powers both of his minde and body, and must be only intentive to that which he collecteth, without any expression of joy or cheerfulnesse, whilest he is at work.[2]

"And for a farewell to our jurisprudent, I wish unto him the gladsom light of jurisprudence, the lovelinesse of temperance, the stabilitie of fortitude and the soliditie of justice." [3]

---

[1] Co. Litt. 71 a.
[2] 4 Inst. Epilogue.
[3] Co. Litt. Epilogue.

VI

The Influence of Biblical Texts Upon English Law

The Influence of Biblical Texts Upon English Law [1]

The subject of this address, "The Influence of Biblical Texts Upon English Law," must appear peculiarly unattractive. It suggests upon one hand a sermon, on the other hand a law lecture; and if there is anything less alluring than a sermon, especially on a week-day, it would be a lecture on law; and if there is anything more repellant than a lecture on law, I suppose it would be a sermon. The combination would be deadly. It was probably for this reason that the committee in charge of this performance did not announce my subject in advance, so I can only give you this brief warning of what you will have to endure. After this, in Biblical phrase, your blood be upon your own head; in legal language, *volenti non fit injuria* — that is, no one can complain who is willing to be hurt.

At the outset it may be proper to say what excuse there may be for selecting such a subject for a Phi Beta Kappa address.

The object of our society is stated in its constitution to be the promotion of literature, and our motto indicates that philosophy, including religion and ethics, is worthy of cultivation as the guide of life. In selecting a topic for this address, I felt that I must not wander too far from this profession of faith, and yet that for practical reasons I was restricted to some subject within the narrower orbit of my own profession. But in a way the study of law will, especially when undertaken from its

---

[1] Address before the Phi Beta Kappa and Sigma Xi Societies, June 14, 1910.

historical side, inevitably lead, through more or less devious windings, into the whole world of learning and literature — for law is the system of rules governing the conduct of men as members of society and their reciprocal rights and duties. The study of the law, therefore, touches and surrounds the problems of history, politics, social economics, ethics, religion and philosophy, as the air which we breathe without feeling its weight envelops the earth and all who dwell thereon. It is a strictly historical science, the product of centuries of development and evolution, and like natural science exhibits a continuous adaptation to surrounding circumstances, with consequent diversification and improvement, leading from lower up to higher and better forms. As has been pointed out, and perhaps the comparison may reconcile the members of the Sigma Xi to the subject of this paper, "the general facts upon which the theory of evolution by natural selection rests, namely, the struggle for existence, the survival of the fittest, and heredity, have all of them their parallels or analogies in the realm of Jurisprudence."

Our law is not like Melchisedec—"without father, without mother, without genealogy, having neither beginning of days nor end of life." The law, like everything we do and like everything we say, is a heritage from the past.

Sir Francis Bacon long ago said, "The law of England is not taken out of Amadis de Gaul, nor the Book of Palmerin, but out of the Scripture, out of the laws of the Romans and Grecians." And again, he said, "Our laws are as mixed as our language."

So just as our English language has sprung from Anglo-Saxon, Teutonic, French, Latin and Greek roots, our English common law with its unsurpassed powers of assimilation, elimination and expansion, has its origins in old local customs, the civil law, the canon law of the

Church, the writings of philosophers and texts of Scripture, interwoven with the accumulation of a thousand years of statutes and judicial decisions. To speak in a parable, it is like the air plant, growing by the wayside in Bermuda, which, even when torn from its native soil, still keeps on growing, deriving its nutrition from every one of the four winds of Heaven; or, again, like the banyan tree, whose branches, wherever they touch the earth, take fresh root and spring anew.

Now every man is presumed to know the law. Bentham, in speaking of judge-made law, called it "dog law." "Do you know," he said, "how they make it? Just as a man makes laws for his dog. When your dog does anything you want to break him of, you wait until he does it, and then beat him for it. This is the way you make laws for your dog; and this is the way the judges make law for you and me." Nevertheless, you are all supposed to know the law, and likewise you are all supposed to know the Bible. What I am to say, therefore, about a certain connection between the law and the Bible, is theoretically supposed to be entirely familiar to you, and indeed to say that the Bible in many ways has exerted a mighty influence on our law is a platitude so profound that I can scarcely hope to be excused for having uttered it.

This influence has been manifested in several very distinct ways, with only one of which we shall deal this afternoon.

First, of course, there is the general influence of the Bible through the medium of the Christian religion upon the law. It has been often said, indeed, that Christianity is part of the common law of England, and this is due in great measure to the authority of Sir Matthew Hale (*King* v. *Taylor*, 1 Vent. 293; 3 Keble 507), Blackstone and other writers, while Lord Mansfield held (*Chamberlain*

of *London* v. *Evans*, 1767) that the essential principles
of revealed religion are part of the common law. The
former proposition has some support also in the decisions
of our own State, but in its broad and general sense is
without adequate foundation, as has been frequently
demonstrated. There can be, however, no doubt that
the principles of the Christian religion have profoundly
affected the law. Christianity supplied, as it were, the
atmosphere of public opinion which surrounded the
English people, the legislature and the courts, but its
precise effect would be an almost impossible task to
determine.

Of course, the Ten Commandments will occur to every
one as examples of Biblical laws which were adopted into
our own. Disbelief in God, as well as disbelief in Christ,
Blasphemy, Sabbath Desecration, Theft, Adultery, Homicide, Perjury, to mention the chief offenses, were either
punished by the spiritual or the civil courts, or by both.
The history of heresy alone in England, with all that it
involved, the hatreds, the persecutions, the judicial
murders which it narrates, forms one of the saddest
chapters in human history. With none of this are we
concerned at present.

Second, there is the special influence of the Church
and the law of the Church upon the common law.

We who live in modern times, when the State is the
supreme and only source of law, and the Church is absolutely deprived of temporal authority, find it hard to
realize that for many centuries the Church exercised an
authority quite as important as that of the State, that
its jurisdiction extended over and regulated the minutest
detail of the daily life of every man, and that its laws
were administered by courts whose sentence of excommunication practically cut off the culprit from all rights
and privileges as a member of society. He could not be

a juryman, a witness, nor a suitor in the civil courts, and if pertinacious, could be kept in prison indefinitely. The ecclesiastical courts of England have a longer pedigree than those of the common law; for the Church, of which they formed the judicial branch, antedated the Conquest, and through the Church courts, the Popes exerted their authority over all Christendom. The canon lawyers compiled a great system of law, only comparable to that of the Roman or civil law, and this law was held by the Church to be superior to the common law of the land, just as the Church claimed superiority over the State, and the Pope over the King. Even after the Reformation, when Henry VIII boldly asserted the royal supremacy, the canon law of the Catholic Church became the King's ecclesiastical law of the Church of England. The Church courts exercised a corrective jurisdiction over the religious beliefs and morals of both the clergy and laity. All matrimonial questions were settled in these courts, they also granted probate of wills and letters of administration, and to a great extent controlled executors and administrators.

This law of the Church was founded upon the Holy Scriptures as expanded and interpreted by the decrees of the Popes and the glosses of commentators. Its influence upon the system of the common law was greater than is generally supposed, and through it the Bible has had much indirect effect.

But in the third place, and this is the narrower subject of this paper, we find scattered here and there throughout the statutes, law treatises and reports of judicial decisions, many legal rules which were held either to be directly founded upon certain texts of Scripture, or at least profoundly affected and strengthened by them.

The Old Testament was indeed considered as supplemented rather than supplanted by the New, but subject to this qualification, — the Bible, although it consisted not of one book, but of many books, written at periods of time far removed from one another, and from different points of view, in divers tongues, and in the literary forms peculiar to an ancient and Eastern civilization, was considered as the permanent expression of the divine will, and almost every text an inspired oracle for the guidance of all men in all countries and at all times. Interpretation and criticism were practically unknown; the histories of the early Semitic tribes, their prophetic exhortations, their poetry, lyric and dramatic, and their laws, were all received on the same basis; and a text of the Bible, wherever it might be found, and whatever might be its logical connection, was regarded as an infallible authority. Indeed, in the fundamental laws of the Colonies of Massachusetts, Connecticut, New Haven and West New Jersey, the judges were commanded to inflict penalties according to the law of God. The study of the Scriptures was especially associated with the study of law. Chief Justice Fortescue, in his book, *De Laudibus*, said of the judges, that after court "when they have taken their refreshments, they spend the rest of the day in the study of the laws, reading of the Holy Scriptures, and other innocent amusements, at their pleasure."

All through the middle ages, and indeed for long after, men craved authority for all they thought, said and did. The Bible was, of course, first, with the writings of the Fathers of the Church second; but Aristotle, "*The* Philosopher," especially as his works were reconciled with Christianity through the writings of St. Thomas Aquinas, was followed with almost equal devotion; and many of the Latin poets and Cicero served in default of something better. Virgil was particularly esteemed, being regarded as almost a forerunner of Christianity;

indeed St. Paul was supposed to have shed tears over
Virgil's tomb in his regret that he had never seen the
greatest of the poets in life.

> *"Ad Maronis mausoleum*
> *Ductus fudit super eum*
> *Piae rorem lacrimae;*
> *'Quam te,' inquit, 'reddidissem*
> *Si te vivum invenissem,*
> *Poetarum maxime.'"*

We will now consider briefly some of the more striking
instances of the influence exercised by specific texts.

That husband and wife are in law one person was an
axiom of the common law, and the old joke was that the
one person was the husband. "This is now bone of my
bones and flesh of my flesh"; . . . "And they shall be
one flesh." Gen. 2: 23. Such texts as these and the
inferior position of the wife in the Old Testament had a
powerful effect upon the law of married women. The
law of the Church followed these texts, and, by emphasiz-
ing the sacramental character of the marriage relation,
produced a result which harmonized well with the feudal
system. For many centuries the laws governing married women in regard to the marriage bond itself, her
dealings with the outside world in matters of contract
and of tort, her capacity to own real and personal property, were all grounded upon this theory, and so continued
until very recent times.

Another text which had great importance in the law
of marriage was that in Matthew 19: 6–9, Mark 10: 9,
where Christ, after repeating the text from Genesis,
added, "What therefore God hath joined together, let
not man put asunder," to which he added the rule which
is understood to allow divorce only on the grounds of
infidelity. These commands of Christ, given also in the

Sermon on the Mount and contained besides in the Gospel of St. Luke, are the foundation of our law of marriage.

The political thought of the Middle Ages affords a curious instance of the application of Biblical texts to the theory of a corporation. A body corporate was a phrase which instantly suggested or was, perhaps, suggested by the language of St. Paul in speaking of the Church as Christ's body: — "We being many are one body in Christ," Romans 12: 4, 5; "Now ye are the body of Christ and members in particular," I Corinthians 12: 27. Indeed the whole of that chapter is based upon the comparison, and St. Paul in other of his epistles refers to the same idea, which is reflected in the theory that a corporation is an artificial body composed of divers constituent members, but without a full and independent personality. The most usual corporations were of course ecclesiastical, to which St. Paul's metaphor directly applied, but the idea was naturally extended to civil corporations, notably the State itself, and then generally to all. The members of a corporation were its limbs, its officers were its organs, its franchises were compared to the ligaments. Such a body must have a head, or it could not act; the death of an abbot, for example, worked a serious inconvenience. All this entered into the discussion which was waged between the nominalists and realists of the day, whether corporations were real or ideal, actual or fictitious things, and the echoes of the controversy are reverberating to the present time.

Slavery was a matter of course in ancient times in all countries. The Old Testament form of it was particularly mild and humane. In theory, at least, a slave was a member of his master's household, or might become such by having his ear pierced with an awl and thus fastened to the door post. This made his slavery permanent, as it annexed him to the home, or it may be that by the "door post" was meant the gate of the camp or city, which gave formal publicity to the proceeding. And in Deut. 23:15, a fugitive slave was to be protected when he fled from his master. St. Paul, on the other hand, sent back Onesimus to his master, Philemon, though with an injunction to treat him kindly, and in his Epistle to the Ephesians exhorted slaves to be obedient to their masters. Yet in numerous passages he speaks of the distinction between slave and freeman as having no meaning in their relationship to God. He himself was a bond servant to Christ. The condition of slavery, in other words, was only external, having no existence in the spiritual life "where there is neither Greek nor Jew, bond nor free, but Christ is all and in all." And on Mars' Hill St. Paul declared that God had made of one blood all nations of men, for in Him we live, move and have our being, quoting what the poet Aratus said, "For we are also his offspring."

The early Fathers, and the Church down to modern times, recognized slavery in the same way. St. Gregory repeated the theory inherited from the Greek philosophy that all men are by nature equal, and reconciled it with the institution of slavery by holding the latter to be a concession to necessary conditions of human life and one of the consequences of sin. He who commits sin is the servant of sin.

In the bitter controversies over slavery and the Fugitive Slave Laws which preceded our Civil War, no authority was quoted with greater confidence than was St. Paul, and he who argued against the injustice of slavery was held to be an opponent of the revealed will of God; while on the other hand, Emerson, in his speech on the Fugitive Slave Law, unhesitatingly affirmed that an immoral law was void and appealed for support to the Bible, which he said was a part of every technical law library.

So St. Paul said, "Let every soul be in subjection to the higher powers: the powers that be are ordained of God." "Fear God, honour the king." These and similar texts in later times became the ground of the formal theory of the Divine Right, which made so much mischief in the history of our constitutional law. But in other well-known passages St. Paul holds that the end of civil government is to be the avenger for wrath to him who doeth evil; its divine institution was for that purpose, and only so far as that purpose was fulfilled did government retain its sacred character. In short, the Bible contains an arsenal of texts, from which the advocates of the Divine Right on one side, and the defenders of human freedom and equality on the other, freely selected their weapons.

The medieval doctrine of the unlawfulness of usury, that is, the charging of interest for the loan of money, produced a profound impression upon social and economic progress. The texts which forbade it are familiar. Exodus 22: 25, and Levit. 25: 36 prohibited the exaction of interest from the poor, which practically included at that time every one who wanted to borrow; and while the later code of Deut. 23: 19 allowed the Jews to charge interest on loans to foreigners, the XVth Psalm described a citizen of Zion as one who putteth not out his money to usury; and Christ himself in the Sermon on the Mount, Luke 6:35, directed his disciples to lend, "hoping for nothing again." Aristotle, moreover, declared that money being by nature barren or unproductive, to extract offspring from it must necessarily be contrary to nature, it being remembered that the Greek word τόκος meant both "child" or "offspring" and, derivatively, interest. There could be no question as to the iniquity of a practice forbidden by both Aristotle and the Bible, so all through the Middle Ages and

long afterwards, usury was regarded with peculiar abhor-
rence as a mortal sin, although avarice, triumphant over
piety, continually evaded the law by ingenious devices.
And indeed in those days men borrowed not so much
to use money in business or commerce as to relieve
pressing necessity; the debtor was a poor man who borrowed as a last resort to support himself and his family,
and the creditor in recovering his loan would take all that
his victim owned. Money lending, therefore, was left
to the Jews, who being without the pale of the Church
were not regarded as subject to its laws, and it was
thought were damned already, though, of course, the
practice was not legal with them any more than it was
with Christians. The natural effect was to increase
vastly the rate of interest charged in order to insure the
contingent losses of an illegal and vastly unpopular business. He who ran the risk of odium and temporal loss
in this world, and damnation in the next, naturally made
the most while he could out of his iniquitous enterprise;
the rates of interest rose to enormous percentages and the
restrictions on trade and commerce became, as trade and
commerce increased, unbearable. The practical wisdom of
Elizabeth's Parliament repealed the earlier acts in 13 Elizabeth 8, and avoided all contracts for interest over 10%.

The curious and horrible history of witchcraft in England, Old and New, is due to the misapplication of the
well-known text in Exodus 22: 18, "Thou shalt not suffer
a witch to live." This injunction was reinforced by the
references in Deut. 18: 9 to sorcerers, charmers and con-
sulters with familiar spirits, and in Levit. 20: 27; such
offenders were doomed to be stoned. The Hebrews, like
all ancient people, were profoundly superstitious, and
firm believers in such things. Saul himself is stated in
I Samuel 28: 9 to have driven the wizards and mediums
from the country, yet in his last extremity he consulted

the Witch of Endor, who procured for him a *séance* with the prophet Samuel. The evil effects of witchcraft upon a superstitious people may be fairly estimated by what we see in present times of their modern representatives, and the penalty of death, though apparently severe, was doubtless not an unreasonable police regulation some eight centuries before Christ. But the command, "Thou shalt not suffer a witch to live," was transplanted to England after an interval of over two thousand years, as though it were intended to apply everywhere and for all time, and "these awful words," says Mr. Lea, in his History of the Inquisition, "have served as a justification for more judicial slaughter than any other sentence in the history of human jurisprudence." Statutes were passed upon the subject during the reign of Henry VIII and Elizabeth, and in the following century, James I, who firmly believed in Demonology, procured the passage of a drastic act in the first year of his reign. The best-known examples of persecution for witchcraft were the case of the Lancashire witches in 1634, and the case of the Norfolk witches ten years later, in which latter affair about fifty persons were executed. One pathetic feature of this unhappy time is that it was the fervently religious people who believed most implicitly in the guilt of the wretched old women who were accused. Sir Matthew Hale was one of the brightest ornaments of the English Bench, yet it was he who presided in 1665 at the trial of witches in Bury St. Edmunds, where Sir Thomas Browne, the author of the *Religio Medici*, gave his expert testimony against the defendants. Bacon, Raleigh, Selden and other famous and brilliant men were all infected with the same terrible error, and in fact the acts were not repealed until 1736.

Blackstone IV, 60, says at a later date, "To deny the possible, nay the actual existence of witchcraft and sorcery is at once flatly to contradict the revealed word of God in various passages both of the Old and New Testament."

Those who read the testimony as set forth in *Hutchinson on Witchcraft, Potts' Discoverie*, and the case of *Temperance Lloyd* in the State Trials, 8, 1018, will be saddened and amazed at the record of credulity and superstition. In New England the case of the Salem witches is well known, but in Pennsylvania there is no such sad record. Only one trial for witchcraft appears to have taken place in this Province, and in that the verdict was "not guilty," though coupled with a finding that the defendant was guilty of "having the common fame of a witch."

While it would be too much to assert that all of this was due to the Biblical texts referred to, it is certain that for many years doubters were silenced by the supposedly Divine authority.

There was an ancient rule that any animate or inanimate thing that caused the death of a human being should be *deo dandum*, that is, "given to God," which in practice meant that the deadly thing or its value was handed over to the king as the price of blood, to be, at least theoretically, devoted by his almoner to pious uses, or objects of charity. The law seems to have especially applied in cases where the death was caused by something in motion, like a horse that throws its rider, or a cart that runs over a man. Mrs. Green thus describes the law: "If a peasant were kicked by his horse, if in fishing he fell from his boat, or if in carrying home his eels or herrings he stumbled and was crushed by the cart wheel, his wretched children saw horse, or boat or cart with its load of fish, which in olden days had been forfeited as deodand to the service of God, now carried off to the king's hoard." And for centuries in every indictment for homicide the value of the weapon which caused the death was always stated.

This rule is very ancient and most likely antedated the time when the Bible had any very great influence in shaping the law, but Lord Coke, followed by Blackstone, grounds it expressly upon the law of God as stated in Exodus 21: 28: "If an ox gore a man or a woman that they die, then the ox shall be surely stoned and his flesh shall not be eaten." It is a strange example of the persistence of ancient law that deodands were not abolished in England by statute until 1846. (9 and 10 Vict. c. 62.) It is, however, worthy of consideration whether modern conditions do not call for a revival of the law. If every automobile or trolley car, for instance, which causes the death of man, woman or child, were forfeited by the owner, it is very likely that the number of accidents would suddenly decrease.

A curious parallel with the law of deodands was drawn from the covenant with Noah in Genesis 9: 5: "And surely your blood of your lives will I require; at the hand of every beast will I require it, and at the hand of man"; and from the requirement that a homicidal animal should be put to death. These texts were considered by the medieval Church as authority for the prosecution and punishment of delinquent animals. In France, Germany and other continental countries many curious indictments were preferred against rats, mice and other destructive vermin, as well as vicious animals who killed or injured men, but as no such prosecutions seem to have been brought in England, the subject lies beyond our limits.

The famous privilege claimed and enjoyed for centuries by the priesthood, known as Benefit of Clergy was, according to Blackstone, founded upon the text, "Touch not mine anointed and do my prophets no harm." (4 Blacks. 365, Keilwey 181.)

Benefit of Clergy was one of the most important heads of medieval criminal law, and meant briefly that an ordained clerk or clergyman who committed any of the graver crimes known as felonies could only be tried by an ecclesiastical court, and only be punished by such punishment, that is, penance, as such court might decree. The result was that when any one in holy orders committed a crime, he could plead his clergy, and the civil courts were then obliged to turn him over to the ecclesiastical authorities; and as he was entitled before them to be discharged by what was called compurgation, upon his swearing that he was innocent and procuring others who would swear as a matter of form that they believed him, the clerical criminal became practically immune from punishment. The doctrine soon developed that all who were sufficiently learned to be able to read were considered clerks, and entitled to benefit of clergy, and this produced a condition of things for which the only excuse is that the frightful barbarity of the criminal was mercifully tempered. Indeed the privilege was finally extended to all who could read what was called the "neckverse," a single verse of the Bible by custom taken from the fifty-first Psalm. "Have mercy upon me, O God, according to thy loving kindness; according unto the multitude of thy tender mercies, blot out my transgressions." In the reign of Henry VII, burning in the hand was substituted for the ecclesiastical compurgation in order that the advantage of committing crime might not be enjoyed a second time, the theory apparently being that every educated man was entitled to commit one felony in the course of his life. At its best, benefit of clergy was a clumsy device to mitigate the severity of the criminal law; at its worst, it nullified the law in favor of those persons who had least excuse for breaking it. And yet Benefit of Clergy was not formally abolished until 1827. (7 and 8 George IV, c. 28.)

Among the ancient Hebrews the law of blood revenge caused the institution of the altar asylum. You will remember how Cain feared the Avenger after killing Abel, and how Joab in I Kings 2: 28 fled to the Tabernacle of the Lord and caught hold of the horns of the altar. So there were also set aside cities of refuge as places where the innocent manslayer might flee for protection from the avenger of blood, the victim's next of kin, who might in accordance with Numbers 35: 19 slay the murderer. According to the narrative in Deut. 19: 1 and 4: 41 Moses selected Bezer in the wilderness, Ramoth in Gilead and Golan in Bashan, and in Numbers 35: 14, three cities were provided in Canaan and three on the other side of Jordan. But intentional murder was not protected. In Exodus 21: 14 it is provided that if a man slay his neighbor with guile, "thou shalt take him from mine altar that he may die." In English law there was an interesting parallel to this legislation in what was called the privilege of sanctuary, which was closely connected with that of Benefit of Clergy. Through Benefit of Clergy the criminal escaped through the fact or fiction that he had taken orders and was a holy man; by the privilege of sanctuary he was protected by his refuge in a holy place. Felons who had fled to a church were allowed to leave it unmolested on taking oath to abjure the realm within a certain time. In other words, they were permitted to escape punishment if they went to a foreign country, taking with them their criminal habits, and leaving behind them everything else they possessed. The custom dated from Anglo-Saxon times, and by a statute of 32 Henry VIII, c. 12, certain towns were constituted "places of tuition and privilege" in lieu of expatriation. There were eight in all, in various parts of the kingdom, including Westminster, but the privilege was confined to the minor offenders. Later statutes nominally abolished all privilege of sanctuaries, but they persisted for a long time, especially in London. Southwark was notorious for them, and all readers of Scott's masterly *Fortunes of Nigel* will remember the hero's adventures in Alsatia, near the Temple, which derived its pretended privilege of sanctuary from the monastery of White Friars which formerly stood there.

Whether or not tithes were due by Divine Right, was a question that was warmly debated between the ecclesiastical and the common lawyers. Naturally those who demanded tithes claimed that the well-known texts in Numbers and Deuteronomy sufficiently proved the Divine will; those who had to pay the tithes just as naturally denied it. But it seems quite clear that this important right of the Church was established in direct imitation of the Hebrew law.

There are few rules of our law more familiar than that which requires a will to be proved by two witnesses, and this is only one of the many cases where the so-called "two-witness" rule applies. Although it is as difficult to trace the pedigree of a legal doctrine as the genealogy of a family, it is reasonably clear that this one is derived from Biblical authority. In Numbers 35: 30 it is said: "One witness shall not testify against any person to cause him to die." In Deut. 17: 6: "At the mouth of two witnesses, or three witnesses, shall he that is worthy of death be put to death; but at the mouth of one witness he shall not be put to death." In Deut. 19: 15: "At the mouth of two witnesses, or at the mouth of three witnesses, shall the matter be established." And in St. John, 8: 17, Christ said: "It is also written in your law that the testimony of two men is true." The same rule, "In the mouth of two or three witnesses every word may be established," is also quoted by Christ in St. Matthew 18: 16, and by St. Paul in II Corinthians 13: 1, and

I Timothy 5:19. By the time of the Emperor Constantine, the rule that a single witness was insufficient in law had been adopted by the Roman law and was further developed by the canon law of the Church. The common law of England never adopted it as a systematic rule, but as the Church courts had jurisdiction over wills, they required two witnesses for probate, on the ground that this was agreeable to the law of God, and this rule has become a part of our law of wills.

The general principle that two witnesses are necessary to prove a legal fact was adopted also by the Court of Chancery and produced there very important results in equity practice and pleading, which affect our law to this day, although of a nature too technical to be interesting, and we also owe to it the rule that requires two witnesses to convict a defendant of perjury, and the provision in the Constitution of the United States, Art. 3, Sec. 3, that "no person shall be convicted of treason unless on the testimony of two witnesses to the same overt act or on confession in open court."

The command, "Whosoever sheddeth man's blood, by man shall his blood be shed," Genesis 9:6, was probably a fragment of the law of retaliation, or talion, stated more fully in Exodus 21:23: "And if any mischief follow, then thou shalt give life for life, eye for eye, tooth for tooth, hand for hand, foot for foot, burning for burning, wound for wound, stripe for stripe"; and in Leviticus 24:18: "And he that killeth a beast shall make it good, beast for beast. And if a man cause a blemish in his neighbor, as he hath done so shall it be done to him." It has indeed been surmised that the law of "eye for eye," etc., was a milder substitute for an older law which made death the universal penalty, for the natural impulse is to kill the aggressor for any serious injury inflicted by him. As Whitmore says in Shakespeare's Henry VI, Pt. 2, Act. IV, Sc. 1:

> "I lost mine eye in laying the prize aboard
> And therefore, to revenge it, shalt thou die."

At any rate, "eye for eye" is in accordance with the primitive ideas of retributive justice, tit for tat, to make the punishment fit the crime; but Christ, in his Sermon on the Mount, Matthew 5:38, expressed his disapproval of the principle, and it was perhaps for this reason never adopted by the common law. In fact, it never seems to have obtained in any of the Germanic systems. The traces of it in Anglo-Saxon times, notably in the laws of King Alfred, were merely copied from Exodus. In cases of intentional homicide, however, the death penalty survives in most civilized countries because it still harmonizes with the general sense of justice, and men still turn back, as did Coke and Blackstone, to the texts in the Old Testament which enjoin it, while they follow the New Testament in its abrogation of the general application of the rule. As Stephen says, "A murderer should be destroyed just as a wolf or tiger"; and Æschylus in one of his dramas says:

> "There is a law that blood, once poured on earth
> By murderous hands, demands that other blood
> Be shed in retribution."

Compare with this the verse in Genesis 4:10, "What hast thou done? the voice of thy brother's blood crieth unto me from the ground."

So as to marriage and divorce. The text that makes man and wife one flesh is found in Genesis 2:23, but according to the Deuteronomic code, Deut. 24:1, divorce appears to have been absolutely at the pleasure of the husband. He might, in the quaint phrase of the Wyclif version of Matthew 19:7, give his wife "a litil boke of forsakynge and leave off," and this little book was called in the Hebrew tongue by the simple but expressive monosyllable, "Get." In the Gospel of Matthew, it is said that "Moses, because of the hardness of your hearts, suffered you to put away your wives, but from the beginning it was not so." That men's hearts continued too hard for the full realization of this ideal Christian theory of marriage is a commonplace of history, illustrated copiously in the ecclesiastical law which could so frequently discover sufficient reasons for holding marriages void *ab initio*. It is always a very easy matter to distinguish and refine upon texts which do not suit one's personal views upon the subject, and rely triumphantly upon others which are more agreeable.

In like manner the two-witness rule probably derived its real power from the facts, however dimly recognized, that the cumulative force of the testimony of two or more witnesses increases almost in the geometrical ratio of their number, and that the second witness can hardly tell so consistent a story that, if either be false, cross-examination will fail to detect the falsehood. The Apocryphal story of Susanna is a well known illustration.

Thus, also, in cases where the injunctions and penalties prescribed by the Hebrew law did not satisfy the consciences of our ancestors, they were frankly disregarded. The prohibition of swine's flesh as food was never taken seriously by a nation devoted to breakfast bacon, and the punishment of death by stoning for Sabbath breaking, Numbers 15: 36, and disobedience to parents, Deut. 21: 18, were passed over as belonging to the "old dispensation."

So the early law of the Province of Pennsylvania gave a double portion to the eldest son, in imitation of the Hebrew code in Deut. 21: 17, but this was soon abandoned in favor of equality of distribution.

But the Bible was quoted by all the earlier law writers and judges not merely as authority, but also by way of illustration or analogy. In many cases it is difficult to determine just how much weight was intended to be attached to the quotations. It may perhaps be interesting to observe some such instances. I have therefore culled a few flowers from Lord Coke's writings and Blackstone's *Commentaries*, authors who have probably exerted more influence upon our law than any others.

Thus, in reference to the segregation of lepers in England, Coke cites the provisions of Leviticus 13: 44, and Numbers 5: 1 as the law of God upon the subject. In speaking of twelve as the number of the jury, he observes that this number is much respected in Holy Writ, as twelve apostles, twelve stones taken by Joshua from the midst of Jordan, twelve tribes, etc., and it is interesting to note that Coke himself had twelve children. On partition by lot, he cites Numbers 26: 55 and 33: 54, where the Lord directed Moses to divide the land by lot. He holds that predictions of the end of the world are unlawful because, according to Acts 1: 7, "It is not for you to know the times or the seasons." He illustrates the offense of bribery by the text, "A gift doth blind the eyes of the wise and pervert the words of the righteous," Deut. 16: 19. On duelling, he refers to the words of Christ in Matthew 26: 52, "Put up again thy sword into his place, for all they that take the sword shall perish with the sword," and the text, Deut. 32: 35, "To me belongeth vengeance and recompense." He holds the modern doctrine of international law that political refugees should not be delivered up, and says that this is grounded by some on the law in Deut. 23: 15, "Thou shalt not deliver unto his master the servant which is escaped from his master unto thee." In his chapter on Buildings, in 3 Inst., he quotes with approval the direction in Deut. 22: 8, "When thou buildest a new house, then thou shalt make a battlement for thy roof, that thou bring not blood upon thine house if any man fall from thence," which probably had a deeper meaning than Lord Coke supposed. He illustrates the law forbidding a subject of the King of England to receive a pension from a foreign king by the text from Matthew, 6: 24, "No man can serve two masters." Duelling he condemns because God said, "Vengeance is mine, I will repay." "No man," says Coke, "ought to be condemned without answer," that is, the opportunity to defend himself. He calls this the Divine law, and refers to the saying of Festus in Acts 25: 16, "It is not the manner of the Romans to deliver any man to die before that he which is accused have the accusers face to face and have license to answer for himself concerning the crime laid against him," and the saying of Nicodemus, St. John 7: 51, "Doth our law judge any man before it hear him, and know what he doeth?" In mentioning the relief from jury service of men over 70 years of age, under the Statute of West. II c. 38, he repeats, "The days of our years are three score years and ten," Psalms 90: 10. The circuits of the judges he derives from I Samuel 7: 16, where Samuel "went from year to year in circuit to Beth-el and Gilgal and Mizpeh, and judged Israel in all those places." Chapter 25 of Magna Charta concerns weights and measures; and Coke says this is founded on the law of God, citing Deut. 25: 13, "Thou shalt not have in thy bag divers weights, a great and a small."

The Statute of Westminster, I c. 34, against slander of the king or the great men of the realm, is said to be in accordance with the law of God, Exodus 22: 28, "Thou shalt not revile the gods nor curse the ruler of thy people," and Jude 8, "These filthy dreamers speak evil of dignities." And Lord Coke, in his admiration for Moses, frequently alludes to him as a judge, and the first writer of law.

These examples from Lord Coke might be multiplied indefinitely, so we shall pass to Blackstone, who, writing over a century later, uses Scripture texts in much the same way, although not to the same extent. He founds the right of property upon God's gift to Adam, Genesis 1: 28, of dominion over the earth and every living thing, that moveth upon it (II 2); and refers (II 6) to Isaac's reclamation of the wells which Abraham had digged, Genesis 26: 15, and to the partition made between Lot and Abraham.

He illustrates the English law of inheritance by showing that males were preferred to females by the Jewish law in Numbers 27, the case decided by Moses, of the daughters of Zelophehad. In treating of the use of seals in conveyances by deed, he cites (II 305) the purchase by Jeremiah of the field of Anathoth from his nephew, where the evidence of the sale was signed and sealed. Livery of seisin he illustrates (II 313) from the story of Ruth, 4: 7, "Now this was the custom in former time in Israel concerning redeeming and concerning changing, for to confirm all things a man plucked off his shoe and gave it to his neighbour." He refers (II 446) to the sale of Machpelah to Abraham for 400 shekels of silver, current money with the merchants, Genesis 23: 16, and illustrates the antiquity of wills by Jacob's bequest to Joseph in Genesis 48: 22.

In bringing to a close these superficial and desultory remarks upon certain influences of Biblical texts upon the law, it is right to add that no one should receive an erroneous impression from the harmful use of the Bible which many of the examples might without this caution seem to indicate. In law, as in religion, the letter killeth, but the spirit giveth life. Biblical texts, dragged from their context and applied without any consideration of the times in which they were written, the circumstances in which they were employed, or the purposes for which they were intended, have certainly done an immense amount of harm in law as elsewhere, if regarded in the spirit of Browning's Spanish Cloister:

> "There's a great text in Galatians,
>   Once you trip on it, entails
>   Twenty-nine distinct damnations,
>   One sure, if another fails."

Or as a means of divination by the *sortes sanctorum*, where the Bible was opened at hazard, and the first verse of the opened page was taken as the oracle. But no one should overlook what many writers have so often shown in words far better than any of mine, the benign and ameliorating influence of so much in the Old Testament and so much more in the New. Our attention this afternoon has been directed only to the consideration of one of the elements which has entered, in a curious way, into the growth of our complex system of jurisprudence.

A word more. The Bible as a law book has not received the careful study to which it is entitled. Its theological importance, and, in later times especially, its literary interest have absorbed the attention of its readers, but there are other aspects from which it should be studied. I have confined myself to a small part of its influence in specific cases upon the development of our own law; but the student of comparative law can find in this most accessible place a rich store of material, comparable only with those systems upon which Sir Henry Maine has thrown so much light. Thus Judge Sulzberger has written upon the Hebrew Parliament, and Mr. David W. Amram, in a series of articles in the *Green Bag*, and in his book, *Leading Cases in the Bible*, has shown how the Hebrew legal system was developed from the patriarchal type, and founded upon the family as the social unit, which, like a corporation, survived the death of its head.   We find among the ancient Hebrews the blood feud, the liability of the head of the family for the crimes of his children, the correlative power which the family head had over the children even to deprive them of life and liberty; these archaic ideas, and the corresponding status of women, the custom of polygamy, the rights and obligations of inheritance which are described in the Old Testament have their counterparts in the ancient laws of the Romans, the ancient Aryans and our own ancestors.

The study of our law, especially by the historical method, should indeed be reckoned a part of a liberal education, and as such it is consistent with the purposes of our society.   If it teaches nothing more, it teaches this: that imperfect as all our human institutions are, a comparison with the past shows how great has been their improvement.   Every one should know something of our law, not with the minute study which the practising lawyer is obliged to give it, but enough to enable him to appreciate what law is, what are its elementary principles, and how it came to be what it is through its long centuries of development; for our law is the protector of society, the safeguard of our rights, and the rule of our daily life.   As one last quotation from the Book, it is said in Joshua 8:35, "There was not a word of all that Moses commanded, which Joshua read not before all the congregation of Israel, with the women and the little ones, and the strangers that were conversant among them."   And in William Penn's Great Law of the Province of Pennsylvania, passed at Upland, on December 7,

1682, it was provided that the laws of the Province "should be printed and taught in the schools."

Bentham at a later date likewise suggested that what was good in the common law should be enacted as a statute and read in the churches and used for school exercises. So far, however, the law has not supplanted the Gospel in the churches and has not been popular in the schools or colleges.

It is not a dull, dry study. It concerns, as I said, and greatly enlivens every phase of history, politics, economics, philosophy and literature, and the student can be assured in Milton's words, that in this study, "There be delights, there be recreations and jolly pastimes that will fetch the day about from sun to sun, and rock the tedious year as in a delightful dream."

VII

The Historical Method of the Study of the Law, illustrated by the Master's Liability for his Servant's Tort

The Historical Method of the Study of the Law, illustrated by the Master's Liability for his Servant's Tort[1]

I propose to talk to you this evening upon "The Historical Method of the Study of the Law." We all know that it is not enough to study the statute books and the decisions of the Courts. These must be the basis of our legal education, of course, but the knowledge of them alone is not enough to make us lawyers, though it may afford the equipment of a successful practitioner. We should learn what the law is, but, unless we learn more than that, we shall not know of the law more than of the wind, whence it cometh or whither it goeth.

To study law as a science we must inquire: How did the law come to be what it is? and this inquiry will lead to a second: Why should the law be what it is, or What political or ethical justification is there for it?

Philosophical writers upon the law, such as Austin, Holland and others, occupy themselves, for the most part, with the scientific analysis of legal ideas, and aim to develop a general system of jurisprudence. Others, like Bentham, endeavor, by criticism of the law as they find it, to reform it in accordance with their theory of ethics. Without underrating the importance of such studies, it would seem clear that no correct appreciation of them can be gained by any one of them who has not traced the history of the law, and observed its development, and,

---

[1] Delivered to the students of the Philadelphia Law School of the Temple College on February 25, 1902.

therefore, the historical method of study is not only of
fundamental importance, but is especially appropriate for
the student. He will find that the law grew by a process
of evolution, in accordance with the necessities of the
people, and is founded upon their customs and social conditions. He will find that his investigations lead inevitably to the discovery and analysis of primitive and
changing conceptions of politics and morals. He will find
that, in many instances, the law was founded upon a religious basis. Thus, in the early history of many nations,
the lawgivers were the priests. The Hebrew law is found
in the Pentateuch. Until comparatively modern times,
the English Chancellor, the keeper of the king's conscience, was an ecclesiastic. Still more recently, the
Puritans of Massachusetts Bay established a virtual
theocracy; and, at the present time, with the followers
of Mohammed, Law and Religion are one.

And, in tracing the development of legal principles, the
student will find instances where their origin cannot be
definitely ascertained. In many cases legal rules will be
found to rest upon mistaken premises or false reasoning.
In many cases the task will be found impossible, and we
must content ourselves with surmises and probabilities.
To speak metaphorically, the stream cannot be traced
to a distinct source, but will be found to rise from many
widely separated springs, so that it is impossible to say
which one is the true *fons et origo*.

But, in every case, the student will derive both pleasure
and advantage from his investigations. He may not
succeed in finding the primary object of his search, but
he will be led imperceptibly into many side tracks, paths
leading nowhere in particular, and yet enabling him to
get a good general view of the whole province which he is
exploring, and perhaps affording many interesting and
valuable discoveries by the way.

Just here let me say that Blackstone's *Commentaries* are, for this reason, the best elementary book ever written for the student. They are concise, stimulating, written in a most delightful, and, indeed, inimitable style, and, notwithstanding that later scholarship has discovered many historical inaccuracies, and discarded much of his reasoning, yet, upon the whole, the *Commentaries* are a legal classic, and should be carefully read by every student even if it is the fashion nowadays to disregard them as out of date.

I would further commend to you the works of Sir Henry Maine, especially his *Ancient Law.* Published in 1861, nearly fifty years ago, this book gave to the rational investigation of the law an interest which is fresh at the present day, and, I believe, will never become stale, flat or unprofitable, even though his work, also, has been supplemented, and, in part, corrected by more recent writers.

And, some years ago, Mr. Bryce, the author of *The American Commonwealth*, published a most interesting volume of *Studies in History and Jurisprudence*, including a very valuable essay on the "Methods of Legal Science."

Without dwelling further upon this general subject, I propose, in the time allotted me, to illustrate, by a practical example, the historical method of the study of the law, and to show, if I can, its interest and usefulness. I shall not attempt to give you anything which you could not find out for yourselves. My object is merely to stimulate in you a desire for personal research and investigation.

The example I have selected is taken from the law of Master and Servant, and is expressed in the rule that the master is liable for the injury caused by his servant's torts, committed within the scope of his employment.

A most familiar rule, for our reports are crowded with cases wherein it has been applied in actions of negligence, and yet it is subject to many exceptions, its origin is obscure, and the reasons given for its justification are various and conflicting.

Before proceeding to the general investigation of the subject I would, by way of illustration, refer to some cases decided in our own Courts and taken almost at random.

The first is the *Philadelphia, Wilmington & Baltimore R. R.* v. *Brannen*, 17 W. N. C., 227. The engineer of a railroad train, running his engine along a street in Philadelphia, blew the whistle and frightened a horse. After the horse had quieted down, the engineer blew two more blasts on the whistle, which so frightened the horse that it ran away and knocked down the plaintiff, who sustained serious injuries. The rules of the company forbade the sounding of the whistle except to prevent accident. Although the act of the engineer was regarded as a clear violation of his orders, yet the Supreme Court held the railroad company liable, giving as a reason that the act of the engineer was within the general scope of his employment, and that, while the public can see and know the general scope of employment of the servant, they have no means of knowing the secret orders given to him.

Another case is *McClung* v. *Dearborne*, 134 Pa., 396. The plaintiff had purchased an organ on the "installment plan," and failed to make his payments according to the contract, so that the title to the organ remained in the defendant. In order to recover his property, the defendant sent two men to the plaintiff's house, expressly instructing them to use no violence. The defendant's employes obtained access to the house by a trick, forcibly removed the organ, and, in the course of the scuffle, assaulted the plaintiff's wife and son. The trial Court held that this was a wilful trespass, for which the employer was not liable, but the Supreme Court reversed, because the defendant had sent his employes on an errand that he knew was likely to result in trouble, and he took the chances of his employes being able, under excitement, to retain their self-control and follow his instructions.

I suppose every one would agree that, if a tort is committed in accordance with an express command, the person who gave the order should be responsible. If an early authority is asked for, you will find an old case, 22 Ed. III, about 1349, in 2 Rolle Abr. 555. Translated from the old law French it reads, "If a man commands another to assault me, and he does it accordingly, he is a trespasser, just as though he had done it himself." This, as I say, would seem clear, but, at first blush, it would seem illogical that a man should be held responsible for the torts of another not committed by his command, or even, as we have just seen, in direct violation of his orders: or that an employer, who has exercised every reasonable precaution in the selection of his servant, should have to answer for his servant's carelessness or negligence. Such, however, is the rule of law which, as Judge Sharswood observed in *Hays* v. *Millar*, 77 Pa., 238, "is often attended with much seeming hardship," and "is apt to strike the common mind as unjust."

It is safe to say that a rule of law which has been maintained so long and so persistently as this must have some solid historical basis, and it is equally safe to affirm that its seeming injustice must be counterbalanced by weighty considerations of public policy. "Every important principle which is developed by litigation," says Judge Holmes in *The Common Law*, page 35, "is, in fact and at bottom, the result of more or less definitely understood views of public policy, most generally, it is true, under our practice and traditions, the unconscious result of instinctive preferences and inarticulate convictions, but none the less traceable to views of public policy in the last analysis."

Let us then first examine the historical origin of the rule, and then consider the arguments of public policy which sustain it.

We are so accustomed to regard the individual, and the individual alone, as responsible for his own acts, that every form of vicarious responsibility may readily seem, to our modern view, absurd, or, at least, unjust. Even children are liable for their torts. You will find a case in Pennsylvania, *McGee* v. *Willing*, 31 Leg. Int. 37, where a child of six years was held civilly liable for striking his nurse in the eye with a tack hammer; whilst on the other hand, a parent is not responsible for his child's tortious act, unless he expressly authorized or commanded it.

But, in order to estimate fairly this principle of vicarious liability, we must lay aside our pre-judgment, and take ourselves, in imagination, far back in time; not, perhaps, to the period when our long-armed and hairy ancestors had no idea of redress beyond vengeance, or of justice beyond mere individual reprisal, but to the times of which we have reliable written records. We find that the civilization and the laws of the ancients were founded upon the family as the unit of society, and the rights and liabilities of the individual were, generally speaking, considered as belonging to the family of which he was a member. Let us take some examples from a Book supposed to be familiar to all. There we find that the sins of the fathers are, according to the Second Commandment of the Decalogue, visited upon the children unto the third and fourth generations. In Esther 10: 13, 14, not only Haman, but his ten sons were hanged. Not only Korah, but, according to a fair reading of the text, his family were swallowed up. Not only Naboth, but his sons also were included in the death sentence after Naboth had been convicted of treason. Ahab's sins were visited not on him, but on his children. "And the word of the Lord came to Elijah the Tishbite, saying, Seest thou how Ahab humbleth himself before me? Because he humbleth himself before me I will not bring the evil in his days, but in his sons' days will I bring the evil upon his house" (1 Kings 21: 28, 29.). Here the actual offender, by repentance, saved himself, but the *crime* was unexpiated, and its punishment was inflicted on his descendants. In the Book of Deuteronomy, 24: 16, it is written, "The fathers shall not be put to death for the children, neither shall the children be put to death for the fathers; every man shall be put to death for his own sin," which clearly implies that the law had been otherwise, and now was changed. Or, as the prophet Jeremiah expressed the same idea in morals by his poetical, semi-humorous figure in 31: 29, 30, "They shall say no more, the fathers have eaten a sour grape, and the children's teeth are set on edge. But every one shall die for his own iniquity; every man that eateth the sour grape, his teeth shall be set on edge."

This primitive theory of liability is not confined to the Hebrew law. It seems to be general. Thus, Henry C. Lea, in his essay on the Wager of Law (*Superstition and Force*, chapter 1), says, "In early times, therefore, the wrong doer owed no satisfaction to the law or to the State, but only to the injured party. That injured party, moreover, was not a mere individual. All the races of the great Aryan branch of mankind have developed through a common plan of organization, in which each family was a unit, with respect to similar aggregations in the tribe or nation. . . . Within these units, as a general rule, each individual was personally answerable for all, and all were answerable for each." And he sums up significantly, "This solidarity of the kindred is the key to much that would otherwise appear irrational in their legislation, and left, as we have seen, its traces late in the customary law."

You will find the same thought in Spencer's *Sociology*, chapter ix of Part III, on The Family.

Doubtless many special proofs might be collected of the truth of this generalization. Indeed, some interesting examples go further. Thus, in Vol. X of the Selden Society's publications, we find cases where injured parties sought redress, not from the person actually offending, but against some other person or persons, who were merely inhabitants of the same town, and had accidentally come within reach. For example, in case 34, A.D. 1398, some citizens of Bristol seized a ship from Waterford, in revenge or reprisal for some wine taken from a Bristol ship by citizens of Waterford.

Upon instances such as this, I will not dwell longer, but merely call your attention to a striking illustration of vicarious liability in English law, which survived until a comparatively recent period.

By the common law, a criminal, upon sentence of death or judgment of outlawry, became *attaint*, that is, stained or blackened, and one of the consequences of attainder was expressed in that terribly realistic phrase, "corruption of blood." The attainted person could neither inherit nor transmit to his heirs.

Thus you will recall the familiar scene in King Henry VI, Part I, Act II, Scene 4, where Somerset and Plantagenet meet in the Temple Garden. Plantagenet picks the white rose, and Somerset the red, which incident is the traditional origin of the name given to the Wars of the Roses. And, as they continue their quarrel, Somerset taunts Plantagenet by calling him "yeoman":

> "Was not thy father, Richard, Earl of Cambridge,
> For treasons executed in our late king's days?
> And by *his* treason stands't thou not attainted,
> Corrupted and exempt from ancient gentry?
> *His* trespass yet lives guilty in *thy* blood,
> And till thou be restored thou art a yeoman.

Plantagenet:

> My father was attachèd, not attainted,
> Condemned to die for treason, but no traitor.
> And that I'll prove on better men than Somerset —
> Were growing time once ripened to my will."

In the next Act, Scene 1, King Henry says:

> "Therefore my loving lords, our pleasure is
> That Richard be restored to his blood . . .
> If Richard will be true, not that alone,
> But all the whole inheritance I give
> That doth belong unto the House of York,
> From whence you spring by lineal descent . . .
> Rise, Richard, like a true Plantagenet
> And rise created princely Duke of York."

The conclusion to be drawn is, that the idea of vicarious liability is not necessarily *un*natural; on the contrary, that, in the history of early family law, it must have seemed both natural and reasonable. As Sir Henry Maine says, "The unit of an ancient society was the family, and, of a modern society, the individual."

We are now prepared to examine the explanations advanced for the origin of the rule in English law. Judge

Holmes, in his brilliant treatise on the Common Law, traces it back to the Roman law of *noxæ deditio*, the surrender of the hurtful thing, animal or slave. By this rule the animal, child or slave who did the damage was to be surrendered by the owner or parent to the injured person, or else the damage paid for. Judge Holmes is of the opinion that the option of surrender was not introduced by way of limitation of a liability, which was, in the first instance, general, but that payment was introduced by way of a privilege, as the alternative of a failure to surrender, and this, he asserts, was the law of Greece as well. In other words, the liability of the owner was merely a way of getting at the slave or animal which was the immediate cause of offense, and therefore primarily liable.

I shall not attempt to discuss the Roman law upon this point, for I am no civilian, and can only claim, with Robert Louis Stevenson, to know that emphyteusis is not a disease nor stillicide a crime. Whether the law of Greece sustains Judge Holmes' view, is, perhaps, also a question. The passage from Plato which he cites may or may not sustain his view, and it may interest you to hear it. I quote from Jowett's translation of the laws, chapter xi, 936, "If a slave . . . injure anything . . . the master of the slave who has done the harm shall either make full satisfaction, or give up the slave who has done the injury. . . . And, if a beast of burden, or horse or dog, or any other animal, injure the property of a neighbor, the owner shall, in like manner, pay for the injury."

Holmes then traces the order of development in the Germanic tribes, and finds it, in his opinion, entirely similar to that of the Roman law. Passing to England, he says, "The principle introduced on special grounds in a special case, when servants were slaves, is now the

general law of this country and England, and, under
it, men daily have to pay large sums for other people's
acts in which they had no part or share, and for which
they are in no sense to blame." But Judge Holmes
admits that he cannot find, until a comparatively late
period in England, the unlimited liability of master for
servant, though he is of the opinion, maintained with a
wealth of illustration and suggestive analogy, that it
was established through the influence of the Roman law.

The theory which would provide the rule with a direct
Roman ancestry, and trace its descent to modern times
through the villeinage of ancient English law, is certainly
attractive. But a careful examination of the English
cases and abridgements fails to disclose sufficient historical evidence of it. Surely, if Holmes were correct,
some cases could be found of a lord held liable for the
acts of his villein; but, so far as I can find, none exists —
and his theory is disapproved by Pollock & Maitland
in their monumental *History of English Law*, II, 528,
who assert that a more hopeful line of tradition may lie
within the responsibility of a householder for the members of his household, to which we shall presently refer.

Mr. Wigmore, in his learned examination of the subject in 7 *Harvard Law Review*, 330, writing after
Holmes, arrives at the opposite conclusion, so far, at
least, as the Germanic and early English systems are
concerned. He shows that, according to Germanic law,
the housemaster was responsible to third persons for
those attached to his house. This responsibility was
absolute to render full satisfaction, and, in course of
time, the Wer gild, or compensation money, was considered expiated, or paid, by the surrender of the slave.

In England a similar liability appears at an early date
to be due from a householder, with respect to all who were
members of his mainpast. This word (in Latin, *manu*

pastus, hand fed) was equivalent to household in the broad sense, and included all who were hand fed by the master of the house. In the fourth volume of the Selden Society's publications appear some interesting precedents, or rather, forms. This book is a translation of a form book compiled in the thirteenth century, so that the cases are not necessarily actual cases (though they may be), but typical examples, and, for our purposes, quite as valuable.

I will read a case on page 36: "Sir Steward, the Bailiff, Robert by name, who is here, complaineth of William of the street, who is there, that against the peace of the lord, he sent Thomas, his son, on such a day, at such an hour, in the year that now is, over the wall newly built and erected, and commanded him to carry off of every manner of fruit at his will, and when the bailiff heard the fruit being knocked down, he marvelled who this could be, and at once entered the lord's garden, and found the boy right high on a costard tree, which he had cultivated for the lord's use, because of its goodness; he made him come down, and attached him without doing any villany, and debonairely asked him by whose commandment and whose sending he entered the lord's garden over walls well closed on all sides, and the boy answered and said, that William, his father, who is present there, bade him enter the garden, and urged him on to the tree with the best fruit." William denies that his son committed the trespass by his command, but the steward says, 'At least thou canst not deny that he is thy mainpast, nor that he was attached in the lord's garden for the outrage and for the trespass.' William then admits his liability, 'Sir, for the deed of my son, and the trespass, I am ready to do thy will, and I ask thy favour.' "

We have not time to review the evidence. I will cite only one more authority from the same volume, page 55:

"William, the Lorimer, thou art attached to answer in this Court for that J. & T., who are thy servants, were found mowing the lord's stubble in such a place against the general prohibition made every year in this Court; and the stubble they carried off whither thou hadst commanded them, with which stubble the lord's reeve might have covered the cowshed and dairy, which now are uncovered, whereby the lord hath damage 40 shillings in the matter of this covering.

"Sir, (to prove) that never did my folk, J. & T. by name, cut the stubble of that place by my commandment, nor carry it off, I am ready to acquit myself by a law with so many folk as were awarded me at the last Court.

"And this was conceded by the steward. He was acquitted by his law, and therefore went quit."

In an alternative version, defendant denies that J. & T. were his mainpast, alleging that they were laborers hired but from day to day, and, of this, he puts himself on the jury.

Some interesting precedents may also be found in 2 Selden Society *Select Pleas in Manorial Court*, pp. 149-158.

It is but fair to say that the householder's liability seems, from other cases, to be only that of amercement, in case the offender is not produced.

Upon the whole, however, the more probable conclusion seems to be, as stated in the article in the *Harvard Law Review* already mentioned, that, although a constant effort was made to avoid liability on the ground that no command or consent had been given, yet, so far as civil actions were concerned, "the moral sense of the community" was inclined to enforce the householder's liability.

The question may here be asked: Why should the householder be thus liable? It is not easy for us, imbued with modern ideas, to find a sufficient answer to the question, but we must look for it in the social necessities of that early period. Where a family was a social unit, and every member of it a mere part, and often an insignificant part, of a great whole, it very probably followed that, unless the injured man had this remedy, he had none at all.

It is impossible, even in this cursory examination of the subject, to leave it without allusion to the view of frankpledge, and the liability for harboring strangers. By the law of frankpledge, it was the duty of the township in which any man lived who was accused of crime, to produce him on pain of amercement. And, so far as strangers were concerned, I will illustrate the liability by citing a case, which occurred on May 28, 1321, and is found in the *Coroner's Rolls*, printed and translated in the ninth volume of the Selden Society's publications, page 74: "A certain poor beggar-woman was found dead at Buckby, on Thursday next after the feast of St. Augustine, in the fourteenth year of King Edward; her throat had been cut, and so she had died forthwith. . . . Inquest was taken before Simon, of Kelmarsh, the coroner, by the oath of twelve men. . . . They say, on their oaths, that, on the preceding Wednesday, before sunset, Michael Darling, of Buckby, sheltered two beggars, a man and a woman, whose names are unknown, in a certain house in his yard, and, during the night, the man cut the woman's throat, and she died forthwith; after committing the act, he fled to some place unknown. Being asked if any other person aided or abetted the act, they say, no. The pledges of Michael Darling, for having given them shelter, Richard Gamel and Walter, son of John. The knife was worth a penny, for which the township of Buckby will account."

Cases of this kind are very numerous in the old records, and show that, in these days, such rules as the view of frankpledge were a necessary part of the domestic police system.

Analogous cases of liability, such as have been mentioned, may have had some influence in shaping the rule we are discussing, but our time is not sufficient to make more than this passing allusion.

Returning to the main subject, — I would call your attention to the extraordinary series of events which marked the fourteenth century, and may have had a part to play in the historical development of the rule.

The Black Death, as it was called, appeared in England about the middle of the fourteenth century. It is supposed to have been the same as the oriental plague, and undoubtedly came from the East. The mortality was tremendous. One-third, some authorities say one-half, of the population perished. Its immediate consequence was a dearth of labor and a corresponding increase of wages. Labor rents were necessarily commuted by the lords, and the practical effect was a subversion of the whole social system. The well-known Statutes of Laborers, passed by Parliament after Parliament, with more and more stringent penalties, proved ineffectual to keep wages at their old rate. As has been said by Thorold Rogers, "All at once, and as by a stroke, the labourer, both peasant and artizan, became the master of the situation in England. The change was as universal as it was sudden." Indeed, Professor Freeman calls the Black Death of 1349 the greatest of all social landmarks in English history. (Thorold Rogers' *Economic Interpretation of History*, c. i and ii; Jusserand's *English Wayfaring Life in the Fourteenth Century*. Stubbs' *Constitutional History*, ii, 416; Freeman in *Encycl. Brit.*, Vol. 8, p. 325; Cheyney's *Industrial History of England*, c. v.).

Other forces were at work beside the discontent caused by the Statute of Laborers. The increase of taxation,

on account of the war in France, the increasing importance of the Guilds, the influence of Wiclif and the preach-
ing of his Lollard disciples, unsettled every stratum of
society.   John Ball, the celebrated travelling priest,
traversed England, taking for his text, "At the beginning
we were all created equal," and its well known rhyming
paraphrase:

> "When Adam dolve and Eve span,
> Who was then the gentleman?"

And then, in 1381, broke out the "peasants' revolt,"
led by Wat Tyler (from whom it is said President Tyler
claimed descent.)   The rebellion was soon quelled.
Tyler and Ball were slain, but their purpose was accomplished, for the ruling classes began to yield to the spirit
of the times.   The reign of Status drew to its end, and
the system of Contract gradually succeeded.

Although I have not seen it anywhere noticed by
others, it may not be impossible that this social and
political revolution produced its effect upon questions
such as we are considering.   Certain it is that the decisions rendered in the fifteenth century, on the subject of
the master's liability, rest distinctly upon a contractual
basis.   Thus we find the cases laying down as a test
of liability the command or implied assent of the master
as employer.

Time permits the citation of only a few typical authorities.   The well-known case of *Beaulieu* v. *Finglam*,
1401, Y. B., 2 H. IV, 18, pl. 6, may be found translated
by Judge Holmes, and also by Wallace in his entertaining
and valuable book on *The Reporters*, p. 84.   It was an
action for damage caused by the defendant's fire.   Markham, J., said, "A man is held to answer for the act of his
servant, or of one of his household, in such a case; for,
if my servant, or one of my family, puts a candle in a

bracket, and the candle falls into the straw and burns up my house and the house of my neighbor also, in this case I shall answer to my neighbor for the damage which he has," which was allowed by the Court. Hull, the defendant's counsel, then said, "That will be against all reason to put blame or default on a man where there is none in him, for negligence of his servants cannot be called his feasance." Then Markham, J., "I shall answer to my neighbor for him who enters my house by my leave or my knowledge, for him who is my guest or my servant's, if he does, or any of them does, anything, as with a candle or other thing, by which the house of my neighbor is burned, but if a man from outside my house, against my will, does so . . . for that I shall not be held to answer to them . . . for this cannot be said to be through ill doing on my part, but against my will."

In 1431, Y. B., 9 H. VI, 53, pl. 37, occurs an action for selling bad wine. Plea, that he sold it through his servant, Martin, Justice, to the defendant, "Of your own knowledge you have deceived him" (the plaintiff). Rolf, for the defendant: "If I have a servant who is my merchant, and he goes to a fair with an unsound horse to sell it, shall the party have action of deceit against me? No." Martin, Justice, "You are right; for you did not order him to sell the thing to the other, nor to any particular person; but if your servant, by your covin and commandment, sells bad wine, the buyer shall have action against you; for it is your own selling, and if the case is that you did not command your servant to sell to that person, then you may allege that you did not sell to the plaintiff."

This, I think, was the opinion of the Court, and not of counsel for the defendant, as Mr. Wigmore asserts, for Martin was judge of the common pleas at this time, and his remarks seem to have been accepted as a statement of the law. You will observe, of course, the prominence given to the express command of the master.

Numerous other cases of this period may be found collected in the article referred to, 7 *Harvard Law Review*, 394-5.

The next stage in the history of the doctrine appears to be the rule that the master's assent is to be implied from the general authority given to the servant.

The first distinctively modern case in which the rule is stated is the well-known one of *Michael* v. *Alestree*, 2 Lev. 172; 1 Ventris, 295; 3 Keble, 650 (1676), an action on the case against a master and servant for bringing horses to be broken or trained in Lincoln's Inn Fields, whereby the plaintiff was injured. It was said in one of the reports of the case (3. Keb. 650), "The master is as liable as the servant, if he gave order for it," and in another (2 Lev. 172), "It shall be intended that the master sent the servant to train the horses there."

It would seem, upon the whole, that the master was considered liable, because he sent his servant on what he must have known was a dangerous business, viz., to break a horse in a public place, and he must, consequently, be understood to have assumed the risk of the business so far as the public were concerned. You may, perhaps, see the analogy to the case of *McClung* v. *Dearborne*, before cited, where the master sent his servant on an errand likely to provoke a breach of the peace, and was held liable for an assault committed in express violation of his orders.

Tuberville v. *Stamp* is another oft-quoted case, decided in 1698. It was an action for a fire started by the defendant's servant in a field; Skinner, 681. It was argued for the defense that, "it does not appear in this case to be done by the command of the master, and then, it being out of his house, he is not responsible."

In another report (Comb. 459), Holt, C. J., said:
"And though I am not bound by the act of a stranger
in any case, yet if my servant doth anything prejudicial
to another, it shall bind me, where it may be presumed
that he acts by my authority, being about my business,"
and according to 1 Ld. Raym. 264, Holt, C. J., further
said: "So, in this case, if the defendant's servant kindled
the fire in the way of husbandry and proper for his employment, though he had no express command of his
master, yet the master shall be liable .   .   . for it
shall be intended that the servant had authority from
his master, it being for his master's benefit."

Cases might be quoted for the remainder of the evening, but I intended to cite only a few of the principal
authorities, and shall merely mention Blackstone, who
says (*Commentaries* I, 429): "In the same manner,
whatever a servant is permitted to do in the usual course
of his business is equivalent to a general command. . . . .
A wife, a friend, a relation, that use to transact business
for a man, are *quoad hoc* his servants, and the principal
must answer for their conduct, for the law implies
that they act under a general command, and without
such a doctrine as this no mutual intercourse between
man and man could subsist with any tolerable convenience."   .   .   .

And finally, down to the present day, the theory becomes that the employer is liable for the torts of his
employe, committed within the scope of his employment.

We will now but briefly consider the various reasons
assigned for the rule.   Let me say, first, that the oft-
quoted maxim, "*Qui facit per alium, facit per se,*" is
merely a way of stating the rule, but affords no explanation, and the other maxim, "*Respondeat superior,*" is
even more bald.   But some explanations, founded on
public policy, are worthy of notice.

1. While, of course, the master cannot relieve himself from liability by showing that he has exercised every precaution in the selection of his servant, yet his obvious interest is to make all possible effort in this direction, in order to prevent such accidents as far as possible. This is the explanation of Bentham and, if not of itself sufficient, is, nevertheless, of considerable force.

2. We must not overlook the wonderful increase in the number of corporations, which, considered as artificial persons, must necessarily act through their servants or employes in much of their business. The popular tendency to regard the corporation's servant as the visible, tangible representative of the corporation is too strong to be resisted, and this alone might account for the preservation and extension of the rule.

3. Bacon's *Abridgment* (Master and Servant, K.) says, "For, as in strictness, everybody ought to transact his own affairs, and it is by the favor and indulgence of the law that he can delegate the power of acting for him to another, it is highly reasonable that he should answer for such substitute, at least *civiliter*."

A very learned writer (Pollock, *Essays on Jurisprudence*, p. 125) has elaborated, on independent lines, a like explanation, and considers this form of liability as analogous to a group of other cases. Thus, the owner of land is bound to keep it fenced, and is responsible for the damage caused by his straying cattle. He is likewise responsible for the damage caused by the breaking of his dam or reservoir, in which he has stored water, or the falling of a building which overhangs a public road. The diligence which such a person is bound to observe is measured by the degree of hazard in his undertaking. Now, as a man's business is his property, in the broad sense, and as the means by which he carries it on, as vehicles or machinery, are his property, in the strict sense, analogy leads to the rule that the employer's obligation is, that reasonable care, as regards the public, shall be used in the conduct of his business, and this, whether he attends to it himself, or, for his own convenience, through his servants.

4. Finally, there is an ever-recurring feeling in the popular mind that the master ought to be liable, because, in ninety-nine cases out of a hundred, the servant is not financially able to pay the damage caused by his negligence. This sentiment has appeared in at least one judicial decision in England (and there may be others). Said Willes, J., in *Limpus* v. *London Omnibus Co.*, 1 H. & C. 539, "There is virtually no remedy against the driver of an omnibus and, therefore, it is necessary that, for an injury resulting from an act done by him in the course of his master's service, the master should be responsible, for there ought to be a remedy against some person capable of paying damages to those injured by improper driving." So it was said in our own case of *McClung* v. *Dearborne*, 134 Pa. 406, before cited: "Servants and employes are often without the means to respond in damages for the injuries they may inflict on others by the ignorant, negligent or wanton manner in which they conduct the business of their employer. The loss must be borne in such cases by the innocent sufferer, or by him whose employment of an ignorant, careless or wanton servant has been the occasion of the injury, and, under such circumstances, it is just that the latter should bear the loss." That is to say: The damage, which would overwhelm the person injured if he were forced to bear it himself, is shifted on to the shoulders of another, better able, in the majority of cases, to bear the loss. It resembles a sort of accident insurance, in which the public are policy holders, and the employer is obliged to assume the rôle of an insurer.

To recapitulate, we find that the rule of the employer's liability probably had its origin in ancient times, when the servant or slave was a member of the employer's household; that it at first depended upon status, or the legal relationship of the parties, and was founded upon primitive conceptions antedating the contractual ideas of modern times. That, gradually, as the social system changed, and men became liable for their own acts, and not for those of others unless they had previously authorized or subsequently ratified them, the rule was maintained on a contractual theory, really because it was agreeable to public policy, although the reasons assigned for it by the Courts varied from time to time. From direct command to implied authority, and from this to the principle of scope of employment, we find a gradual development of this important rule of law to the present time.

I will not pretend to assert that other and different conclusions may not be drawn from the data preserved. And, indeed, the decisions are so numerous, so obscure, so shifting in the reasons assigned for them, that no one can confidently claim to have correctly interpreted them, or to have discovered all which bear upon the subject. In fact, to find early cases really bearing upon a question such as this is like looking for a needle in a haystack, and you know the only way to find a needle is to sit down on it suddenly when you are looking for something else. And then, remember what Captain Cuttle said, "Which when found, make a note of." But whether the conclusions offered you this evening are exactly right or not is, for our present purpose, unimportant. It is enough if you will assent to what was said at the beginning, that such investigations of the origins of our law will lead to a study of history, politics, sociology and a clearer understanding of legal reasoning.

I had intended, when I began my preparation for this talk to you, to treat in like manner of several other rules and trace them to their historical origins, but even this superficial discussion has consumed my time and I must close.

This reminds me of an incident I witnessed once in the Court of the Master of the Rolls, in London, when I was spending a few weeks' holiday some years ago. Lord Esher was sitting, a Judge more distinguished for legal ability than for urbanity. A Q. C., after addressing the Court for some time, to the manifest annoyance of the Judge, who was fidgety and anxious to be off, finally said, in winding up his argument, "And now, my lord I think I have said upon this subject all I have to say," when Lord Esher interrupted him with the cruel remark, "If you have said all you have to say, you had better sit down." It is needless to say that counsel very soon acted upon this broad hint.

So having said all I have to say, I think I will sit down also, but not before I plead guilty to violating a promise which I made when I was requested to address you. I then said I would not give you any advice, and yet I fear I have been advising you throughout, and cannot leave without expressing the hope that you will pursue your legal studies in the historical spirit, and by the historical method; and I will say with Lord Chesterfield, in one of his letters to his son, "I wish to God that you had as much pleasure in following my advice as I have in giving it to you, and you may the easier have it, as I give you none that is inconsistent with your pleasure."